Moroccan Interiors
Intérieurs marocains

Lisa Lovatt-Smith

Moroccan Interiors
Intérieurs marocains

TASCHEN

KÖLN LONDON LOS ANGELES MADRID PARIS TOKYO

Illustration page 2 / Reproduction page 2 / Abbildung Seite 2:
Home of Alessandra Lippini and Nadir Naldi (see pp. 160–171): bedpost
Maison d'Alessandra Lippini et Nadir Naldi (voir pp. 160–171): colonne de lit
Haus von Alessandra Lippini und Nadir Naldi (s. S. 160–171): Bettpfosten
Photo: Nadir Naldi

Illustration page 7 / Reproduction page 7 / Abbildung Seite 7:
Home of Boul de Breteuil (see pp. 78–85): a niche in one of the salons
Maison de Boul de Breteuil (voir pp. 78–85): une niche dans un des salons
Haus von Boul de Breteuil (s. S. 78–85): eine Nische in einem der Salons
Photo: Pascal Hinous/Agence Top

To stay informed about upcoming TASCHEN titles, please request our magazine at www.taschen.com
or write to TASCHEN, Hohenzollernring 53, D–50672 Cologne, Germany, Fax: +49-221-254919.
We will be happy to send you a free copy of our magazine which is filled with information about all of our books.

© 2005 TASCHEN GmbH
Hohenzollernring 53, D-50672 Köln
www.taschen.com
Original edition: © 1995 Benedikt Taschen Verlag GmbH
Edited and designed by Angelika Muthesius, Cologne
Cover design: Sense/Net, Andy Disl and Birgit Reber, Cologne
Text edited by Jutta Hendricks, Cologne
Photographic co-ordination by Sophie Baudrand, London
French translation by Philippe Safavi, Paris, and Jacqueline Gheerbrant, Neffiès (pp. 8–25)
English translation by Christine Wilson, Norwich (pp. 26–45)
German translation by Martin Hielscher, Cologne, and Birgit Lamerz-Beckschäfer, Datteln (pp. 26–45)

Printed in China
ISBN 3-8228-4752-6
ISBN 3-8228-4845-X (edition with French cover)

Contents
Sommaire
Inhalt

Preface/Préface/Vorwort

Texte: Lisa Lovatt-Smith
Illustrations: Hervé van der Straeten

"Always without formulating the concept, I had based my sense of being in the world partly on an unreasoned conviction that certain areas of the earth's surface contained more magic than others."

Paul Bowles

These words were inspired by a first glimpse of the North African coast. They are from the autobiography of Paul Bowles (*1926), Morocco's most celebrated expatriate, who has long been a resident of Tangier. He continues: *"Had anyone asked me what I meant by magic, I should probably have defined the word by calling it a secret connection between the world of nature and the consciousness of man, a hidden, but direct passage that bypassed the mind."* My own attraction to Morocco was no less visceral, and this book was born out of an instinctive love and admiration of the country and its people.

The first time I set foot in Morocco was in Marrakesh, in the month of May. In the trance-like state induced by heat and emotion, I experienced an overwhelming sense of fulfilment; I had discovered a land so perfectly concordant with my innermost desires that I recognised it as my home. Even after lengthy periods of intensive travelling in Morocco, this unmediated perception has lost none of its strength. The first attraction was imaginative. The notion of "Orientalism", of Islamic culture filtered through the perceptions of the West, had captivated me. There was no lack of sources. North Africa in general and Morocco in particular has inspired a phenomenal quantity of travel literature, from Leo Africanus, who wrote a comprehensive study, *A Description of Africa,* in the 16th century, to the present day. Now, six years on, a detailed knowledge of the people and their customs, architecture and lifestyle has cemented my fascination.

I learnt that there are many Moroccos, from the white-painted villages of the Mediterranean coast to the earth constructions on the fringes of the Sahara desert. The snow-capped peaks near Ifrane, the great cedar forests between Fez and Marrakesh and the Spanish-speaking towns of the north endow the country with a variety that is often little known to tourists. The climate varies enormously,

C'est ainsi que Paul Bowles (*1926), le plus célèbre
citoyen d'adoption du Maroc, qui vit à Tanger depuis
des années, relate dans un récit autobiographique
sa première impression des côtes nord-africaines.
Il poursuit: «Si l'on m'avait demandé ce que j'enten-
dais par magie, j'aurais probablement défini le mot
comme une connivence entre le monde de la nature et
la conscience de l'homme, une voie cachée, mais di-
recte, qui ne passait pas par le cerveau.» On ne saurait
mieux résumer la commotion que provoque la
découverte du Maghreb. Celle que j'ai éprouvée,
violente, viscérale et torrentielle, m'a marquée à tout
jamais. Ce livre est donc aussi un témoignage de reconnaissance, l'expression de l'amour et de l'admiration que je porte au Maroc et à ses habitants.

Je me rappelle encore cette journée de mai où
j'ai pour la première fois posé le pied sur le sol marocain. Le soleil brillait sur Marrakech. Je débarquais
d'un autre monde. Et là, submergée par la chaleur
et l'émotion, je découvrais soudain une terre qui ré-
pondait exactement à mes désirs les plus profonds,
une terre dans laquelle je reconnaissais spontané-
ment ma patrie spirituelle. J'étais enfin comblée (aujourd'hui encore, malgré d'innombrables séjours au
Maroc, cette première impression n'a rien perdu de
sa vigueur). J'avais voulu visiter le Maroc par goût
de l'ailleurs: l'orientalisme, cette vision occidentale
de la culture musulmane, m'intriguait. J'avais lu
Pierre Loti. Je savais que l'Afrique du Nord, et notamment le Maroc, avait inspiré d'innombrables récits de voyage, depuis la «Description de l'Afrique»
de Léon l'Africain en 1550 jusqu'aux reportages de
nos globe-trotters modernes. Six années ont passé.
J'ai appris à connaître le pays, ses habitants, ses
coutumes, son architecture et ses mœurs. Et il me
fascine toujours autant.

J'ai découvert qu'il y avait plusieurs Maroc.
Celui des maisons blanches de la côte méditerra-
néenne et celui des constructions en pisé des portes

Es war der erste Eindruck von der nordafrikanischen
Küste, der zu diesen Worten inspirierte. Sie stammen aus der Autobiographie von Paul Bowles
(*1926), Marokkos berühmtestem Ausländer, der
schon seit langem in Tanger lebt. Weiter heißt es:
»Wenn mich jemand gefragt hätte, was ich denn mit
Magie meine, dann hätte ich das Wort wahrscheinlich
so definiert, daß ich es als eine geheime Verbindung
zwischen der Welt der Natur und dem Bewußtsein des
Menschen bezeichnet hätte, einen verborgenen, aber di-
rekten Weg, der den Verstand umgeht.« Ich fühlte
mich ebenso unmittelbar, ja körperlich von Marokko
angezogen, und dieses Buch verdankt seine Entstehung einer instinktiven Liebe voller Bewunderung
für dieses Land und seine Menschen.

Ich erinnere mich daran, wie ich zum ersten
Mal nach Marokko kam, und zwar nach Marrakesch
im Mai. In meinem tranceähnlichen Zustand, der
von der Hitze und meinen aufgewühlten Empfin-
dungen herrührte, hatte ich plötzlich das überwälti-
gende Gefühl der Erfüllung. Ich hatte ein Land entdeckt, das so perfekt mit meinen tiefsten Sehn-
süchten übereinstimmte, daß ich es als meine Heimat erkannte. Auch nachdem ich nun über einen
längeren Zeitraum Marokko kreuz und quer bereist
habe, hat dieser erste unmittelbare Eindruck nichts
von seiner Intensität eingebüßt. Was mich zunächst
anzog, waren eher Phantasien. Die Vorstellung des
»Orientalischen«, von islamischer Kultur, gefiltert
durch die westliche Perspektive, fesselte mich. Diese
Gedanken wurden gespeist von Reiseberichten und
Reiseliteratur über Nordafrika im allgemeinen und
Marokko im besonderen. Sie reichen von Leo Africanus, der im 16. Jahrhundert eine umfassende »Beschreibung Afrikas« verfaßte, bis zum heutigen
Tage. Sechs Jahre später nun ist meine Faszination
durch ein solides Detailwissen über die Marokkaner
und ihre Sitten, ihre Architektur und ihre Lebensweise nur noch gefestigter.

too, as does the landscape, from the fertile coastal plain to the austere Rif mountains. Near Ourika the hills are red and the ochre earth imparts its colour to the great walls of Marrakesh. The fortifications and the medina at Fez are a sandy tone. Casablanca is as white as its Spanish name suggests. The very desert itself can be black, brown or gold. There are cities specialised in each kind of craft, huge regional variations in costume, and a whole Berber subculture that is a closed book to many travellers, and indeed to many Moroccans themselves. The recent introduction of certain programmes in Berber dialects on national television is symptomatic of the increased respect for these traditionally rural people. The Berbers, according to the classic text *Races of Africa* by C.G. Seligman are ethnically Hamites with a suspected Nordic strain and make up the most important percentage of the population.

Young Morocco

One of the most surprising facts for the visitor is how quickly modern Morocco has evolved. Less than a hundred years ago, during the rule of the last two independent sultans, the country was in the grip of corruption and decadence. As Walter Harris, *The Times'* eccentric correspondent in Tangier from 1887 to 1933, wrote: " ... the rotten old edifice had stood for many years in a state of imminent collapse."

Europe acknowledged France's "special interest" in the country, and in 1912 the last Sultan, Moulay Hafid, was persuaded to abdicate and the French protectorate was established. Harris, like many other European writers of the day, thought highly of Marshall Louis Hubert Lyautey, the Resident General, and his attitude towards the Moroccan people: "They experienced, for the first time in centuries, security. The ever-present fear of death, confiscation, and imprisonment, under the shadow of which they had lived their whole lives, as had their parents and their ancestors before them, disappeared." Nationalists, by contrast, saw in Lyautey

du désert. Le Maroc des hautes montagnes enneigées de la région d'Ifrane, celui des forêts de cèdres géants qui s'étendent entre Fès et Marrakech, celui des petites villes hispanophones du Nord. Bref, toute une diversité qu'en général les voyageurs pressés ne soupçonnent pas. Les climats sont aussi contrastés que les paysages, et l'éternel printemps des plaines côtières est à mille lieues des rudes hivers du Rif. Et que dire des couleurs, tant la palette est riche? Il y a le rouge des collines d'Ourika, l'ocre des grands remparts de Marrakech, la blondeur des murailles de la médina de Fès, la blancheur de Casablanca, le camaïeu noir, brun et doré du désert. Chaque ville possède sa propre tradition artisanale. Chaque région, chaque tribu a ses costumes. Le Maroc est peuplé en majorité de Berbères, un peuple d'origine chamite croisé d'influences nordiques, lit-on dans «Les races africaines» de C.G. Seligman. La passionnante culture berbère mériterait à elle seule de longs développements, et cela d'autant plus que peu d'étrangers y ont accès. Elle commence à conquérir un droit d'expression plus large, comme le prouve la programmation d'émissions en chleuch et en teshelhait (les deux principaux dialectes berbères) par la chaîne de télévision nationale.

Le Maroc jeune

On est toujours étonné de constater combien l'histoire est allée vite au Maroc. Que de chemin parcouru en moins d'un siècle, depuis l'époque décadente et corrompue des derniers sultans! Au début du siècle, la gangrène est si grave que l'excentrique Walter Harris, correspondant du «Times» à Tanger de 1887 à 1933, n'hésite pas à écrire que «le vieil édifice pourri» est depuis des années «au bord de l'effondrement».

Après que les puissances européennes eurent reconnu «l'influence prépondérante» (comme disaient les diplomates) de la France sur le Maroc, le dernier sultan, Moulay Hafid, doit accepter le traité de protectorat en 1912. Comme beaucoup d'autres observateurs européens de l'époque, Walter Harris a une haute opinion du Maréchal Louis Hubert Lyautey, résident général de la Répu-

Ich weiß nun, daß es viele Marokkos gibt, von den weißgetünchten Dörfern der Mittelmeerküste bis zu den Lehmbauten am Rande der Sahara. Auch weiß ich, daß die schneebedeckten Gipfel bei Ifrane, die großen Zedernwälder zwischen Fes und Marrakesch und die spanischsprachigen Städte des Nordens dem Land einen Abwechslungsreichtum schenken, den Touristen hier kaum vermuten. Ganz wie die Landschaft ist auch das Klima sehr unterschiedlich, von dem fruchtbaren milden Küstenstreifen bis zu den kargen rauhen Gebirgszügen des Rif. In der Nähe von Ourika sind die Hügel rot, und die ocker-farbene Erde verleiht den großen Mauern von Marrakesch ihre Färbung. Die Stadtmauern und die Medina von Fes haben einen sandfarbenen Ton. Casablanca ist so weiß, wie sein spanischer Name es suggeriert. Aber auch die Wüste selbst kann schwarz, braun oder golden sein. Jede Stadt hat ihr eigenes Kunsthandwerk, auf das sie sich speziali-siert hat, jede Region hat ihre eigene traditionelle Kleidung. Außerdem gibt es die Kultur der Berber, die vielen Reisenden wie auch Marokkanern selber vollkommen unzugänglich bleibt. Daß seit kurzem nun auch bestimmte Sendungen des staatlichen Fernsehens in Berberdialekten ausgestrahlt werden, zeigt den gestiegenen Respekt gegenüber diesem traditionsreichen Landvolk. Die Berber sind – der klassischen Studie »Die Rassen Afrikas« von C.G. Seligman zufolge – ethnisch betrachtet Hamiten mit einem vermutlich nordischen Einschlag und bilden den größten Prozentsatz der Bevölkerung.

Junges Marokko
Besucher sind meist überrascht, wie jung das moderne Marokko ist. Vor knapp hundert Jahren, während der Herrschaft der letzten beiden unabhän-gigen Sultane, lag das Land noch im Würgegriff von Korruption und Dekadenz. Wie der extravagante Walter Harris, von 1887 bis 1933 Korrespondent der »Times« in Tanger, schrieb: »Das verrottete alte Gemäuer hatte viele Jahre lang dagestanden, als würde es jeden Augenblick einstürzen.«

In Europa akzeptierte man das »besondere Interesse« Frankreichs an diesem Land, und im Jahre 1912 wurde der letzte Sultan, Moulay Hafid,

the worst kind of Imperialist, a "good colonial hand" who genuinely loved the country and was thus less likely to provoke the rebellion they desired. Indeed, Morocco was only to gain back its independence in 1956.

French influence on architecture

The French were energetic colonisers, building roads, railways, hospitals and an administrative structure. From an architectural point of view, the French transformed the country. Modern quarters laid out on grid patterns were built in all the main cities; they stood outside and separate from the medinas. Lyautey had learnt the lesson of French Imperialism in Egypt and French experiences in Algeria and Tunisia. He did not seek to tamper with Moslem life. Wyndham Lewis, whose *Journey into Barbary* was written during the French protectorate, testified to this: "... a really incredible scrupulosity has been shown in leaving *souk,* casbah and village intact – except perhaps for a surreptitious house-drain or two, and numbers painted upon the doors of the houses of the medina, to guide the postman I suppose." In this way the traditional medinas were preserved, and it is here that the great architectural interest of the country resides. Conservation is something of a rarity in the Arab world. Most of the medinas of Saudi Arabia and Egypt have been adulterated or razed and replaced with soulless high-rise blocks and shopping centres. It has become disheartingly clear that the medinas of Morocco are increasingly under threat, without distinction of architectural quality. Decay has set in as the palaces and homes of these ancient native quarters are left empty or rented out. The original proprietors, many of whom still count among the country's most important families, have moved either to the political and economic centres of Casablanca and Rabat or to the *villes nouvelles* constructed during the thirties and forties. On the other hand, rural depopulation has resulted in regular influxes of peasant from the *bled*. The resultant overcrowding has produced conditions that the administration seeks to "clean up" by demolishing whole quarters. Large-scale urban reforms are planned which would effectively destroy

blique française au Maroc, et de sa politique envers les Marocains: «Pour la première fois depuis des siècles, la population se sent en sécurité alors que, de mémoire de Marocain, elle avait toujours vécu dans la crainte des exécutions, des spoliations et de l'emprisonnement.» Les nationalistes, en revanche, voient en Lyautey un impérialiste de la pire espèce, l'un de ces colonialistes au grand cœur qui, à force de paternalisme bon enfant, risque d'anesthésier la révolte qu'ils appellent de leurs vœux (leurs craintes sont d'ailleurs parfaitement fondées, puisque le Maroc ne conquerra son indépendance qu'en 1956).

L'influence française

En colonisateurs énergiques qu'ils sont, les Français construisent des routes, des chemins de fer, des hôpitaux, des bâtiments administratifs. Le pays se métamorphose. On voit surgir dans toutes les grandes villes de vastes quartiers modernes tracés au cordeau. Mais les médinas restent intactes: Lyautey a manifestement tiré les enseignements de l'expérience coloniale en Egypte, en Algérie et en Tunisie, et il tient à préserver la vie musulmane, ce que ne manque d'ailleurs pas de remarquer Wyndham Lewis, qui écrit dans son «Voyage en Barbarie»: «On a pris grand soin de conserver tels quels le souk, la casbah et le village. Hormis peut-être une ou deux gouttières discrètes et les numéros inscrits sur les maisons, les médinas ont été préservées, et avec elles l'immense intérêt architectural du pays.» La chose est assez rare dans le monde arabe pour être signalée. En Arabie saoudite et en Egypte, la plupart des vieux quartiers ont été «modernisés», ou rasés et remplacés par des immeubles médiocres et des centres commerciaux tape-à-l'œil. Mais les médinas marocaines sont menacées. Les palais et les habitations se vident et se dégradent. Leurs propriétaires, dont beaucoup appartiennent encore à de grandes familles, sont partis vivre à Rabat, à Casablanca, ou dans les nouveaux quartiers construits dans les années trente et quarante. A leur place se sont installées des familles rurales pauvres qui s'entassent dans d'étroits logements, d'où une surpopulation et une insalubrité à laquelle les pouvoirs publics essaient de remédier à coups de bulldozers.

dazu gedrängt, abzudanken: es begann die Ära des
französischen Protektorats. Harris – wie viele andere europäische Schriftsteller jener Zeit – hielt sehr
viel von Marschall Louis Hubert Lyautey, dem ersten
Generalresidenten, und seiner Haltung gegenüber
den Marokkanern: »Sie erlebten zum ersten Mal seit
Jahrhunderten so etwas wie Sicherheit. Es ver-
schwand die allgegenwärtige Angst vor dem Tod, vor
Verhaftung und Einkerkerung, in deren Schatten sie,
wie schon ihre Eltern und deren Vorfahren, ihr
ganzes Leben gelebt hatten.« Im Gegensatz dazu
sahen Nationalisten in Lyautey die schlimmste Spiel-
art des Imperialisten verkörpert, nämlich den geschickten Kolonialisten, der das Land aufrichtig
liebte und daher wohl kaum den Aufstand heraufbe-
schwören würde, den sie sich wünschten. So wurde
Marokko denn auch erst im Jahre 1956 unabhängig.

Der französische Einfluß auf die Architektur
Die Franzosen waren tüchtige Kolonialisten. Sie
bauten Straßen, ein Eisenbahnnetz, Krankenhäuser
und richteten eine Verwaltung ein. Unter ihrem Einfluß veränderte sich die Architektur des Landes. In
allen größeren Städten wurden moderne Viertel gebaut, die im Schachbrettmuster angelegt waren. Sie
lagen außerhalb und getrennt von den Medinas.
Lyautey hatte vom französischen Kolonialismus in
Ägypten und von den Erfahrungen der Franzosen in
Algerien und Tunesien gelernt. Er hatte nicht vor,
sich ins moslemische Leben einzumischen. Wyndham Lewis, dessen »Reise zu den Barbaren«
während des französischen Protektorats geschrie-
ben wurde, bezeugt dies: »... eine wirklich unglaub-
liche Gewissenhaftigkeit zeigt sich darin, daß man
souks, Kasbahs und Dörfer intakt gelassen hat – bis
auf vielleicht ein oder zwei verstohlen angebrachte
Abflußrohre und Hausnummern auf Türen in der
Medina, zur Orientierung für den Briefträger, denke
ich.« So hat man die Medinas erhalten und mit ihnen die großartige architektonische Bedeutung des
Landes. Konservierung ist eine Seltenheit in der arabischen Welt. Die meisten Medinas Saudi-Arabiens
und Ägyptens wurden verunstaltet oder abgerissen
und durch seelenlose Hochhausblocks und Ein-
kaufszentren ersetzt. Es ist entmutigend zu beob-

the medinas, and which, if implemented, would do irreparable damage to the architectural heritage of Morocco and the world.

The contrast of the ancient way of life in the medinas, with their bustling *souks* and narrow streets, each dedicated to a particular craft or commerce, and the spacious, modern *villes nouvelles* is a fascinating one. It is a metaphor for another confrontation, that of a traditional Islamic society attempting to embrace the latest technology without losing its religious and national identity. The country has effectively leaped forward several centuries in the space of three generations.

Categories of dwelling
Three categories of dwelling are traditional in Morocco: urban buildings, Berber *pisé* constructions such as the *ksour* of the Dra Valley, and tents. The latter survive only among the nomadic tribesmen of the Atlas mountains. In 1931, when Wyndham Lewis was writing, transhumance and nomadism were still widespread, and tents were a ubiquitous feature of the landscape: "It is the low-slung roofs of coarse, home-spun cloth, made of camel and goat hair, palmetto and other vegetable fibre – high enough for squatting but not standing – that you see all over the Maghreb... Everywhere, throughout the thousand miles from Oran to Casa, groups of *nouala*, or most often the low, dark-brown nomadic tent, are met with incessantly. It is a chain of encampments – or strings of wandering families, in Indian file, with loaded asses."

Today, Moroccans live in the French-designed Art Deco architecture of Casablanca and Rabat, or in the suburbs of these cities, built for the most part in the fifties. Gracious colonial villas in residential areas such as La Montagne in Tangier possess enduring charm. The Palmeraie of Marrakesh, a date oasis of 150 km² size not far from the city, is increasingly built up with luxury villas for foreigners and Moroccans. Throughout Morocco, expatriate aesthetes in the grand tradition of the American millionaire Barbara Hutton maintain a valuable role in renovating traditional *riyâds* and small palaces in the medinas; this is particularly true of Tangier and Marrakesh.

Le grand plan d'urbanisme qui se mijote dans certains cabinets d'architectes reviendrait à détruire les médinas et à appauvrir irréparablement le patrimoine architectural du Maroc et du monde.

On ne peut qu'être frappé par le contraste entre les vastes espaces ordonnés des quartiers modernes et cet inextricable lacis qu'est le souk, avec ses foules bigarrées et ses minuscules échoppes où s'affairent boutiquiers et artisans. Ce double visage du Maroc illustre parfaitement l'histoire d'un pays musulman qui a su entrer dans la vie moderne sans pour autant renier son identité et ses traditions, et qui a réussi un bond en avant de plusieurs siècles en trois générations.

Types d'habitat
On trouve trois types d'habitat au Maroc: la maison de ville, la construction en pisé des Berbères, telles qu'on peut encore la voir dans les ksour de la Vallée du Draa, et la tente, à laquelle seules les tribus nomades du Haut Atlas sont restées fidèles. En 1931, à l'époque où Wyndham Lewis sillonnait l'Afrique du Nord, la transhumance était encore bien vivante, et les campements nomades faisaient partie du paysage. «Partout au Maghreb», écrit-il, «on voit ces tentes basses faites de grandes tapis tissés en poil de chameau et de chèvre, de feuilles de palmiers et autres fibres végétales, des tentes dans lesquelles il faut vivre accroupi. Elles s'égrènent sur des milliers de kilomètres, d'Oran à Casa, et l'on rencontre constamment des groupes de *nouala*, ou plus souvent une tente brun foncé solitaire, posée au milieu de nulle part. C'est un long ruban de campements, un chapelet de familles nomades qui se déplacent en file indienne avec leurs baudets surchargés.»

Aujourd'hui, les Marocains vivent à Casablanca ou à Rabat dans des maisons Art déco datant de l'époque du Protectorat, ou dans des banlieues construites dans les années cinquante. Des familles fortunées ont élu domicile dans les élégantes demeures coloniales de La Montagne, le quartier résidentiel de Tanger. La palmeraie de Marrakech abrite de luxueuses propriétés appartenant à des Marocains ou à des étrangers. D'un bout à l'autre du pays, des Européens et des Américains amoureux

achten, daß nun auch die Medinas von Marokko zunehmend bedroht sind. Ihre architektonische Bedeutung wird vielfach ignoriert. Verfall breitet sich aus, weil die Paläste und Häuser dieser alten, ursprünglichen Wohnviertel verlassen oder vermietet worden sind. Die ursprünglichen Eigentümer sind entweder in die politisch-ökonomischen Zentren von Casablanca und Rabat gezogen oder in die »Villes nouvelles«, die in den dreißiger und vierziger Jahren angelegt wurden. Andererseits hat die Landflucht einen ständigen Zufluß von Bauern des *bled* zur Folge gehabt. Die daraus resultierende Übervölkerung hat zu Zuständen geführt, die die Verwaltung »sanieren« will, indem sie ganze Viertel niederreißt. Umfangreiche Stadtreformen werden geplant, die letztlich die Medinas zerstören und – falls sie durchgeführt würden – dem architektonischen Erbe Marokkos und der Welt irreparablen Schaden zufügen würden.

Der Kontrast zwischen dem archaischen Leben in den Medinas mit ihren wimmelnden *souks* und engen Gassen, die jede einem bestimmten Gewerbe oder Handel zugeordnet sind, und den großräumigen, modernen »Villes nouvelles« ist faszinierend. Er ist außerdem eine Metapher für ein anderes Spannungsfeld, nämlich das einer traditionellen islamischen Gesellschaft, die den Versuch unternimmt, moderne Technologie zu integrieren, ohne ihre religiöse und nationale Identität dabei aufzugeben. Das Land hat sich in der Tat in einem Zeitraum von nur drei Generationen um mehrere Jahrhunderte weiterentwickelt.

Wohnformen

Es gibt drei traditionelle Wohnformen in Marokko: Stadthäuser, Piseebauten der Berber wie die *ksour* des Dra-Tales und Zelte. Letztere findet man nur noch bei den Nomaden im Atlasgebirge. Im Jahre 1931, zu der Zeit, als Wyndham Lewis schrieb, waren Herdenwanderung und Nomadenleben noch sehr verbreitet, und Zelte waren ein allgegenwärtiger Teil des Landschaftsbildes: »Es sind die niedriggeschwungenen Dächer aus grobem, selbstgesponnenem Stoff, aus Kamel- und Ziegenhaar, aus Palmen und anderen Pflanzenfasern – hoch genug, damit

Following this example, some of the Moroccan families who had chosen not to live in their traditional palaces are starting to restore them and even consider inhabiting them again.

A new construction boom

Morocco is now entering the second phase of a construction boom during which some of the most beautiful of its natural sites have been ruined for lack of building regulations. Over the last four decades, traditional structures have been abandoned in favour of modern suburban villas. Property speculation, with its concomitant pressures, is rife. The Chechaouen valley in the Rif mountains remained closed to foreigners as late as 1920; now it is the site of apparently random construction. The Amelan valley in the south contains some of the country's finest architectural ensembles, but their fragile *pisés* are being allowed to disintegrate while prosperous villagers build themselves ugly houses of reinforced concrete next door. The Atlantic coast, where the writers Truman Capote and Tennessee Williams and the British photographer Cecil Beaton picnicked, has been disfigured by vast "pleasure palaces" that arise almost overnight without a thought for architectural harmony. A plan has been made to run a road right through the medina in Fez, under the supervision of the "official" architect Michel Pinseau; the threat is all the more dangerous as the UNESCO is considering to declassify the site, to the horror of the world's architectural élites.

King Hassan II has championed his country's traditional crafts and traditions, but the protection of landscapes, villages and *pisé* buildings is an altogether more difficult challenge. The country's architectural integrity is at stake. It is not a question of delaying economic growth, still less of transforming the country into a museum for the benefit of the tourist industry but rather of subsidising restoration rather than demolition, and to impose well thought-out regulations for sites of outstanding natural or architectural beauty. Morocco does, after all, have the example of several predominantly European architectural sites which have suffered badly from excessive building in the very recent past.

d'art et d'architecture rénovent des *riyâds* et les petits palais des médinas, notamment à Tanger et à Marrakech, comme le fit avant eux la millionaire américaine Barbara Hutton.

Le boom immobilier

Hélas, le «progrès» immobilier a déjà défiguré quelques-uns des plus beaux sites du pays. Depuis une quarantaine d'années, les habitations traditionnelles sont délaissées en faveur des villas de banlieue. La spéculation immobilière, attisée par l'absence de véritables règlements d'urbanisme, fait des ravages. La vallée du Chechaouen, dans le Rif, qui fut inaccessible aux étrangers jusque dans les années vingt, se développe dans l'anarchie la plus totale. Les notables des magnifiques villages de la vallée d'Amelan construisent impunément des verrues en béton à côté de leur belle habitation en pisé qui tombe en ruines. La côte atlantique, où les écrivains Truman Capote et Tennessee Williams et le photographe anglais Cecil Beaton aimaient tant pique-niquer, se couvre de tentaculaires complexes bâtis à la va-vite et au mépris de toute considération pour le site. Un plan d'urbanisme élaboré sous la direction de l'architecte «officiel» Michel Pinseau prévoit même de percer une route en plein cœur de la médina de Fès; la menace est d'autant plus sérieuse que l'UNESCO parle de déclasser la ville, ce qui provoque un tollé chez les architectes du monde entier.

La roi Hassan II a maintes fois prouvé qu'il voulait préserver l'artisanat et les traditions de son royaume, mais la nécessité de protéger les paysages, les villages et les maisons en pisé est un tout autre problème. Pourtant, c'est tout le patrimoine architectural du pays qui est en jeu. La conservation ne doit évidemment pas se faire au détriment de la croissance économique; elle ne doit pas non plus figer le pays en un vaste musée pour touristes. Mais il est urgent de restaurer les bâtiments au lieu de les démolir, et d'imposer des règlements cohérents pour protéger les plus beaux sites naturels et bâtis du pays. Le Maroc ne doit pas reproduire les erreurs commises récemment dans certaines villes européennes, massacrées par un bétonnage tous azimuts.

man sich hinhocken kann, aber stehen kann man nicht – , die man im ganzen Maghreb sieht... Überall, auf den ganzen tausend Meilen von Oran bis Casa, trifft man unaufhörlich auf Gruppen von *nouala* oder meistens auf niedrige, dunkelbraune Nomadenzelte. Es ist eine einzige Kette von Lagern – oder von Familien, die mit ihren beladenen Eseln im Gänsemarsch dahinziehen.«

Heute wohnen die Marokkaner in den von Franzosen entworfenen Art-déco-Häusern in Casablanca und Rabat oder in den Vororten dieser Städte, die zum größten Teil in den fünfziger Jahren gebaut wurden. Anmutige Kolonialvillen in Wohnvierteln wie »La Montagne« in Tanger besitzen einen unvergänglichen Charme. Die Palmeraie von Marrakesch – eine ca. 150 km² große Dattelpalmenoase in unmittelbarer Nähe der Stadt – wird immer mehr mit Luxusvillen für Ausländer wie auch Marokkaner zugebaut. In ganz Marokko spielen ausländische Ästheten in der Tradition der amerikanischen Millionenerbin Barbara Hutton eine wichtige Rolle bei der Renovierung von alten *riyâds* und Palästen in den Medinas; das gilt besonders für Tanger und Marrakesch. Einige marokkanische Familien, die aus ihren Palästen ausgezogen waren, folgen nun jenem Beispiel und restaurieren die Gebäude, um sie möglicherweise sogar selber wieder zu bewohnen.

Ein neuer Bauboom

Marokko befindet sich derzeit in der zweiten Phase eines Baubooms, in dessen Verlauf einige seiner schönsten natürlichen Wohnlagen wegen fehlender Bauvorschriften ruiniert worden sind. Während der letzten vier Jahrzehnte sind traditionelle Strukturen zugunsten moderner Vorortvillen vernachlässigt worden. Die Grundstücksspekulation und der damit einhergehende sozialökonomische Druck greifen um sich. Das Chechaouen-Tal im Rif-Gebirge war bis ins Jahr 1920 für Ausländer unzugänglich. Inzwischen ist es zum Schauplatz einer offenbar vollkommen willkürlichen Bautätigkeit geworden. Im Tal der Ammeln im Süden befinden sich einige der schönsten Architekturdenkmäler des Landes. Aber die fragilen Piseebauten verfallen, während sich wohlhabende Dorfbewohner häßliche Betonhäuser dane-

Admittedly, the social connotations are complex. For most Moroccans, the prospect of building a new house with all mod cons is more enticing than restoration. Such an attitude is not without historical precedent. The Sultans, in particular, were fond of building over their predecessors' buildings. In Fez, a few walls are all that remain of the fabulous Merinides Palace, and the first act of despotic Moulay Ismail, when he seized power in 1672, was to destroy the 16th-century Saadien Palace in Marrakesh, one of the most extraordinary buildings in Moroccan history. The country's architectural and landscape heritage is once again in the balance. It is encouraging to note that strong local administrations and enlightened entrepreneurs have largely succeeded in saving the beauty of Essaouira and Taroudant; in such places, and in the marvellous kindness of its people, lies much of the charm of Morocco.

Looking for beautiful houses
In my meandering voyages, often through isolated regions, armed only with a few words of Arabic and invariably loaded down with an enormous amount of luggage, I again and again encountered the traditional Moroccan hospitality. My *modus operandi* involved knocking on countless unknown doors. As I wandered through villages or medinas in my quest for beautiful houses, I was welcomed into the homes of people who then went to great lengths to help me visit all the interesting houses they could think of, plied me with tea and often prevailed on me to share their dinner. Since meals are eaten with one's right hand out of a communal dish, to be invited to join a family's meal suggests a trusting relationship which it is a point of honour to respect. The guest becomes a member of an extended family. Never happier than when squatting over a charcoal stove, being initiated into a new kind of *tajine*, I often ended up sharing the communal sleeping arrangements in the best salon. On two memorable occasions, my daughter, the photographer and I were bedded down on piles of rugs in the homes of mountain cave dwellers.

Certes, cette frénésie de construction est aussi un fait de société. La plupart des Marocains préfèrent construire une maison moderne plutôt que de rénover une ruine. C'est du reste une vieille tradition dans le pays. Les sultans ne faisaient-ils pas bâtir leurs palais sur ceux de leurs prédécesseurs? C'est ainsi qu'aujourd'hui le fabuleux palais de Mérinides à Fès se résume à quelques murs. Et lorsque le despote Moulay Ismail prit le pouvoir en 1672 il commença par faire démolir l'un des trésors de l'architecture marocaine, le Palais saadien de Marrakech, construit un siècle auparavant. Reste que le patrimoine architectural et naturel du pays est aujourd'hui très menacé. Mais tout n'est peut-être pas perdu: certains riches Marocains qui avaient délaissé le palais de leurs ancêtres commencent à le restaurer, voire à s'y réinstaller. Les responsables locaux et une poignée d'hommes d'affaires éclairés ont réussi à sauver la beauté d'Essaouira et de Taroudant; ce sont des localités comme celles-ci, et bien sûr la merveilleuse gentillesse des habitants, qui font le charme du Maroc.

A la recherche de belles maisons
Au cours de mes pérégrinations, je me suis souvent retrouvée au fin fond du pays, avec pour tout viatique quelques mots d'arabe et mon (gros) sac à dos. Et j'ai toujours été accueillie à bras ouverts. Dès que j'arrivais dans un village, je frappais aux portes en quête d'une jolie maison, et immanquablement je trouvais une famille qui se mettait en quatre pour me trouver un gîte chez des amis ou des voisins, m'offrait le thé et insistait pour que je reste à dîner.
Cette invitation est une marque de confiance que l'étranger se doit d'honorer. Il devient ainsi un membre de la famille élargie. Que de soirées n'ai-je pas passé ainsi, à piocher délicatement avec les doigts (de la main droite, l'autre étant considérée comme impure) à même le grand plat commun! Que de nouvelles recettes de tajine n'ai-je pas découvertes, accroupie devant un brasero, au milieu d'un cercle de visages amicaux! Bien souvent, je finissais par dormir à la bonne franquette dans le salon. A deux reprises, ma fille, le photographe et

ben bauen. Die Atlantikküste, wo die Schriftsteller Truman Capote und Tennessee Williams und der britische Fotograf Cecil Beaton picknickten, ist von riesigen Vergnügungspalästen verunstaltet, die beinahe über Nacht aus dem Boden schießen, ohne daß auch nur ein Gedanke an ein dem Ort angemessenes harmonisches Architekturkonzept verschwendet wird. Es gibt Pläne, unter der Oberaufsicht des »offiziellen« Architekten Michel Pinseau eine Straße mitten durch die Medina von Fes zu bauen. Diese Bedrohung ist umso ernster, als die UNESCO erwägt, dem Ort seine Klassifizierung als Kulturdenkmal zu entziehen, zum Schrecken von führenden Architekten in aller Welt.

König Hassan II. engagiert sich für das traditionelle Handwerk und die Bräuche seines Landes, aber der Schutz von Landschaften, Dörfern und Piseebauten ist eine insgesamt sehr viel größere Herausforderung. Die architektonische Integrität des Landes steht auf dem Spiel. Dabei geht es wirklich nicht darum, das Wirtschaftswachstum des Landes zu gefährden, und erst recht nicht darum, das Land wegen der Profite aus der Tourismusindustrie in ein Museum zu verwandeln. Dringend geboten ist es vielmehr, Restaurierungen zu finanzieren und wohldurchdachte Konzepte für besonders schöne und wertvolle Landschaften und Gebäude durchzusetzen. Marokko hat schließlich das Beispiel mehrerer, hauptsächlich europäischer Orte vor Augen, die in der jüngsten Vergangenheit durch exzessives Bauen schwer gelitten haben.

Die sozialen Probleme im Zusammenhang mit dem Erhalt der alten Architektursubstanz sind kompliziert. Für die meisten Marokkaner ist die Vorstellung, ein neues Haus mit allem modernen Komfort zu bauen, verlockender als eine Restaurierung. Diese Haltung kann sich auf historische Vorbilder berufen. Besonders den Sultanen gefiel es, die Häuser und Paläste ihrer Vorgänger jeweils durch eigene Bauten zu ersetzen. In Fes erinnern nur noch ein paar Mauern an den berühmten Meriniden-Palast, denn als der Despot Moulay Ismail 1672 an die Macht kam, war seine erste Tat, eines der prachtvollsten Gebäude in der marokkanischen Geschichte, den Saadier-Palast aus dem 16. Jahrhundert in Mar-

My experiences echoed those of previous generations of travellers. Elias Canetti, in his classic travel novel *The Voices of Marrakesh* (1967), describes a visit to a Jewish family in the mellah: "A door was opened on to the far side of the courtyard, and I was invited to enter. It was a smallish room, scrupulously tidy and clean, but it was furnished in the European style … It was undoubtedly the best room; any other room in the house would have interested me more, but they thought to honour me by offering me a seat here." The generosity lavished on the guest can be overwhelming. I have often left Moroccan homes with my arms overflowing with home-baked biscuits, paper bags full of dried fruit, trinkets, scarves and photographs of family members, and this despite a firm resolution not to accept presents. In the words of the cookery writer Paula Wolfert: "Arab hospitality is legendary – an embarrassment of riches, total satisfactions, abundance as an end in itself and a point of pride with the host."

I have travelled extensively during Ramadan, the Islamic holy month in which a fast is observed during daylight hours. This can be burdensome for foreign travellers because it is difficult to procure any lunch. But the sense of sharing, as the fast is broken at dusk, is rewarding in itself. In the course of photographing some of the neo-traditional turn-of-the-century palaces during Ramadan I was, of course, invited to share the *harira* (the soup traditionally consumed at the break of the fast) along with dates, boiled eggs rolled in cumin and honey cakes, all from the master table laid with embroidered linen. But the energy of the moment is best understood in the streets, as the whole nation waits for the muezzin's cry to ring out. The anticipation is palpable. Traffic becomes suicidal as everyone races through the clear, violet light of the Moroccan sunset. Tempers are short, nerves are frayed. Then, all of a sudden, the streets are deserted. In the few cafés that are open, visitors to the city sit before the steaming bowls of soups awaiting the signal. Everyone else waits at home in the bosom of the family. A lone beggar stands on the kerb holding an old tin full of steaming soup. Now the usually

moi avons même dormi sur des piles de tapis dans des habitations troglodytes.

Des générations de voyageurs ont avant moi goûté l'hospitalité marocaine. Dans «Les voix de Marrakech» (1967), Elias Canetti fait un récit savoureux de sa visite à une famille juive de la mellâh: «Une porte s'ouvrit au fond de la cour, et on m'invita à entrer. Je pénétrai dans une pièce assez petite, parfaitement propre et rangée, mais meublée à l'européenne. C'était manifestement la plus belle pièce de la maison; n'importe quelle autre m'aurait intéressé davantage, mais ils pensaient me faire honneur en me recevant dans celle-ci.» L'invité est traité avec une générosité presque embarrassante. Au moment de prendre congé, et malgré ma ferme résolution de ne pas accepter de cadeaux je me suis souvent retrouvée les bras chargés de biscuits, de sacs en papier remplis de fruits secs, de babioles, de foulards et de photos de famille. Mais comme l'observe la chroniqueuse gastronomique Paula Wolfert, «la légendaire hospitalité arabe aime l'excès – l'hôte mettra un point d'honneur à vous prodiguer mille attentions et à vous couvrir de présents».

J'ai souvent voyagé pendant le mois du Ramadan. Je jeûnais … faute de trouver un endroit quelconque pour déjeuner. Mais dès que la nuit tombait, le Maroc tout entier se mettait à table et alors c'était la fête. Si j'avais passé la journée à photographier quelque palais néo-traditionnel du début du siècle, j'étais évidemment invitée à partager la *harira* (la soupe consommée traditionnellement pour rompre le jeûne), accompagnée de dattes, d'œufs roulés dans le cumin et de gâteaux au miel, assise avec les autres à une grande table recouverte d'une nappe brodée. Mais l'intensité d'une fin de journée de Ramadan est surtout tangible dans la rue. Le muezzin va bientôt annoncer la fin du jeûne. Il y a de l'électricité dans l'air. Les automobilistes se transforment en kamikazes. La foule s'agite dans la lumière violacée du soleil couchant. L'énervement est à son comble. Et soudain, les rues se vident. Dans les quelques cafés encore ouverts, les voyageurs attablés attendent le signal devant leur bol de *harira* fumante. Le mendiant se tient debout au coin de la rue avec sa gamelle pleine de soupe. La mé-

rakesch, zu zerstören. Das architektonische und landschaftliche Erbe des Landes hängt wiederum an einem seidenen Faden. Es ist jedoch ein ermutigendes Zeichen, daß es starken Behördenvertretern und klugen Unternehmern vor Ort weitgehend gelungen ist, die Schönheit von Essaouira und Taroudannt zu bewahren. In solchen Orten und vor allem in der großartigen Freundlichkeit ihrer Bewohner liegt der Charme Marokkos.

Auf der Suche nach schönen Häusern

Auf meinen mäandernden Reisen, die mich – mit nur ein paar Worten Arabisch ausgerüstet und unweigerlich total bepackt – oftmals in abgelegene Gegenden führten, ist mir immer wieder die traditionelle Gastfreundschaft begegnet. Zu meinem Modus operandi gehörte, daß ich an zahllose Haustüren mir unbekannter Menschen klopfen mußte. Während ich auf der Suche nach schönen Häusern durch Dörfer und Medinas wanderte, wurde ich von Menschen hereingebeten, die sich dann sehr viel Zeit nahmen und mir halfen, alle interessanten Häuser zu besichtigen, die ihnen einfielen, mir endlos Tee nachschenkten und mich oft auch noch dazu überredeten, mit ihnen zu Abend zu essen. Da man die Mahlzeiten mit der rechten Hand aus einer Gemeinschaftsschüssel ißt, ist es ein großer Vertrauensbeweis, von einer Familie zum Essen eingeladen zu werden, eine Ehre, die man unbedingt respektieren sollte. Der Gast wird zum Mitglied der erweiterten Familie. Für mich gibt es nichts Schöneres, als an einem Holzkohleherd zu hocken und in das Geheimnis einer neuen *tajine* eingeweiht zu werden. Oft endete es damit, daß ich im besten Salon auch noch die gemeinsame Schlafstätte mitbenutzte. Bei zwei unvergeßlichen Gelegenheiten wurden meine Tochter, der Photograph und ich in der Wohnstätte von Höhlenbewohnern in den Bergen auf einem Haufen Teppiche gebettet.

Meine Erfahrungen entsprechen denen früherer Generationen von Reisenden. Elias Canetti beschreibt in seinem klassischen Reiseroman »Die Stimmen von Marrakesch« (1967) den Besuch bei einer jüdischen Familie in der *mellâh*: »Man öffnete eine Tür in ein Gemach, das auf der fernen Seite des

chaotic medina falls silent. The musical chants that lead up to prayer have ceased. Even the swallows, twittering protagonists of the late afternoon, are silent. You can feel the concentrated desire of the people, primitive in its power. Suddenly, much louder than you have expected, the signal streams out over the town's still air. The voice of the muezzin of the great mosque mixes with the noise of the siren, and from minaret to minaret the cry is taken up. It is a moment of great purity. The nation breathes a sigh of relief: the feast day that marks the end of the fast, is one day closer.

From my room at the Palais Jamai in Fez, looking out over one of the most fascinating agglomerations of housing anywhere in the world, I could imagine families squatting around the laden tables, drinking long draughts of milk flavoured with almonds. Each household has its own "break-fast" menu and recipe for *harira*, with dozens of intensely nutritious ingredients: dates, egg, chicken, meat, lentils, chickpeas and vermicelli. Once I was caught by nightfall on the station platform in Rabat. It is a small, attractive station, set between two banks of red earth. The palm trees turned slowly black against a sky that had progressed from flame to mauve to dove grey. The station master was a solitary figure, walking across the platform with his large bowl of *harira*. An ancient Berber woman in a dusky pink caftan pulled out her Ramadan picnic and invited me to join her; no Moroccan would let anyone stay hungry at the break of the fast.

Foreigners in Morocco

About half the homes in this book belong to foreigners who, for one reason or another, have chosen to spend most of their time in Morocco. Their homes are particularly interesting for showing how traditional techniques can be reinterpreted. This is best seen in the work of the Marrakesh-based decorators and architects such as Bill Willis, the doyen of the *métier* (see pp. 150–159). In Tangier, there has been a marked resurgence of the lively local palette.

dina est muette. Les chants se sont tus. Même les hirondelles, dont les cris aigus avaient salué le crépuscule, se tiennent coites. Le temps est comme suspendu. Des milliers d'hommes et de femmes attendent, immobiles et silencieux. Et soudain, une mélopée puissante d'élève dans l'air limpide du soir. La voix du muezzin de la grande mosquée, reprise de minaret en minaret, se mêle à la clameur des sirènes. La tension retombe, les visages s'éclairent, les yeux sourient: encore un jour de moins avant le jour, qui marquera la fin du Ramadan.

De ma chambre du Palais Jamai à Fès, mon regard plonge sur les petits immeubles serrés les uns contre les autres. J'imagine des familles entières accroupies autour des tables chargées de victuailles, buvant du lait parfumé aux amandes et goûtant une robuste *harira* faite des meilleurs ingrédients – dattes, œufs, poulet, agneau, lentilles, pois chiches, vermicelle ... Et me revient en mémoire ce jour de Ramadan à Rabat. Je me trouvais dans la gare, un joli petit bâtiment posé comme un bijou entre deux bandes de terre rouge. La nuit allait tomber. La masse sombre des palmiers se détachait sur le ciel pourpre qui virait rapidement au mauve puis au gris. Son bol de *harira* à la main, le chef de gare faisait les cent pas. C'est alors que, m'apercevant, une vieille femme vêtue d'un caftan rose tira de son sac quelques biscuits et m'invita à rompre le jeûne avec elle. Un musulman ne saurait laisser quiconque avoir faim en période de Ramadan ...

Les étrangers au Maroc

La moitié environ des maisons présentées dans cet ouvrage appartiennent à des étrangers qui, pour une raison ou une autre, ont choisi de vivre une grande partie de l'année au Maroc. Leurs intérieurs ont ceci d'intéressant qu'ils réinterprètent la tradition. Ce syncrétisme est particulièrement net chez l'architecte-décorateur Bill Willis, le doyen de la profession (voir pp. 150–159). L'éclatante palette traditionnelle est reprise et actualisée (les Marocains, eux, n'ont jamais méprisé les teintes vives, comme le prouvent les bleus outremer ou les jaunes canari des devantures des cafés ou des portes des garages). David Herbert (voir pp. 252–259) vit depuis quarante ans

Hofes lag, und bat mich einzutreten. Das ziemlich kleine Zimmer, peinlich ordentlich und rein, war nach europäischer Weise eingerichtet... Sicher war es ihr bestes Zimmer. Jedes andere im Hause hätte mich mehr interessiert, aber sie meinten mich zu ehren, indem sie mir hier Platz anboten.« Die Großzügigkeit, die dem Gast zuteil wird, kann einen überwältigen. Oft verließ ich marokkanische Familien vollbepackt mit selbstgebackenen Keksen, Papiertüten voller Trockenfrüchte, Souvenirs, Schals und Photographien von Familienmitgliedern – und das trotz des festen Entschlusses, keine Geschenke anzunehmen. In den Worten der Gastronomie-Schriftstellerin Paula Wolfert: »Arabische Gastfreundschaft ist legendär – beschämende Reichtümer, vollkommene Zufriedenstellung, Überfluß um seiner selbst willen ist eine Ehrensache für den Gastgeber.«

Ich bin oft und ausführlich während des Ramadan herumgereist, dem heiligen Monat der Moslems, in dem tagsüber gefastet wird. Das kann sehr anstrengend werden, weil es schwierig ist, sich ein Mittagessen zu besorgen. Aber dann gemeinsam zu essen und mit anderen zu teilen, wenn bei Einbruch der Dämmerung das Fastengebot aufgehoben wird, ist eine wunderbare Belohnung. Als wir während des Ramadan einige der neotraditionellen Paläste der Jahrhundertwende photographierten, wurde ich wie selbstverständlich eingeladen, gemeinsam mit den anderen die *harira* zu essen (die Suppe, die traditionsgemäß gegessen wird, wenn das Fastengebot aufgehoben wird), dazu Datteln, gekochte, in Kreuzkümmel gewälzte Eier und Honigkuchen, alles an einem großen Tisch, der mit einem bestickten Leinentuch gedeckt war. Aber die Energie, die in diesem Moment freigesetzt wird, versteht man am besten auf der Straße, wenn das ganze Land auf den Ruf des Muezzins wartet. Die angespannte Erwartung ist geradezu körperlich spürbar. Der Straßenverkehr ist regelrecht selbstmörderisch, weil jeder durch die klare, violette Luft des marokkanischen Sonnenuntergangs rast. Alle sind gereizt, die Nerven liegen bloß. Dann sind die Straßen ganz plötzlich verlassen. In den wenigen Cafés, die geöffnet haben, sitzen die Gäste von auswärts vor den dampfenden

Moroccans have never been afraid of brilliant colour combinations and even roadside cafés and garage doors are often painted with the brightest hues. Under the vivacious influence of David Herbert (see pp. 252–259), who has been living in his pink and green house on the mountain of Tangier for over forty years, many foreigners have embraced luminous colour schemes. The decorator Stuart Church (see pp. 304–309), on the other hand, has been instrumental in the rediscovery of simple, wooden Berber furniture. The grand colonial style – London or Paris transposed – is beautifully exemplified by Richard Timewell's Villa Léon l'African in Tangier (see pp. 232–237).

The foreigner who elects residence in Morocco is to some extent a cultural voyeur. American writer Edith Wharton in 1920 has remarked on "the dream-like feeling that envelopes with every step". There is still a strong sense of being part of the civilisation of the ancient world. The rites and rituals of everyday life are still unchanged in many areas. The eternal aspects of mankind are always present. There is a purity that belongs to an older age, and everywhere there is a direct communication with the past: in family relationships, in local dress, in the prevalent code of manners. Morocco is and has always been a deeply mystical land. For all its modernity, its skyscrapers and telecommunications, there is a strong sense of still belonging to the civilisation of the ancient world. Thus for the Romantic, its appeal has always been to the soul no less than to the senses. As Jérôme and Jean Tharaud wrote in 1930 about Fez: "It is the site of a miracle – that of suppressing the passage of time."

dans une maison rose et verte accrochée à flanc de colline à Tanger, et beaucoup de résidents étrangers ont comme lui découvert la gaîté et le charme des couleurs locales. Dans un tout autre registre, le décorateur Stuart Church (voir pp. 304–309) a redonné ses lettres de noblesse au sobre mobilier berbère. Et le style colonial classique – Londres ou Paris transposés outre-méditerranée – est magnifiquement illustré par la villa Léon l'Africain de Richard Timewell à Tanger (voir pp. 232–237).

L'étranger qui choisit de vivre au Maroc est un grand romantique. L'écrivaine américaine Edith Wharton ne notait-elle pas en 1920 qu'une atmosphère de rêve enveloppait chacun de ses pas? Au Maroc, il se replonge dans une civilisation ancestrale aux rites et aux coutumes inchangés. Ici vit l'humanité telle que l'éternité l'a faite. Ici règne une pureté d'un autre âge. Le passé vit – dans les relations familiales, dans les vêtements, dans les règles de politesse. Le Maroc est une terre profondément mystique qui, malgré ses gratte-ciel et ses téléphones, n'a jamais oublié ses racines. Il séduit donc autant l'âme que les sens. En 1930, Jérôme et Jean Tharaud disaient de Fès que c'était un lieu miraculeux qui avait aboli le temps. Le miracle, aujourd'hui encore, s'appelle Maroc.

Suppenschüsseln und warten auf das Signal. Alle anderen warten zuhause im Schoße der Familie. Ein einsamer Bettler steht mit einer alten Blechbüchse voll dampfender Suppe an der Bordsteinkante. Und nun schweigt die sonst chaotische Medina. Die Gesänge, die zum Gebet anleiten, sind verstummt. Sogar die Schwalben, die zwitschernden Hauptdarsteller des späten Nachmittags, schweigen. Man kann die konzentrierte Begierde fühlen, primitiv in ihrer Kraft. Plötzlich, viel lauter als man erwartet hätte, durchdringt das Signal die Stille. Die Stimme des Muezzins der großen Moschee vermischt sich mit den Sirenen, und von Minarett zu Minarett wird der Ruf weitergetragen. Es ist ein Augenblick von großer Reinheit. Ein Seufzer der Erleichterung geht durch das Land: der Tag, der das Ende der Fastenzeit markiert, ist wieder nähergerückt.

In meinem Zimmer im Palais Jamai in Fes, von dem aus ich auf eines der faszinierendsten Häusermeere der ganzen Welt blickte, konnte ich mir die Familien vorstellen, wie sie um den schwerbeladenen Tisch herumsaßen und in tiefen Zügen Mandelmilch tranken. Jeder Haushalt hat sein eigenes Rezept für *harira* und sein eigenes Menü mit Dutzenden von äußerst nahrhaften Bestandteilen: Datteln, Eier, Huhn, Fleisch, Linsen, Kichererbsen und Fadennudeln. Einmal war ich bei Einbruch der Nacht auf einem Bahnsteig im Bahnhof von Rabat. Es ist ein hübscher kleiner Bahnhof, zwischen zwei roten Erdwällen gelegen. Die Palmen zeichneten sich allmählich schwarz vor dem Himmel ab, der sich von einem flammenden Rot über Mauve zu Taubengrau verfärbt hatte. Die einsame Gestalt des Stationsvorstehers ging mit einer großen Schüssel *harira* den Bahnsteig hinunter. Eine alte Berberfrau in einem mattrosa Kaftan holte ihr Ramadan-Picknick heraus und lud mich dazu ein; kein Marokkaner würde irgendjemanden hungern lassen, wenn das Fastengebot aufgehoben wird.

Ausländer in Marokko

Etwa die Hälfte der in diesem Buch abgebildeten Häuser gehört Ausländern, die es aus dem einen oder anderen Grunde vorziehen, den Großteil ihrer Zeit in Marokko zu verbringen. Ihre Häuser sind besonders interessant wegen der Interpretation überlieferter Techniken. Das ist am besten anhand der Arbeiten der in Marrakesch ansässigen Innenausstatter und Architekten zu sehen, wie etwa Bill Willis, dem Doyen des Metiers (s. S. 150–159). In Tanger kann man ein Wiederaufleben der alten Farbenpracht des Ortes beobachten: Die Marokkaner hatten noch nie Angst vor starken Farbkontrasten, und selbst Straßencafés und Garagentüren sind oft in den grellsten Farben bemalt. Unter dem temperamentvollen Einfluß von David Herbert (s. S. 252–259), der seit über vierzig Jahren in seinem rosa-grünen Haus auf dem Hügel von Tanger lebt, haben sich viele Ausländer zu leuchtenden Farbanstrichen anregen lassen. Der Designer Stuart Church (s. S. 304–309) seinerseits war an der Wiederentdeckung von einfachen Berbermöbeln beteiligt. Ein wunderschönes Beispiel für den grandiosen Kolonialstil – London oder Paris nach Marokko versetzt – ist Richard Timewells »Villa Léon l'Africain« in Tanger (s. S. 232–237).

Ein Ausländer, der seinen Wohnort in Marokko wählt, ist bis zu einem gewissen Grad ein kultureller Voyeur. Schon 1920 umschrieb die amerikanische Schriftstellerin Edith Wharton das »Gefühl, sich in einem Traum zu bewegen, das einen bei jedem Schritt umgibt«. Der Eindruck, der Zivilisation der alten Welt anzugehören, ist immer noch sehr stark. Ritus und Ritual des Alltags, der in vielen Bereichen unverändert geblieben ist, die ewigen Aspekte des menschlichen Daseins sind einem immer gegenwärtig. Es gibt eine Reinheit, die einem früheren Zeitalter angehört, und überall gibt es die direkte Kommunikation mit der Vergangenheit: in den Familienbeziehungen, in der landesüblichen Kleidung, in dem herrschenden Verhaltenskodex. Marokko ist und war immer schon ein tief mystisches Land. Trotz all seiner Modernität, seiner Wolkenkratzer und seiner modernen Kommunikationsmittel hat man hier das starke Gefühl, zu der Kultur der alten Welt zu gehören. Für die Romantiker spricht Marokko daher die Seele nicht weniger an als die Sinne. Wie Jérôme und Jean Tharaud 1930 über Fes schrieben: »Es ist die Stätte eines Wunders – nämlich des Auslöschens der Zeit.«

On Islamic Architecture in Morocco

Text: Serge Santelli
Illustrations: Hervé van der Straeten

Sur l'architecture islamique au Maroc

Texte: Serge Santelli
Illustrations: Hervé van der Straeten

Zur islamischen Architektur in Marokko

Text: Serge Santelli
Illustrationen: Hervé van der Straeten

Morocco undoubtedly has the richest and most remarkable urban architectural heritage in North West Africa. To be convinced of this, one need only walk through the narrow winding streets of the medina of Fez, with their high unbroken walls, enter the superb Merinid *medersas*, or visit the ancient houses and palaces of Marrakesh, and wander there among the *riyâds* with their many subtle fragrances. The ornamental splendour of the inner courtyards and their façades of ceramics, plaster and wood still bear witness to the splendour of the town-houses of imperial Morocco. Their beauty finds a less ostentatious and less ornate echo in the houses of small towns or villages.

The floor plan of a Moroccan house

The Moroccan house in the Arab-Islamic style is the most striking expression of a culture and a society which makes the private residence and its inner courtyard one of the most valued and important features of the medina or town. Its layout and architectural style are similar to those of Tunisian and Algerian houses. Indeed, the floor plan of the family house is basically the same throughout the Maghreb, whether it is a large residence, a palace, a modest working-class home, a town-house or rural dwelling. Rooms lead off an inner courtyard or garden, the central area onto which they open and which determines their shape. The walls of the courtyard are the principal façade of the house, as there is no formal frontage on the street. The streets form blank walls interrupted only by doors. The contrast between the silent architecture of the residential streets and alleys of the medina – "outside there are only blank, flat, unbroken, hostile walls" (Jean Gallotti) – and the extraordinary exuberance of the interior of the Moroccan house is therefore quite startling.

   In general the courtyard is surrounded on all four sides by the living rooms *(bayt)*, each of which occupies one wall of the courtyard. The rooms are not deep, measuring two or three metres, but they are very long since their length is generally equal to that of one side of the courtyard. One enters by a central doorway which divides the room into two narrow parts; a bed stands in an alcove at the far

Le Maroc possède certainement le patrimoine archi- tectural et urbain le plus riche et le plus remarquable du Maghreb. Pour s'en convaincre il suffit de se pro- mener dans les rues étroites et sinueuses aux hauts murs aveugles de la médina de Fès, de pénétrer dans ses superbes medersas mérinides, ou de visi- ter les anciennes maisons et palais de Marrakech, de flâner dans ses jardins *(riyâds)* aux parfums mul- tiples et raffinés. La splendeur décorative des cours intérieures aux façades revêtues de faïence, de plâtre et de bois, témoigne encore aujourd'hui de la ri- chesse passée des demeures des villes impériales marocaines. Richesse que l'on trouve également, avec moins d'ostentation et moins de décor, dans les maisons des petites villes ou villages du Maroc.

Le plan d'une maison marocaine

La maison marocaine de type arabo-islamique est l'expression la plus remarquable d'une culture et d'une société qui font de la maison, et de sa cour in- térieure, l'un des éléments les plus précieux et les plus importants de la médina. Elle partage avec les maisons tunisiennes et algériennes une même structure spatiale et une composition architecturale similaire. Il n'y a d'ailleurs qu'une seule famille typologique de maisons au Maghreb, que la maison soit une grande demeure, un palais, une maison modeste ou populaire, une habitation rurale ou une maison citadine. Les pièces sont distribuées par une cour ou un jardin intérieurs, espace central sur lequel elles s'ouvrent et s'ordonnancent. Leurs fa- çades sur cour constituent ainsi les façades princi- pales de la maison, qui ne possède, par conséquent, aucune véritable ouverture sur la rue. De l'extérieur, on ne voit qu'un mur aveugle percé de portes déco- rées. Le contraste est ainsi saisissant entre l'archi- tecture silencieuse des rues et ruelles résidentielles de la médina – «au dehors, il n'y a que des murs nus, plats, aveugles, hostiles» (Jean Gallotti) – et l'extraordinaire exubérance décorative des espaces intérieurs de la maison marocaine.

En général, la cour est entourée sur les quatre côtés par des pièces d'habitation *(bayt)* dont cha- cune occupe un côté entier de la cour. Les pièces sont peu profondes, entre deux et trois mètres, mais

Marokko besitzt zweifellos das reichste und ein- drucksvollste architektonische und städtebauliche Erbe des gesamten Maghreb. Davon überzeugt schon ein Spaziergang durch die Medina von Fes, ein Besuch der wundervollen merinidischen Meder- sen in dieser Stadt oder eines der alten Häuser und Palastgebäude von Marrakesch, ein Schlendern durch die *riyâds,* jene von zahllosen feinen Düften durchwehte Gärten. Die prachtvolle Ausstattung der Patios, deren Wände mit Fayencekacheln, Stuck oder Holz verkleidet sind, zeugt noch heute von der einstigen Pracht der Wohnhäuser in den marok- kanischen Königsstädten. Ähnlich prachtvolle Häu- ser findet man in den kleinen Ortschaften und Dörfern, wenn auch in weniger reich verzierter Form.

Der Grundriß eines marokkanischen Hauses

Das marokkanische Wohnhaus vom arabisch-islami- schen Typ ist beredter Ausdruck einer Kultur und einer Gesellschaft, für die das Haus und sein Innen- hof zu den kostbarsten und wichtigsten Elementen der Medina gehören. Es weist die gleiche Raumauf- teilung und architektonische Anlage wie tunesische und algerische Wohnhäuser auf. Im übrigen gibt es im Maghreb typologisch nur einen Grundriß für ein Familienhaus, das sich als großes Wohnhaus, als Palast, als bescheidenes oder volkstümliches Ge- bäude, als ländliches oder städtisches Haus darstel- len kann. Die Räume sind um einen Innenhof oder -garten herum angeordnet; auch die Fenster öffnen sich auf das innere Zentrum. Die Wände des Innen- hofs bilden deshalb die eigentlichen Fassaden des Hauses, das folgerichtig zur Straße hin keine deko- rative Frontseite hat. Die Außenwand ist fensterlos und bei öffentlichen wie privaten Gebäuden nur durch die Eingangstüren unterbrochen. Da nun im Gefüge arabischer Städte die Innenfassaden der Ge- bäude ihre Hauptfassaden darstellen, besteht ein starker Kontrast zwischen der verhaltenen Architek- tur der Straßen und Gassen im Wohngebiet der Medina – »außen gibt es nur nackte, flache, fenster- lose, feindliche Mauern« (Jean Gallotti) – und der überaus dekorativen Pracht der Innenräume marok- kanischer Wohnhäuser.

end of one of these. Opposite the entrance is the *bahou*, a kind of recess built into the thickness of the wall and in line with the entrance. Furnished with couches on three sides, it acts as a day-room and reception area. During the day, when the room is no longer occupied by those who slept there at night, the door onto the courtyard stays open. Sitting with his guests in the *bahou* opposite the entrance, the owner can admire his house through the "door that is always open to the imagination" (André Ravereau). Almost all the façades would be visible through this door and the two windows which open onto the courtyard.

The courtyard *(wast ad-dar)* is regular in shape, square or rectangular. In a typical Moroccan house there are no doors between rooms. To go from one room to another one must cross the courtyard. This enhances the significance of the courtyard whose functions and existence are ever-present in the life of the house. The service rooms – kitchen, hammam (if the owner is rich enough) and laundry (more of a store-room) – are generally on the side of the courtyard nearest the street. The main room, the biggest and generally the most ornate – it often possesses a *bahou* opposite the door – is found furthest from the entrance and public area.

The entrance to the house is a very important room whose angled configuration allows the family's privacy to be respected. In Rabat, this room, known as the *setwan*, is a long corridor bordered on either side by an arcade of engaged columns, that ensures there is no direct line of sight into the courtyard. In this room the owner can receive guests without disturbing the private life of the house. This angled disposition allows it to act as a discreet but efficient filter between public life in the street and the domestic life of the residence. The distinction is essential in Moroccan town-life. The visitor is always amazed by the contrast between the neglected, austere aspect of the street or *impasse* and the charm and serenity that prevail within the house. The contrast is even more marked where the inner courtyard is replaced by a *riyâd,* with its trees and central fountain, its profusion of scents and ripple of running water.

très larges, puisque leur plus longue dimension correspond en général à celle du côté de la cour. On y pénètre par une porte centrale qui divise la salle en deux parties étroites de part et d'autre, le fond étant occupé par un lit niché dans une alcôve. Face à l'entrée se trouve le *bahou*, sorte de renfoncement plus ou moins profond construit dans l'épaisseur du mur. Meublé de banquettes sur les trois côtés, il sert de lieu de séjour et de réception. Dans la journée, quand la chambre n'est plus occupée par ceux qui y ont dormi pendant la nuit, la porte reste ouverte sur la cour. Assis avec ses invités dans le *bahou*, face à l'entrée, le propriétaire peut admirer, à travers la «porte pensée ouverte» (André Ravereau), sa maison dont il peut voir la presque totalité des façades.

La cour *(wast ad-dar)* est de forme régulière, carrée ou rectangulaire. Remarquons que dans la maison marocaine typique les pièces ne communiquent pas et qu'il faut nécessairement traverser la cour pour aller de l'une à l'autre, ce qui rend la présence, l'usage et la signification de la cour extrêmement importants. Les espaces de service – la cuisine, le hammam (quand le propriétaire est suffisamment riche) et la buanderie (plutôt un débarras) – sont en général du côté de l'entrée, proches de la rue. La pièce principale, la plus grande et en général la plus décorée – se trouve ainsi éloignée de l'entrée et de l'espace public.

L'entrée de la maison est une pièce très importante, dont la configuration en chicane permet de ménager l'intimité visuelle de la famille. A Rabat, cette pièce que l'on appelle le *setwan* est un long corridor, bordé sur chaque côté de colonnes adossées supportant des arcades, qui permet l'accès coudé à la cour. C'est dans cette pièce que le propriétaire peut recevoir des étrangers sans perturber la vie privée de la maison. Sa disposition spatiale est importante pour la maison traditionnelle puisqu'elle constitue une espèce de filtre, discret mais efficace, entre la vie publique de la rue et la vie domestique de la demeure. Cette distinction est essentielle dans la ville marocaine dont le visiteur est toujours ébloui par le contraste existant entre le caractère austère et délaissé de la rue ou de l'impasse, et le charme, la sérénité qui se dégagent de l'inté-

Der Patio ist in der Regel auf vier Seiten von den Wohnräumen *(bayt)* umgeben, die jeweils eine ganze Hofseite einnehmen. Die Zimmer sind nicht sehr tief, lediglich zwei bis drei Meter, jedoch sehr lang, da ihre Ausdehnung in jener Richtung meist den Abmessungen der jeweiligen Hofseite entspricht. Man betritt den Raum durch eine mittig gelegene Tür, die ihn zu beiden Seiten in zwei schmale Bereiche unterteilt; im hinterem Teil steht jeweils ein Bett in einem Alkoven. Der Zimmertür genau gegenüber liegt der *bahou*, eine mehr oder weniger ausgedehnte Vertiefung in der dem Eingang entgegengesetzten Außenmauer. Der *bahou* ist entlang seinen drei Seiten mit Bänken bestückt und dient als Wohn- und Empfangsraum. Tagsüber, wenn ein Zimmer nicht als Schlafzimmer genutzt wird, bleibt die Tür zum Innenhof hin offen. Der Hausherr sitzt mit seinen Gästen im *bahou* gegenüber der Eingangstür und kann durch die »Tür des offenen Denkens« (André Ravereau) sein Haus bewundern: durch die Tür und die beiden Fenster zum Patio kann man praktisch alle Fassaden sehen.

Der Innenhof *(wast ad-dar)* weist eine gleichmäßige quadratische oder rechteckige Form auf. Im typischen marokkanischen Wohnhaus fällt auf, daß die Räume nicht miteinander verbunden sind, so daß man den Hof überqueren muß, um von einem Zimmer ins andere zu gelangen. Dadurch werden Existenz, Sinn und Zweck sowie die Bedeutung des Hofes überaus deutlich. Die Nutzräume – die Küche, der *hammam* (wenn der Hausherr reich genug ist) und die Waschküche (eher ein Vorratsraum) – sind meist auf der Eingangsseite in der Nähe der Straße untergebracht. Der wichtigste, größte und oft der am schönsten geschmückte Raum – meist derjenige, der einen *bahou* gegenüber der Tür aufweist – liegt somit weit entfernt vom Hauseingang und vom öffentlichen Lebensraum. Die Eingangshalle des Hauses ist ein sehr wichtiger Raum; durch ihre versetzte Anordnung bleibt die Intimität der Familie optisch gewahrt.

In Rabat bildet der Raum, den man hier *setwan* nennt, einen langen, zu beiden Seiten von Halbsäulen mit Arkaden gesäumten Korridor, durch den man den Innenhof um die Ecke betritt. Hier kann

The courtyard is the most significant part of the Moroccan house, as indeed it is of all Arab-Islamic buildings. Mosques, *fondouks* and *medersas* are all constructed around a central courtyard onto which the building's principal rooms open. The hammam itself does not have an internal courtyard and is constructed around a rest-room with a similar layout to that of the courtyard. In the house, the court is often surrounded by a colonnade, each side consisting of three arches, the central arch being higher and wider. The oldest colonnades have flat lintels which are sometimes corbelled. The more recent have either keel or horseshoe arches. Where the house has two stories, as many 19th-century houses do, the first-floor colonnade is identical. The gallery that is created as a result of this ensures that access to the rooms is protected from sun and rain. In the absence of a colonnade, the façades of the rooms are sheltered by a wooden canopy which juts out over the courtyard. The repetition of these architectural features – colonnades, arches, canopies – on all four sides emphasises the inward and intimate character of the courtyard. But this is not complete without ornaments, and the house is unfinished if craftsmen have not covered the walls with those magnificent materials, ceramic tiles and sculpted plaster.

Decoration

Decorative surfaces are essential to the Moroccan house. They create a distinction between the unembellished dwellings of the poor and the homes of the rich, in which every inner wall, floor and ceiling is sheathed in colour and ornaments. A house can seem almost saturated by this ornamental cladding and not one inner wall of the main rooms of the house is spared this treatment. External walls are whitewashed a dazzling white, or, in the South, covered in cob, which gives a smooth, austere appearance. Interior walls are covered with rich, bright materials: mosaics, sculpted plaster and painted wood. The courtyard is paved with white or grey flagstones whose joints are embellished with bands of polychrome mosaic tiles. Floors are covered with mosaic tiles. The walls of courtyard and room alike are invariably decorated with the same repetitive vertical

rieur de la maison. Ce contraste est encore plus fort lorsque la cour intérieure est remplacée par un jardin *(riyâd)* avec ses arbres et sa vasque centrale, ses senteurs et le murmure de l'eau qui coule.

La cour est l'espace fondamental de la maison marocaine comme elle l'est de tout édifice arabo-musulman. Mosquées, medersas, fondouks: toutes sont des édifices qui se structurent autour d'une cour centrale sur laquelle s'ouvrent les espaces principaux du bâtiment. Le hammam lui-même, qui ne possède pas de cour intérieure, se déploie autour d'une salle de repos dont la configuration rappelle celle d'une cour. Dans la maison celle-ci est souvent entourée d'un portique dont chaque côté est composé de trois arcades, l'arcade centrale étant plus large et plus haute. Les plus anciens portiques sont à linteaux droits, quelquefois à encorbellements. Les plus récents sont formés d'arcs ogivaux outrepassés ou à retombées verticales. Lorsque la maison possède un étage, ce qui est souvent le cas dans les maisons construites au siècle passé, le portique du niveau supérieur est identique à celui du rez-de-chaussée. La galerie ainsi créée permet de protéger les chambres du soleil ou de la pluie. En l'absence de portique, les façades des pièces sont abritées par un auvent en bois qui déborde largement sur la cour. Portique, arcades, auvents, autant d'éléments architecturaux qui, en se répétant sur les quatres côtés de la cour, renforcent le caractère central, intérieur et intime, de la maison. Mais celle-ci n'est pas complète si elle n'est pas décorée et la maison n'est pas finie si les artisans n'ont pas recouvert les murs des matériaux somptueux que sont la céramique ou le plâtre ciselé.

Décoration

Les revêtements décoratifs sont essentiels à la maison marocaine. Ils permettent de différencier la maison du pauvre, sans décor, et la maison du riche, dont toutes les parois, sols et murs, sont systématiquement recouvertes d'une peau décorative. Ce type de revêtement a une telle importance que la maison paraît saturée par le décor, aucune des parois des pièces nobles de la maison n'échappant à cette luxueuse nécessité de parement. A l'ex-

der Hausherr Fremde begrüßen, ohne daß die Privatsphäre des Hauses gestört würde. Der Flur ist ein wichtiges Element des traditionellen Hauses, eine Art Filter, der ebenso diskret wie wirkungsvoll zwischen das öffentliche Leben auf der Straße und das häusliche Leben im Inneren des Gebäudes geschoben wird. Diese Unterscheidung ist für die marokkanische Stadt von wesentlicher Bedeutung. Der Besucher ist stets verblüfft über den Gegensatz zwischen dem strengen Eindruck, den die leicht heruntergekommene Straße oder Gasse machen, und dem Charme und der Heiterkeit im Inneren der Häuser. Dieser Kontrast ist noch ausgeprägter, wenn das Haus anstelle des Innenhofes einen Garten mit Bäumen und einer Brunnenschale in der Mitte besitzt, der mit Düften und plätscherndem Wasser betört.

Der Patio ist, wie bei allen arabisch-islamischen Gebäuden, auch beim marokkanischen Wohnhaus das wesentliche Element. Moscheen, Medersen und *fondouks* sind durchweg Gebäude, deren wichtigste Räume sich zu einem zentralen Innenhof hin öffnen. Auch der *hammam,* der selbst keinen Innenhof besitzt, ist um einen Ruheraum herum angeordnet, dessen Anlage in etwa der eines Patios entspricht. Im Haus ist der Innenhof meist von einer Säulenhalle umgeben, die auf jeder Seite drei Arkaden aufweist. Der mittlere Bogen ist jeweils am breitesten und höchsten. Die ältesten Säulenhallen besitzen gerade Türstürze, manchmal mit vorkragenden Teilen; die neueren bestehen dagegen aus Hufeisen- oder Spitzbögen mit vertikalen Anfangssteinen. Ist das Haus zweigeschossig, was bei Häusern aus dem letzten Jahrhundert durchaus vorkommt, entspricht die Säulenhalle in der oberen Etage genau der im Erdgeschoß. Die so entstandene Galerie schirmt die Wohnräume gegen Sonne und Regen ab. Fehlt eine solche Säulenhalle, sind die Räume durch ein weit in den Innenhof hineinragendes Wetterdach aus Holz geschützt. Der Säulengang mit Arkaden und das Wetterdach sind architektonische Elemente, die sich auf allen vier Hofseiten wiederholen und den zentralen, nach innen gerichteten, intimen Charakter des Hauses unterstreichen. Vollständig ist ein Haus jedoch erst dann, wenn es verziert

patterns. The lower part of the wall is covered with mosaic tiles *(zelliges)*, the upper part with a cornice of sculpted plaster *(tagguebbast)* and the crowning glory – the cornice and ceiling – is made of painted wood. The middle part of the wall, between the *zelliges* and the plaster, is left plain, smoothed over and painted white. Sculpted plaster is very often used around doors and windows, on the inside edges of arches, and for the capitals. Above each door, one or three little vaulted lattice-work windows *(chamachât)* in carved plaster ensure ventilation. Also worthy of note is the wrought ironwork used to protect the courtyard windows and for the balustrades of the first-floor colonnade.

The motifs used in the *zelliges* and sculpted plaster are always geometrical and abstract. They are of complex composition and use either *testir,* geometrical interlacing radiating from a central star-shape (the »Prophet's spider-web«), *tourik*, plant-like ornamentation composed of floral interlacing, foliage or palmettes, or *mukarna,* the famous bee-hive pattern, made in plaster to decorate the intrados of arches and the squinches of cupolas. The techniques of the craftsmen are ancient, passed down and perfected from generation to generation. In *zelliges* the artist uses pieces of ceramic broken to fit standardised geometrical designs with evocative names such as the soldier, the olive-pit, the fig-leaf, the snail etc. The panels are constructed on a board on the ground, in reverse, before being applied to the wall. At the end of the 19th century craftsmen had attained remarkable virtuosity and made astonishing advances in technique. This is the more surprising since the country, its economy and crafts were generally written off as decadent at the turn of the century, and its artistic traditions described as moribund. Plaster is worked *in situ* and the sculptures are angled gently downward into the spectator's line of sight in order to exhibit the depth of the motif.

Garden and fountain

Finally, no description of the traditional Moroccan house is complete without mentioning the importance of fountains and gardens. In the grand houses

térieur les murs sont régulièrement enduits d'une chaux à la blancheur éclatante, ou, dans les régions du sud, d'un mortier de terre à l'aspect lisse et austère. A l'intérieur, les murs sont recouverts de matériaux à l'aspect riche et éclatant: carreaux de mosaïque, plâtre sculpté et bois peint. Le sol de la cour est revêtu de dalles de marbre blanc ou gris aux joints rehaussés de bandes de carreaux de mosaïque polychrome. Les sols des chambres sont recouverts de carreaux de mosaïque. Les murs de la cour et des chambres sont recouverts par un registre vertical décoratif toujours identique: dans la partie basse des carreaux de mosaïque (zelliges), dans la partie haute une corniche de plâtre ciselé (tagguebbast) couronnée par une corniche. La couronne, entre la corniche et le plafond, est en bois peint. La partie médiane du mur, entre le zelliges et le plâtre, est laissée sans revêtement, lissée et peinte en blanc. Le plâtre sculpté est largement utilisé autour des portes et des fenêtres, à l'intrados des arcs et pour les chapiteaux. Au-dessus et dans l'axe de la porte de la chambre un ou trois petits claustra cintrés, les chamachât, assurent la ventilation haute de la chambre. Ils sont en plâtre ciselé. Il ne faut pas oublier de mentionner le fer forgé, utilisé pour protéger les fenêtres sur cour et réaliser les balustrades du portique de l'étage.

Les motifs décoratifs utilisés dans les revêtements de zelliges et de plâtre ciselé sont toujours géométriques et abstraits. Leur composition est complexe et utilise soit les testir, entrelacs géométriques irradiant autour d'une étoile centrale (la «toile d'araignée du Prophète»), soit les tourik, ornements de caractère végétal composés d'entrelacs floraux, de rinceaux ou de palmettes, soit encore les très célèbres nids d'abeille en plâtre, mukarnas, qui décorent l'intrados des arcs et les trompes de certaines coupoles. Les techniques des artisans sont très anciennes, transmises et perfectionnées de génération en génération. Pour les zelliges, l'artisan utilise des morceaux de céramique cassés selon des dessins géométriques spécifiques aux appellations évocatrices: soldat, noyau d'olive, feuille de figuier, escargot, etc. Les panneaux sont composés sur le sol, à l'envers sur une planche, avant d'être dressés

ist. Es gilt also erst dann als fertig, wenn Handwerker die Wände mit edlen Materialien wie Keramikkacheln oder feinen Stuckornamenten überzogen haben.

Ornamentale Verzierungen

Schmuckverkleidungen sind ein zentrales Element marokkanischer Wohnhäuser. Sie bilden das wichtigste Unterscheidungsmerkmal zwischen den schmucklosen Wohnstätten der Armen und den Häusern der Reichen, bei denen alle Wand- und Fußbodenflächen mit einem dekorativen Kleid überzogen sind. Eine solche Verzierung ist so wichtig, daß das Haus wie mit Mustern überschüttet aussieht. In den Repräsentationsräumen des Hauses bleibt keine Wand von diesem Schmuck ausgespart. Die Außenseite des Gebäudes wird in der Regel blendendweiß gekalkt oder, im Süden des Landes, mit Lehmmörtel beworfen und wirkt glatt und streng. Im Inneren jedoch sind die Wände mit prächtigen, glänzenden Werkstoffen überzogen, seien es Mosaiksteine, Kacheln, Stuckornamente oder bemaltes Holz. Der Fußboden des Hofes ist mit weißem oder grauem Marmor gefliest, wobei die Fugen mit bunten Mosaikbändern betont werden. In den Zimmern sind die Böden mit Mosaiken versehen. Die Wände werden sowohl im Hof als auch in den Zimmern stets in der gleichen vertikalen Abfolge verziert: Im unteren Teil ist die Wand mit Mosaikkacheln (zelliges) verkleidet, im oberen Teil befindet sich ein Kranzgesims mit fein ausgeschnittenen Stuckornamenten (tagguebbast). Für den Abschluß zwischen Kranzgesims und Zimmerdecke verwendet man bemaltes Holz. Der mittlere Teil der Wand zwischen zelliges und Stuckornamenten wird ohne Verkleidung belassen, lediglich geglättet und weiß gestrichen. Stuckornamente finden sich vor allem auch noch rund um Türen und Fenster, in den Bogenlaibungen und an den Kapitellen. Symmetrisch oberhalb der Zimmertür sind ein bis drei kleine Belüftungssteine mit Rundbögen angebracht, die aus Stuck gefertigten chamachât. Sie sorgen für die Belüftung des Raumes von oben. Nicht zu vergessen sind überdies die schmiedeeisernen Geländer, mit denen die Fenster zum Hof und der Säulengang im ersten Stock gesichert werden.

there is either a fountain built against one of the courtyard walls, richly decorated with *zelliges* and sculpted plaster, or a marble fountain basin in the centre of the courtyard, of which the tiled bottom in polychrome geometrical motifs creates a jewelled effect. Often the flagstoned courtyard is replaced by a *riyâd* crossed by two paths which cut the courtyard area into four equal parterres. In grand houses and palaces, the *riyâd* is a walled garden that adjoins the main residence and forms an addition to the central courtyard. In this form it is a pleasure garden, generally oblong in shape, on the short sides of which is a building that consists of a room fronted with a portico of three arches or more. The room, a sort of pavilion, often possesses a *bahou* where the owner and his guests can sit and admire the magnificent view through the arches onto the garden. Between garden and pavilion is a flagstoned platform. In the centre of this, water gushes into a fountain bowl or basin *(sahrîdj)* that reflects the garden's beautiful architecture.

Four parterres of flowers and trees, set lower than the transverse paths which cross it, fill the garden. They are planted with orange and lemon trees, pomegranates and figs, and various scented plants such as mint, geranium, basil and jasmine. The visitor can therefore wander about, slightly above the garden, and have direct visual and olfactory contact with the fruits and flowers of the season. A fountain, protected by a kiosk or painted wooden bower, occupies the centre of the garden where the main pathways cross. Some of the larger palaces feature isolated pavilions *(menzeh)* of one or two floors, Arab "follies" that consist of a main room and a few service rooms. These constructions have no purpose other than to enhance the enjoyment of the beauty of the place and the freshness of the air. *Riyâds* of this kind are found only in Morocco and in Andalusia.

Historical changes
This entire domestic world, enclosed and protected until the turn of the century, was shattered by the arrival of the French in the early 1900s. The rapid construction of new European towns, the importing

sur le mur. A la fin du XIXe siècle les artisans avaient atteint un degré de virtuosité remarquable et leurs techniques avaient progressé de manière étonnante. D'autant plus étonnante que les traditions artistiques étaient soi-disant moribondes. Le plâtre était ciselé in situ et les sculptures étaient creusées en biais, dans le sens de l'axe visuel du spectateur, afin de mieux révéler la profondeur du motif.

Le jardin et l'eau
Enfin, on ne peut décrire la maison marocaine traditionnelle sans parler de l'importance de l'eau et du jardin. Dans les belles demeures il y a soit une fontaine adossée à un mur de la cour, richement décorée de zelliges et de plâtre sculpté, soit une vasque-fontaine en marbre au centre de la cour, merveilleusement mise en valeur par le sol de céramique aux motifs géométriques polychromes. Souvent la cour dallée est remplacée par un *riyâd* traversé par deux allées médianes qui découpent l'espace de la cour en quatre parterres égaux. Dans les riches demeures et les palais le *riyâd* est un jardin clos qui jouxte la demeure principale et s'ajoute à la cour centrale de la maison. Il s'agit alors d'un jardin d'agrément de forme le plus souvent oblongue, dont les petits côtés sont occupés par un corps de logis composé d'une pièce précédée d'un portique à trois arcades ou plus. La pièce, l'équivalent d'un pavillon d'agrément, possède souvent un *bahou* où le propriétaire et ses invités peuvent s'asseoir et admirer à travers les arcades du portique la perspective splendide du jardin. Entre celui-ci et le pavillon se développe un terre-plein dallé au centre duquel l'eau jaillit d'une vasque-fontaine ou d'un bassin *(sahrîdj)* dans lequel se reflète la belle architecture du *riyâd*. Quatre parterres occupent le jardin en contrebas des allées qui le traversent selon ses axes transversaux. Ils sont plantés d'orangers, de citronniers, de grenadiers et de figuiers. La menthe, le géranium, le basilic ou le jasmin y forment des tapis subtilement parfumés. Le visiteur peut ainsi se promener en surplombant le jardin et avoir un contact visuel et olfactif direct avec les fruits et les fleurs de la saison. Une fontaine protégée par un kiosque ou une tonnelle en bois peint occupe le centre du jardin, au croisement des

Die Motive, die bei der *zelliges*-Verkleidung und bei den Stuckornamenten verwendet werden, sind immer geometrisch und abstrakt. Ihr komplexer Aufbau umfaßt entweder *testir*, geometrisches, von einem zentralen Stern ausstrahlendes Flechtwerk (das »Spinnennetz des Propheten«), oder *tourik*, Muster aus floralem Flechtwerk, Ranken und Palmetten, oder aber die berühmten Stalaktit- oder Wabenmuster, *mukarnas* genannt, die – aus Stuck modelliert – Bogenlaibungen und Trompen vieler Kuppeln überziehen. Die Techniken der Handwerker sind uralt und wurden von Generation zu Generation tradiert und vervollkommnet. Für *zelliges* setzt der Mosaikleger die in kleine Stücke geschlagenen Keramikkacheln zu vorgegebenen geometrischen Mustern zusammen, die bezeichnende Namen tragen: Soldat, Olivenkern, Feigenblatt, Schnecke und so weiter. Die Mosaike werden mit der Rückseite nach oben auf einer Holzplatte, die auf dem Boden liegt, zusammengesetzt und dann erst an der Wand befestigt. Ende des 19. Jahrhunderts hatten die Mosaikleger mit ihren fortschrittlichen Techniken eine bemerkenswerte Virtuosität erlangt. Um so befremdlicher ist die Tatsache, daß das Land, seine Wirtschaft und sein Handwerk Ende des letzten Jahrhunderts meist als dekadenter Staat mit erlöschenden Kunsttraditionen beschrieben wurde. Die Stuckreliefs werden *in situ* ausgeschnitten und die modellierten Ornamente vom Blickpunkt des Betrachters aus abgeschrägt, so daß die Tiefenwirkung des Motivs besser zur Geltung kommt.

Garten und Wasser

Bei der Beschreibung des traditionellen marokkanischen Wohnhauses darf eine Bemerkung über die eminente Bedeutung des Wassers und des Gartens nicht fehlen. Vornehme Häuser besitzen entweder einen mit *zelliges* oder Stuckornamenten reich verzierten Brunnen, der an einer Wand des Innenhofes angebracht ist, oder eine Marmorschale mit Springbrunnen mitten im Hof, der mit den polychromen geometrischen Mustern seiner Fayencefliesen gewissermaßen das Schmuckkästchen dafür bildet. Oft findet sich anstelle eines gefliesten Hofes ein Garten *(riyâd)*, der von zwei mittig verlaufenden

of new cultural models, new architectural styles and new ways of life presented as superior to those of traditional Moroccan culture, eventually led to the decline of, and some degree of disaffection with, the Arab town and its buildings. And this despite the sensitive and respectful policies of Marshal Louis Hubert Lyautey, Resident General from 1912 to 1925, which favoured the separate development of new towns and the existing Arab towns in the hope of protecting the latter from the horrors of modernity. While the new towns were being rapidly built, major Arab buildings were restored by the Service des Arts Indigènes (Department for Endemic Art). However, the impressive scale of new construction and the economic and financial investment made during the first decades of the Protectorate concentrated all energies and skills in the new towns, to the detriment of the medinas that were left to stagnate and decline. The old towns became the poor quarters of the contemporary Moroccan town.

The architecture created in the new towns under the direction of Henri Prost, Director of the Service Central des plans de ville (central town-planning service), was entirely Western. New public amenities or private blocks were constructed in continuous lines along the boulevards, streets, squares or gardens that formed the civic framework of the town's architecture. Imposing, indeed monumental, façades governed the new relationship between buildings and public space, a space now representative of the power of the "protecting" foreign state. New buildings housed the new offices and modern institutions of the country. Rental properties and suburban residential villas, banks, shops, post-offices, stations, town halls and administrative buildings constituted so many new architectural styles that demonstrated not only the economic and political, but also the cultural power and economic superiority of the coloniser. The new town, with its extrovert façades and rectilinear avenues, was the opposite of the Arab town, built around its internal courtyards and gardens. The novelty of the modern town fascinated Moroccans. For many the medina became an urban anachronism, unsuited to the contemporary world. Today, their original owners

deux allées transversales. Dans certains grands palais on trouve des pavillons isolés *(menzehs)* de plain-pied ou à étage, sortes de «folies» arabes qui comprennent une pièce principale desservie par quelques pièces de service. Ces petits bâtiments ne sont bien sûr utilisés que pour jouir de la beauté du lieu ou de la fraîcheur de l'air. Le *riyâd* est véritablement typique du Maroc et de l'Andalousie.

Transformations historiques
Cet univers domestique, clos et protégé jusqu'à la fin du siècle dernier a été bouleversé par l'arrivée des Français au début de ce siècle. La prolifération des nouvelles villes européennes, l'importation de modèles culturels inconnus jusqu'alors, de typologies architecturales occidentales et de modes de vie présentés comme supérieurs à ceux de la culture traditionnelle marocaine, ont favorisé la décadence et la désaffection relative de la ville arabe et de ses édifices. Et ceci malgré la politique sensible et respectueuse du maréchal Louis Hubert Lyautey, résident général de 1912 à 1925, qui consistait à favoriser le développement des villes nouvelles à côté des villes arabes existantes en vue de protéger celles-ci des affres de la modernité. Pendant que les villes neuves se construisent rapidement les grands monuments arabes sont classés, comme les nombreuses medersas de Fès restaurées sous la responsabilité du Service des Arts Indigènes. Mais l'ampleur impressionnante des constructions neuves et les investissements réalisés durant les premières décennies du Protectorat auront pour effet de concentrer toutes les énergies et les savoir-faire dans les villes nouvelles, au détriment des médinas, vouées à la stagnation et au déclin. La création des villes neuves sonnait le glas des villes anciennes condamnées à devenir les quartiers pauvres de la ville contemporaine marocaine.

L'architecture créée dans les villes neuves, sous la direction de Henri Prost, directeur du Service Central des plans de ville, est totalement occidentale. Les nouveaux équipements publics ou immeubles privés sont construits en alignement sur des boulevards, rues, places ou jardins qui constituent la trame publique de l'architecture de la ville.

Alleen so durchschnitten wird, daß er in vier gleich
große Beete unterteilt ist. Bei reichen Häusern und
Palästen ist der *riyâd* ein an das Hauptgebäude
angrenzender eingezäunter Garten, zusätzlich zum
Innenhof des Hauses. In diesen Fällen handelt es
sich um einen meist länglichen Ziergarten, der an
den Schmalseiten von einem Gebäudetrakt mit
einem Raum und einer davorliegenden Säulenhalle
aus drei oder mehr Arkaden begrenzt wird. Jener
Raum dient als Gartenhaus und ist oft mit einem
bahou ausgestattet, von dem aus der Hausherr mit
seinen Gästen durch die Arkaden der Säulenhalle
hindurch den herrlichen Blick auf den Garten genießen kann.

  Zwischen dem Garten und diesem Pavillon
liegt ein gefliester Streifen; in seinem Zentrum befindet sich eine Brunnenschale oder ein Wasserbecken
mit einem Springbrunnen *(sahrîdj)*, in dem sich die
hübsche Anlage des *riyâd* spiegelt.

  Etwas tiefer als die Wege, die den Garten in
den Querachsen durchziehen, liegen vier Beete mit
Blumen und Bäumen. Die Bepflanzung besteht aus
Orangen-, Zitronen-, Granatapfel- und Feigenbäu-
men, darunter duftende Pflanzen wie Minze, Gera-
nien, Basilikum oder Jasmin. Der Besucher kann so
– je nach Jahreszeit – die Blüten und Früchte von
einer leicht erhöhten Warte aus bewundern und
ihren Duft genießen. In der Mitte des Gartens liegt
im Kreuzungspunkt der beiden Alleen ein Springbrunnen, der durch einen Pavillon oder eine Laube
aus bemaltem Holz geschützt ist. Bei einigen der
größten Paläste finden sich einzelstehende ein-
oder zweigeschossige Gartenhäuser *(menzehs)*,
eine Art arabisches Lustschlößchen mit einem
Hauptraum und einigen Nebenräumen. Die *riyâds*
trifft man ausschließlich in Marokko und in An-
dalusien an.

Historische Veränderungen

Jenes häusliche Universum, das bis zum Ende des
letzten Jahrhunderts in sich geschlossen und geschützt war, wurde durch die Ankunft der Franzosen
zu Beginn unseres Jahrhunderts aus der Bahn geworfen. Die rasche Entstehung neuer Städte nach
europäischem Vorbild, die Übernahme neuer kultu-

long departed, many medinas are lived in by people from the country or suburbs who, in impoverished and over-crowded conditions, occupy the old palaces and historic residences.

The architecture of the Protectorate's new towns was essentially modernist in idiom and made very little reference to Moroccan traditions. The architectural orientalism so frequently encountered in Algeria or Tunisia at the beginning of the century remained the exception in Morocco. Among such exceptions we may cite Lyautey's Resident's Palace, that was built in 1922 by the architect Albert Laprade, well-known for his sketches. His Moroccan salon, with its walls decorated with *zelliges* and its dome of painted wood is a veritable masterpiece of Orientalism, foreshadowing the many contemporary examples of this style in Morocco. However, the large-scale exodus from the medinas by Moroccan families, who have chosen to live in flats or villas in the new suburbs, has not meant the wholesale abandonment of Moroccan architecture. On the contrary: royal directives and the recent publication of André Paccard's monumental work on Moroccan crafts have paved the way for a vigorous renaissance of Moroccan decorative techniques and traditions, making Moroccan craftsmen the most competent and sought-after specialists of Islamic art in the world. It is paradoxical that at a time when so many traditional buildings and complexes, notably the splendid casbahs of South Morocco, are allowed to deteriorate or even disappear, vast numbers of villas are built in the suburbs with salons copiously decorated with *zelliges* and sculpted plaster.

Return to traditional houses

This return to traditional embellishment is paralleled by a predominantly upper middle-class clientele, often of European origin, who are anxious to spend parts of the year in fine residences in the Moroccan style. This trend falls within the Orientalist tradition of the last century, when painters, writers and travellers – Eugène Delacroix, Jean-Léon Gérôme, Pierre Loti, Alexandre Dumas, Guy de Maupassant,

Des façades imposantes, voire monumentales, règlent les nouvelles relations entre l'édifice et l'espace public, véritable espace de représentation du pays Protecteur. De nouveaux édifices accueillent les fonctions et institutions modernes du pays. Les immeubles de rapport et les villas des quartiers résidentiels, les banques et les magasins, la poste, la gare, l'hôtel de ville et tous les bâtiments administratifs sont autant de nouveaux types architecturaux qui témoignent de la puissance et de la domination non seulement économique et politique, mais surtout culturelle, du colonisateur. La ville neuve, avec ses façades extraverties et ses avenues rectilignes, est l'inverse de la ville arabe, refermée sur ses cours et jardins intérieurs. Sa nouveauté fascinera les Marocains pour qui la médina ne sera plus qu'un archaïsme urbain totalement inadapté au monde contemporain. Aujourd'hui, délaissées par leurs propriétaires, les médinas ne sont plus habitées que par des populations d'origine rurale ou suburbaine qui occupent, dans des conditions difficiles de surpeuplement, les anciens palais et demeures historiques.

L'architecture de la ville neuve du Protectorat fait très peu référence à l'art marocain, dont seuls quelques éléments sont utilisés dans un langage architectural de facture moderniste. L'influence orientaliste, si marquée en Algérie ou en Tunisie au début du siècle, reste marginale au Maroc. Parmi ces édifices il faut citer la résidence générale de Lyautey construite en 1922 par l'architecte Albert Laprade, l'auteur talentueux des fameux croquis. Son salon marocain au revêtement de zelliges avec sa coupole de bois peint traditionnel est un véritable chef-d'œuvre orientaliste, qui préfigure les nombreuses réalisations contemporaines de ce style au Maroc.

L'abandon massif des médinas par les familles marocaines, qui ont choisi d'habiter immeubles ou villas des nouveaux quartiers, ne signifie pas l'abandon définitif du style marocain en architecture, au contraire. Les directives royales et la publication récente du livre monumental d'André Paccard sur l'artisanat marocain ont fait renaître les techniques et les traditions décoratives marocaines, si bien que les artisans marocains sont aujourd'hui

reller Vorbilder, neuer Architekturmodelle und neuer
Lebensweisen, die als der traditionellen marokkanischen Kultur überlegen dargestellt wurden, begün-
stigten den mehr oder weniger rapiden Verfall der
arabischen Stadt und ihrer Gebäude, und dies trotz
der einfühlsamen, respektvollen Politik Marschall
Louis Hubert Lyauteys, der von 1912 bis 1925 Gene-
ralresident von Marokko war. Er förderte die Entstehung neuer Städte, abseits der existierenden arabischen Orte, die er vor den schlechten Einflüssen der
Moderne zu bewahren hoffte. Während rasch neue
Stadtviertel gebaut wurden, wurden die großen arabischen Bauwerke unter der staatlichen Aufsicht des
Service des Arts Indigènes (Amt für einheimische
Kunst) restauriert. Die beeindruckenden Ausmaße
der neuen Gebäude und die wirtschaftlichen wie
finanziellen Investitionen, die während der ersten
Jahrzehnte des Protektorats gemacht wurden, hatten
allerdings eine Konzentration aller Energien und des
gesamten Know-hows auf die neuen Viertel zur
Folge, zum Nachteil der Medinas, die man der Stagnation und dem Verfall preisgab. Die Gründung
neuer Städte läutete das Ende der alten ein, die mitt-
lerweile zu den Armenvierteln der heutigen Städte
verkommen sind.

        Unter der Aufsicht von Henri Prost, dem
Leiter des Service Central des plans de ville (Amt für
Stadtplanung), entstanden ganz und gar westlich
ausgerichtete Neustädte. Moderne öffentliche und
private Gebäude wurden Wand an Wand entlang der
Boulevards, Straßen, Plätze oder Gärten errichtet,
die das sichtbare Raster der städtischen Architektur
bildeten. Imposante, oft sogar monumentale Fassaden bestimmten die neuen Beziehungen zwischen
Gebäude und öffentlichem Raum, der zu einer
Bühne für die Selbstdarstellung des Protektorlandes
wurde. Neue Gebäude dienten neuen Funktionen
und den modernen Institutionen des Landes. Mietshäuser und Eigenheime in den Wohnvierteln, Ban-
ken und Geschäfte, Post, Bahnhof, Rathaus und alle
Verwaltungsgebäude stellten durchweg neue Architekturmodelle dar, die von der wirtschaftlichen und
politischen Macht und vor allem aber von der kulturellen Überlegenheit der Kolonisatoren sprachen.
Die Neustadt mit ihren extrovertierten Fassaden und

and many others – discovered the Orient in the Maghreb, its customs, way of life, architecture and ornate interiors. They were fascinated by luxury and refinement, and some of them attempted to reproduce in their homes the interiors that they had discovered in North West Africa and the Near East. From early in the Protectorate, French painters and architects fired with enthusiasm for local traditions, made Morocco and its towns famous throughout Europe. The Compagnie Générale Transatlantique opened hotels in Meknes, Rabat and Marrakesh – where, in 1929, the Hotel Transatlantique (now the Hotel La Mamounia) opened to a select, cosmopolitan elite. Well-known European artists and personalities built second homes or restored old houses in Tangier and Marrakesh, the two Moroccan towns most favoured by this international society.

In investing large sums of money in the restoration or construction of these houses, and in calling upon the talents of architects and decorators, the owners of these grand residences were inspired by the domestic Moroccan tradition, and thus enhanced its standing. If the house was old, the rooms and their décor were carefully restored. If the house was new, the designers respected the austere, enclosed aspect of the house, and planned the layout of the different rooms around a central courtyard or a covered living-room. Reference to Moroccan architectural style was not confined to the living-room, but extended throughout the house to recreate an environment and an atmosphere which grew directly out of Moroccan architectural tradition.

Often new decorative and functional features, such as the fireplace, unknown in the Moroccan house, were introduced. The swimming pool was a further addition and is now standard. In the grander houses it is treated as a simple pool, integrating perfectly with the traditional presence of water in Moroccan Arab residences and gardens. Interior decoration owes everything to the expertise of craftsmen in *zelliges*, sculpted plaster and wrought ironwork, to carpenters and painters on wood. *Tadelakt*, the traditional coating of lime mixed with pigments and smoothed on with tablets of soft soap, is mostly

les spécialistes les plus compétents et les plus recherchés de l'art islamique dans le monde. Et alors que de très nombreux édifices ou ensembles urbains traditionnels, comme les très belles casbahs du Sud se dégradent et disparaissent, on construit dans les banlieues les plus récentes une quantité massive de villas dont les salons marocains sont généreusement revêtus de zelliges et de plâtre sculpté...

Retour aux demeures traditionnelles

Ce retour aux sources décoratives marque l'architecture traditionnelle marocaine réalisée depuis longtemps par une clientèle très bourgeoise, souvent d'origine européenne, qui a choisi de vivre dans de belles demeures de tradition marocaine. Ce courant s'inscrit dans une tradition orientaliste du siècle passé, lorsque peintres, écrivains et voyageurs – Eugène Delacroix, Jean-Léon Gérôme, Pierre Loti, Alexandre Dumas ou Guy de Maupassant, pour ne citer que les plus connus – découvraient l'Orient maghrébin, ses coutumes et son mode de vie, ses architectures et ses décors fastueux. Amateurs subtils d'un savoir-vivre dont le luxe et le raffinement les fascinaient, certains tentaient de reproduire chez eux les espaces intérieurs qu'ils avaient découverts avec ravissement dans les maisons arabes du Maghreb et du Proche-Orient. Au Maroc même, dès l'instauration du Protectorat, des peintres et architectes français, amateurs épris des traditions locales, font connaître le Maroc et ses villes par leurs peintures et leurs écrits. Des hôtels de la Compagnie Générale Transatlantique s'ouvrent à Meknès, à Rabat et à Marrakech – dont l'hôtel Transatlantique ouvert en 1929 n'est autre que l'hôtel La Mamounia – et accueillent la fine fleur d'une élite cosmopolite étrangère. D'autre part, des personnalités et artistes européens célèbres se font construire des résidences secondaires ou restaurent d'anciennes demeures à Tanger et à Marrakech, les deux villes marocaines les plus appréciées de cette société internationale.

En investissant beaucoup d'argent dans la restauration ou la construction de ces maisons, et en faisant appel à des décorateurs et architectes de talent, les propriétaires de ces belles demeures

den schnurgeraden Avenuen war das genaue Gegenteil der arabischen Stadt, die den Blick ganz und gar nach innen auf Patios und Gärten richtete. Das Neue faszinierte die Marokkaner; für viele gilt die Medina heute nur noch als ein der modernen Welt nicht mehr angemessener urbaner Archaismus. Inzwischen sind die von ihren einstigen Bewohnern verlassenen Altstädte von Menschen aus ländlichen Gebieten oder Vorstädten übernommen, die nun in schwierigen Wohnverhältnissen auf engstem Raum in den ehemaligen Palästen und historischen Gebäuden leben.

Die Architektur der Neustadt des Protektorats hat äußerst wenig mit marokkanischer Kunst zu tun, von der lediglich einige Elemente in eine architektonische Sprache modernistischer Machart Eingang finden. Die zu Beginn unseres Jahrhunderts in Algerien oder Tunesien so häufig anzutreffenden Arabismen blieben in Marokko die Ausnahme. Erwähnenswert ist die Residenz, die Lyautey 1922 von dem begabten Architekten Albert Laprade errichten ließ. Der marokkanische Salon mit seiner *zelliges*-Verkleidung und der Kuppel aus traditionell bemaltem Holz ist ein echtes Meisterwerk des orientalistischen Stils, das zum Vorbild für zahlreiche moderne Gebäude dieser Art in Marokko wurde.

Die massive Abwanderung marokkanischer Familien aus ihren Wohnhäusern in den Medinas in Mietshäuser oder Eigenheime in den neuen Vierteln bedeutet keineswegs die endgültige Abkehr vom marokkanischen Architekturstil. Im Gegenteil: Königliche Erlässe und das kürzlich erschienene monumentale Buch André Paccards über marokkanisches Handwerk haben zu einer lebhaften Renaissance der dekorativen Techniken und Traditionen Marokkos geführt, und marokkanische Handwerker gehören im Bereich der islamischen Kunst zu den fähigsten und gesuchtesten Fachleuten der Welt. Es ist marokkanische Realität, daß man parallel zum Verfall oder Verschwinden zahlreicher traditioneller Gebäude oder Stadtteile – wie etwa der wunderschönen Kasbahs im Süden des Landes – in den jüngsten Vororten eine Vielzahl von Villen errichtet, deren marokkanische Salons man großzügig mit *zelliges* und Stuckornamenten versieht.

used on the walls of bedrooms and bathrooms. In Marrakesh the architects Charles Boccara (see pp. 120–127) and Elie Mouyal (see pp. 114–119) vied with each other in architectural virtuosity to create domes of earthen bricks, skilful groupings of semi-circular and groined vaults, squinches and pendentives.

Interior designers delighted in mixing oriental furniture with that of the European classical tradition to satisfy the eclectic tastes of their clientele. International interior design magazines have long celebrated these creations which draw for inspiration on the ever-vibrant Moroccan traditions but are also imbued with European traditions of decoration. They have undoubtedly influenced the recent taste of the Moroccan elite for its traditional architecture. Renovation carried out in recent years in the small coastal town of Asilah by owners returning for spring or summer to use their houses as second homes, after having left them empty for many years, is clear evidence of the new affection for the traditional town. Attachment to, and maintenance of, old buildings remains, in sentiment and practice, an unknown concept for most Moroccans whose reversion to architectural tradition takes the form of new building. While the real heritage, the grand residences and ordinary houses which constitute the basic architectural units of the medinas and villages, is in danger of simply disappearing through neglect, houses which rich Europeans and the Moroccan middle-classes are building in the suburbs allow the threatened heritage to be reconstructed. It is to be feared that the traditional houses of the medinas will almost completely disappear. Soon little will survive but important monuments, mosques and *medersas*, in addition, no doubt, to a few large residences converted into tourist restaurants or bazaars. But there will also remain a few of these fine houses in which men and women of refined taste try to revive the art of oriental living in an architectural setting that combines tradition with modern comfort.

s'inspirent de la tradition domestique marocaine, qui s'en trouve ainsi valorisée. Si la maison est ancienne les pièces et leur décor sont soigneusement restaurés. Si la maison est neuve les concepteurs respectent, souvent avec bonheur, l'aspect austère et fermé des volumes extérieurs du *dâr* et conçoivent à l'intérieur la distribution des différentes pièces autour d'une cour centrale ou d'un salon couvert. La référence à l'architecture marocaine ne se réduit donc pas au seul salon marocain. Elle se veut globale et reconstitue un environnement et un cadre spatial issus directement de la tradition architecturale du Maroc.

Souvent de nouveaux éléments décoratifs ou de confort comme la cheminée, inconnue dans la maison marocaine, viennent embellir les salons et les chambres de la maison. La piscine s'y ajoute toujours et fait partie des éléments incontournables du nouveau confort domestique. Dans les plus belles maisons elle est traitée comme un simple plan d'eau s'intégrant parfaitement à la présence traditionnelle de l'eau dans la demeure et le jardin arabes du Maroc. La décoration intérieure est totalement redevable de tout le savoir-faire des artisans des zelliges et du plâtre sculpté, des menuisiers, des peintres sur bois et des ferronniers. Le *tadelakt*, cet enduit traditionnel de chaux mélangé à des pigments de couleur et lissé avec des galets au savon noir, est largement employé sur les murs des chambres et des salles de bains. A Marrakech, les architectes Charles Boccara (voir pp. 120–127) et Elie Mouyal (voir pp. 114–119) rivalisent de virtuosité constructive dans la réalisation de coupoles construites en briques de terre, assemblages savants de voûtes cintrées ou d'arêtes, de trompes et de pendentifs.

L'aménagement intérieur mélange jusqu'à l'excès le mobilier orientaliste et celui de la tradition classique européenne, et fait le délice des décorateurs qui peuvent ainsi satisfaire le goût éclectique de leurs clients. Les revues internationales de décoration intérieure ont d'ailleurs fait connaître depuis longtemps la qualité de ces créations ressourcées à la tradition toujours vivante de l'art de vivre marocain, mais également imprégnées des

Rückkehr zu traditionellen Häusern

Die Rückkehr zu den dekorativen Quellen zeigt die Rückbesinnung auf die traditionelle marokkanische Architektur, die seit langem bei einer großbürgerlichen Schicht, vielfach europäischen Ursprungs, zu beobachten ist; in diesen Kreisen ist man bestrebt, in schönen Häusern traditioneller Bauweise zu wohnen. Diese Strömung steht in einer orientalistischen Tradition des letzten Jahrhunderts, als Maler, Schriftsteller und andere Reisende – etwa Eugène Delacroix, Jean-Léon Gérôme, Pierre Loti, Alexandre Dumas oder Guy de Maupassant, um nur die bekanntesten zu nennen – im Maghreb den Orient mit seinen Bräuchen und Lebensweisen, seiner Architektur und seinem üppigen Zierrat entdeckten. Als Liebhaber eines verfeinerten Lebensstils, dessen Luxus und Raffinesse sie faszinierte, versuchten sie, Innenräume nachzubilden, die sie in den arabischen Wohnhäusern des Maghreb und des Nahen Ostens entdeckten. In Marokko selbst machten seit Einrichtung des Protektorats von lokalen Traditionen faszinierte französische Maler und Architekten das Land und seine Städte in Bildern und Schriften bekannt. Die Compagnie Générale Transatlantique richtete Hotels in Meknès, Rabat und Marrakesch ein – das hier 1929 eröffnete Hotel Transatlantique ist identisch mit dem Hotel La Mamounia –, deren Gäste vornehme, kosmopolitisch orientierte Ausländer sind. Andererseits ließen sich europäische Prominente und Künstler auch Zweitwohnsitze bauen oder alte Wohnhäuser in Tanger oder Marrakesch, den beiden beliebtesten marokkanischen Städten, restaurieren.

Die Besitzer jener schönen Gebäude stecken viel Geld in die Restaurierung oder den Neubau und beschäftigen hervorragende Ausstatter und Architekten in dem Bestreben, an die Traditionen des marokkanischen Wohnhauses anzuknüpfen, die damit zugleich aufgewertet werden. Bei alten Häusern werden die Räume ebenso wie ihre Einrichtung sorgfältig wiederhergestellt. Bei Neubauten respektieren die Planer – oft durchaus gelungen – die Strenge und Geschlossenheit der Außenseiten des *dâr* und behalten im Inneren des Hauses die Raumaufteilung um den Patio oder um einen überdachten

traditions décoratives européennes. Elles ont certainement influencé le goût récent de l'élite marocaine pour son architecture traditionnelle. Les rénovations réalisées ces dernières années dans la petite ville côtière d'Asilah, par des propriétaires qui retournent aujourd'hui dans leur maison pour des séjours de printemps ou d'été (la maison est utilisée comme résidence secondaire), alors qu'ils l'avaient laissée vide pendant de nombreuses années, témoignent clairement de ce nouvel attachement pour la ville traditionnelle. L'amour et l'entretien des vieilles pierres restent un sentiment et une pratique encore inconnus pour la majorité des Marocains, qui vivent leur retour à la tradition architecturale dans la seule construction neuve. Alors que le patrimoine authentique, celui des belles demeures mais aussi celui des maisons ordinaires qui constitue l'essen-

tiel du tissu architectural des médinas et agglomérations rurales, est menacé de disparition massive pour cause d'abandon et manque d'entretien, les maisons que la riche bourgeoisie européenne, et aujourd'hui marocaine, se fait construire dans la périphérie des villes permettent de reconstruire un patrimoine en voie de disparition. Car les médinas sont menacées: il ne restera bientôt que quelques monuments prestigieux, mosquées et medersas, sans doute aussi quelques anciennes grandes demeures transformées en restaurants ou en bazars pour touristes. Mais il restera aussi ces belles maisons dans lesquelles des femmes et des hommes de culture au goût raffiné, tentent de ressusciter un art de vivre oriental dans un cadre architectural sachant concilier la tradition et le confort contemporain.

Salon herum bei. Der Bezug zur marokkanischen Architektur bleibt insofern nicht auf den »Salon marocain« beschränkt, sondern versteht sich als globale Wiederherstellung eines Umfeldes und räumlichen Rahmens, der sich direkt aus der architektonischen Tradition Marokkos herleitet.

Salons und Schlafzimmer werden oft um neue Elemente bereichert, die der Dekoration oder dem Komfort dienen, etwa um einen offenen Kamin, der im marokkanischen Wohnhaus eigentlich nicht vorkommt. Stets findet sich ein Schwimmbecken, eines der unverzichtbaren Attribute des neuen häuslichen Komforts. Bei den schönsten Anwesen werden die Becken als schlichte Wasserfläche angelegt und stehen so in völligem Einklang mit den in Marokko traditionell im Haus und im arabischen Garten vorhandenen Wasser. Die Innenausstattung hängt voll und ganz vom Können der Handwerker ab, die *zelliges* oder Stuckdekorationen anbringen, von den Tischlern, Malern und Kunstschmieden. *Tadelakt*, der traditionelle Kalkputz, der mit Farbpigmenten vermischt und mit Rollen und Schmierseife geglättet wird, findet sich vielfach an den Wänden von Schlafzimmern und Bädern. In Marrakesch überbieten sich die Architekten Charles Boccara (s. S. 120–127) und Elie Mouyal (s. S. 114–119) gegenseitig mit ihren virtuosen Kuppeln aus Ziegeln und Lehm, intelligenten Konstruktionen mit Kreuzgrat- oder -rippengewölben, Trompen und Pendentifs.

Bei der Inneneinrichtung werden orientalisierende und klassisch-europäische Möbel bedenkenlos vermischt, auch von Innenarchitekten, die damit den eklektischen Geschmack ihrer Kunden befriedigen können. Internationale Zeitschriften zum Themenkreis Innendekoration haben übrigens längst die Qualitäten dieser Interieurs entdeckt, die einerseits aus der noch immer lebendigen Tradition marokkanischer Lebensart schöpfen, zugleich aber auch von den dekorativen Gewohnheiten Europas geprägt sind. Sie haben sicherlich zur Rückbesinnung der heutigen marokkanischen Oberschicht auf ihre eigene Architekturtradition beigetragen. Die Renovierungsarbeiten, die in den letzten Jahren in der Küstenstadt Asilah durchgeführt wurden, wo die seit Jahren leerstehenden Häuser inzwischen wieder als

Frühlings- oder Sommersitze genutzt werden, bezeugen eindeutig diese neue Hinwendung zur traditionellen Stadt. Die Liebe zu alten Gemäuern und das Bemühen um ihre Erhaltung bleibt allerdings der Mehrzahl der Marokkaner, die ihre Rückbesinnung auf die Tradition lediglich in Neubauten ausdrücken, meist sowohl emotional als auch praktisch verschlossen. Einerseits ist das authentische architektonische Erbe, welches das Stadtgefüge der Medinas und ländlichen Ortschaften bestimmt, massiv vom Verfall bedroht, weil die Bewohner abwandern und niemand die Bausubstanz erhält. Andererseits bietet sich mit den Villen am Stadtrand, die vom reichen europäischen und neuerdings auch marokkanischen Bürgertum errichtet werden, die Möglichkeit, ein vom Untergang bedrohtes Gut zu erneuern. Es ist zu befürchten, daß die traditionellen Häuser der Medinas praktisch vollständig verschwinden werden. Bald wird es vom architektonischen Erbe nur noch einige prestigeträchtige Bauwerke, Moscheen und Medersen geben und vielleicht ein paar der großartigen alten Wohnhäuser, die man in Restaurants oder Basare für Touristen umfunktioniert hat. Und dann sind da diese wundervollen Wohnhäuser, in denen kultivierte Männer und Frauen von erlesenem Geschmack sich um eine Wiedererweckung der orientalischen Lebensart bemühen, und zwar in einem architektonischen Rahmen, der Tradition und modernen Komfort miteinander versöhnen.

Le Sud

If one believes, with the famously opinionated Wyndham Lewis writing in the thirties that "the best contemporary architecture in the Maghreb is, as a matter of fact, Saharan", then the 'ksour', casbahs and 'agadirs' of the south are a fascinating discovery. Palaces of adobe appear as grandiose extensions of the earth itself, organic and thus supremely perishable. They have been eroded by the very sun that baked them into being. They are a source of wonder. Many are now abandoned as rural depopulation takes its toll. Others, built to serve the purpose of a nomadic or tribal lifestyle, are no longer relevant to modern Moroccans. These Berber constructions glare down blindly from the heights of the Gorges of the Dades, or the Dra, empty windows bordered with lime, as far removed aesthetically from the elaborately embellished Hispano-Moresque of the north as they can possibly be. Their origins and architectural inspiration are unknown although they give off references to Mali, Egypt, Mesopotamia or Mycenae. Built to withstand the successive attentions of nomadic tribes, these fortified country villages are constructed with whatever materials were at hand, sometimes stone but usually 'pisé'. The harmoniously proportioned interiors are partly due to the fact that the use of date palm trunks for internal timbering sets a natural limit to the internal dimension. It is estimated that, without restoration and constant upkeep, these supreme examples of architecture, built without architects, cannot survive more than two hundred years, returning to the dust they were built from.

Dans les années trente, cet incorrigible donneur de leçons qu'était Wyndham Lewis écrivait: «La plus belle architecture moderne du Maghreb est indubitablement saharienne.» Les ksour, les casbahs et les ‹agadir› du sud marocain sont d'exceptionnels chefs-d'œuvre. Véritables palais d'adobes, prolongements grandioses de la terre elle-même – organiques et par là-même périssables – s'effritant sous le soleil qui les a cuits, ils sont une intarissable source d'émerveillement. Beaucoup sont abandonnés tandis que l'exode rural poursuit inexorablement son cours. D'autres, constructions éphémères érigées pour les besoins de la vie nomade ou tribale, tombent en désuétude. Sur le plan esthétique, ces demeures berbères perchées sur les hauteurs des vallées du Dadès ou du Draa, avec leurs fenêtres désertes bordées de chaux, sont aux antipodes du style fleuri hispano-moresque qui domine dans le nord. On ignore l'origine de cette tradition architecturale, mais elle rappelle indiscutablement le Mali, l'Egypte, la Mésopotamie ou encore Mycène. Ce sont généralement d'anciens villages agricoles fortifiés, construits pour résister aux vagues successives de tribus nomades avec les matériaux à portée de main, parfois la pierre mais le plus souvent le pisé. Les proportions harmonieuses des intérieurs sont en partie dues au boisage en troncs de dattiers qui en fixent les limites naturelles. Faute de restauration et d'un entretien régulier, ces superbes exemples d'architecture sans architecte ne survivront sans doute pas plus de deux siècles, après quoi ils retourneront à la poussière et au sable dont ils sont issus.

Wenn man wie der englische Schriftsteller Wyndham Lewis der
Meinung ist, daß »die beste zeitgenössische Architektur des Maghreb
in der Tat die saharische ist«, dann sind die ›ksour‹, Kasbahs und
›agadirs‹ des Südens eine faszinierende Entdeckung. Paläste aus
Lehm, grandiose Auswüchse der Erde selbst, organisch und daher
überaus vergänglich: nun von der Sonne erodiert, die sie ursprünglich
gefestigt hat, bringen sie uns immer wieder zum Staunen. Viele sind
infolge der Landflucht inzwischen verlassen. Andere, für ein Noma-
den- oder Stammesleben gebaut, haben keine Funktion mehr. Diese
Berberbauten starren blind in die Schluchten des Dades oder des
Dra-Tals herab. Sie sind ästhetisch von der kunstvoll verschnörkelten
hispano-maurischen Architektur des Nordens so weit entfernt wie nur
irgend möglich. Ihr Ursprung und ihre architektonischen Inspirations-
quellen sind unbekannt. Früher waren es befestigte Dörfer von Acker-
bauern, so angelegt, daß sie den ständigen Nachstellungen von
Nomadenstämmen widerstanden, und aus dem Material gebaut, das
gerade zur Hand war, manchmal aus Stein, aber gewöhnlich aus
Stampflehm (Pisee). Die harmonisch proportionierten Innenräume
verdanken sich zum Teil der Tatsache, daß ihnen durch Dattel-
palmenstämme als Holzverschalung eine natürliche Grenze gesetzt
wird. Man schätzt, daß diese bedeutenden Beispiele für eine »Architektur ohne Architekten« ohne Restaurierung und dauernde Instand-
haltung nicht mehr als zweihundert Jahre überdauern können und
wieder zu dem Staub werden, aus dem sie einst gebaut wurden.

Moroccan Interiors   La tente berbère   Le Sud

The Berber tent: along with the town house or palace and rural 'pisé' constructions, the tent is considered to be one of the three traditional dwelllings of Morocco. The desert traders and travellers, so beloved of the Orientalist painters of the 19th century, were all tent-dwellers. Nowadays, the Berber tribes of the Atlas mountains, their movement governed by the seasonal migration of their flocks, weave large tents of dark sheep's wool and goat hair such as the one shown here. The tents blend with the dark sands of the desert and are often embellished with embroidered geometric motifs. They are divided into the women's and children's quarters as well as a reception area where the men sleep. The floor is scattered with herbs for health and luck, and the carpets and cushions on which the men sleep are stacked during the day.

La tente berbère

La tente est l'une des trois habitations traditionnelles du Maroc, au même titre que la maison de ville (ou le palais) et les constructions en pisé des campagnes. Traditionnellement, c'était celle des marchands et des voyageurs du désert, chers aux orientalistes de la fin du XIXème siècle. Aujourd'hui, les tribus berbères des montagnes de l'Atlas qui transhument avec leurs troupeaux tissent de grandes tentes en laine sombre de mouton ou de chèvre comme on en voit ci-contre. Elles se fondent dans le sable gris du désert ou le paysage aride, et sont souvent rehaussées de broderies en laine à motifs géométriques. L'intérieur comporte toujours une partie réservée aux femmes et aux enfants et un espace de réception, où dorment les hommes. Sur le sol, on jette des herbes qui assurent bonne fortune et santé. Des tapis et des coussins, empilés pendant la journée, sont étalés le soir en guise de matelas.

Das Berberzelt: Neben dem Stadthaus oder Palast und den ländlichen Piseebauten gilt das Zelt als eine der drei traditionellen Wohnformen in Marokko. Die Wüstenhändler und Nomaden, die bei den Orientmalern des 19. Jahrhunderts als Motiv so beliebt waren, waren allesamt Zeltbewohner. Heutzutage weben die Berberstämme aus dem Atlas, die den jahreszeitlich bedingten Wanderungen ihrer Herden folgen, große Zelte aus dunkler Schafswolle und Ziegenhaar, wie das hier abgebildete. Die Zelte heben sich gegen den dunklen Sand der Wüste kaum ab und sind oft mit aufgestickten geometrischen Mustern verziert. Sie sind aufgeteilt in einen Bereich für die Frauen und Kinder sowie den Empfangsbereich, wo die Männer auch schlafen. Der Fußboden wird mit Kräutern bestreut, die Glück und Gesundheit bringen sollen. Die Teppiche und Kissen, auf denen die Männer nächtigen, werden tagsüber aufeinandergeschichtet.

The harvester's tent: somewhere between Tiznit and Goulimine, isolated in the deserted landscape, Mohammed is brewing his mint tea. The white canvas of his little round tent blends with the pale yellow of the wheat: endless wheat, growing in impossibly parched soil that stretches as far as the eye can see. Apart from a short trip to the nearest town to buy provisions every two days Mohammed lives in complete isolation. Wherever there is harvesting or planting to be done, he and his tent can be found. With his scythe he harvests at an unhurried pace, tying the small bundles of wheat close to his tent at night. His tent, gas burner and the land reclaimed from the desert are contemporary, but his nomadic way of life accurately reflects the not so distant past of many Moroccans.

La tente du moisonneur

Quelque part entre Tiznit et Goulimine, perdu dans un paysage désertique, Mohammed prépare son thé à la menthe. La toile blanche de sa petite tente ronde se fond dans le jaune pâle du blé: les champs, cultivés sur une terre d'une sécheresse inouïe, s'étendent à perte de vue. Hormis deux fois par semaine, quand il se rend à la ville la plus proche pour faire ses provisions, Mohammed vit dans la solitude la plus complète. Il se déplace avec sa tente, au gré des moissons et des semences, sur des lopins de terre que rien ne distingue des parcelles voisines. Il travaille lentement, à la faucille, puis lie le blé en bottes qu'il entasse pour la nuit autour de son habitation. Sa tente, son réchaud à gaz et la terre qu'il a arrachée au désert datent d'aujourd'hui, mais sa vie nomade reflète le passé, pas si lointain, de nombreux Marocains.

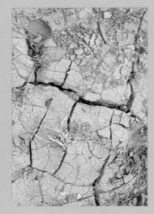

Das Zelt des Erntearbeiters: Irgendwo zwischen Tiznit und Goulimine, allein in der verlassenen Landschaft, brüht sich Mohammed seinen Pfefferminztee auf. Der weiße Stoff seines kleinen runden Zeltes verschmilzt mit dem blassen Gelb des Weizens – endloser Weizen in dieser ausgetrockneten Erde, so weit wie das Auge reicht. Bis auf einen kurzen Ausflug zur nächstgelegenen Stadt alle zwei Tage, um Proviant einzukaufen, lebt Mohammed in vollständiger Isolation. Wo immer geerntet oder gepflanzt werden muß, taucht er mit seinem Zelt wieder auf. Mit seiner Sichel erntet er ohne übertriebene Eile und bindet die schmalen Weizenbündel am Abend dicht bei seinem Zelt fest. Sein Zelt, der Gaskocher und das Land, das der Wüste abgerungen worden ist, stammen aus der Gegenwart, aber seine nomadische Lebensweise zeugt von der noch nicht allzu fernen Vergangenheit vieler Marokkaner.

A traditional house: in the Amelan valley, near Tafraoute, the rockscape is compellingly beautiful. Purple and pink, the steep sides of the valley rise to form the ridge of Jebel Lekst. The villages, twenty-six in all, cling to the lower slopes, the green arable land below having provided for their existence since time immemorial. The indigenous 'pisé' constructions are simple and beautifully thought out. Built of earth and little else, this house is a stunning example of architecture without architect. It is one of the few still in perfect condition and has been painstakingly maintained by a blind Berber and his grandson. The blind man is supported, in accordance with Islamic tradition, by tithes from his fellow villagers, many of whom have emigrated. This may be the last opportunity to admire his 'dâr'. Its immediate neighbours are sun-baked ruins as their owners have preferred to build modern, cement homes, a few metres down the hill.

Maison traditionnelle

Dans la vallée d'Amelan, près de Tafraoute, le paysage rocheux est d'une beauté envoûtante. Les versants escarpés de la vallée – violets et roses – se dressent vers la crête du Djebel Lekst. Les villages, vingt-six en tout, sont accrochés au flanc des collines les moins élevées où la terre arable, verdoyante et fertile, assure leur subsistance depuis des temps immémoriaux. La technique locale du pisé a donné des maisons simples et superbement conçues: construites presque entièrement avec de la terre comprimée, elles constituent un exemple étonnant d'architecture sans architecte. Un vieux Berbère aveugle et son petit-fils entretiennent avec grand soin l'une des rares bâtisses encore en parfait état. Conformément à la tradition musulmane, le vieillard vit de la générosité des autres villageois, dont un grand nombre ont émigré. Il y a fort à parier que son ‹dâr› disparaîtra avec lui. Autour de lui ne subsistent que des ruines calcinées par le soleil, leurs anciens propriétaires leur ayant préféré des maisons modernes en ciment, un peu plus bas sur la colline.

Ein traditionelles Haus: Die Felslandschaft im Tal der Ammeln, in der Nähe von Tafraoute, ist überwältigend schön. Purpurrot und rosa steigen die steilen Hänge vom Tal auf und formen sich zum Gebirgsmassiv des Djebel Lekst. Die Dörfer, insgesamt sechsundzwanzig, schmiegen sich an die niedrigeren Hänge; das grüne fruchtbare Land darunter hat die Bewohner seit ewigen Zeiten genährt. Die einheimischen Piseebauten sind einfach und gut durchdacht: Fast ausschließlich aus Erde erbaut, ist das hier abgebildete Haus ein phantastisches Beispiel für eine Architektur ohne Architekten. Es ist eines der wenigen noch perfekt erhaltenen, weil es von einem blinden Berber und dessen Enkelsohn sorgfältig gepflegt wird. Der blinde Mann wird, wie es die islamische Tradition gebietet, durch die Zahlung des Zehnten von den anderen Dorfbewohnern unterstützt. Allerdings sind viele von ihnen emigriert. Dies ist vielleicht die letzte Gelegenheit, sein ›dar‹ zu bewundern, denn die unmittelbaren Nachbarn sind bereits sonnenverbrannte Ruinen, deren Eigentümer es vorgezogen haben, sich ein paar Meter weiter unten am Hügel moderne Zementhäuser zu bauen.

The house is three storeys high and built into the steep hill. The animals are stabled on the ground floor, near the well. The windows are small slits intended to keep out both enemies and the summer heat. Smooth earthen steps lead up to the next floor. Open to the sky, the kitchen occupies the central courtyard. The corridor-like rooms arranged around it each have their own function. The dining-room is on the landing between the kitchen and the top-floor reception rooms, and the stairway has been cleverly constructed to produce a draft of air that makes this the coolest part of the house. A special visitors' door admits guests directly at this level so that they are not obliged to pass through the stables and kitchen. On the top floor is a room for prayer, and a large reception-room furnished with carpets and cushions.
Right page: the top floor reception room, lined with Berber rugs.

Cette maison de trois étages est construite sur le flanc abrupt d'une colline. Le rez-de-chaussée, près du puits, est destiné aux animaux. Pour assurer la défense du site et le protéger de la chaleur de l'été, de simples meurtrières font office de fenêtres, plongeant l'intérieur de la maison dans une pénombre constante. Des marches en terre battue mènent à l'étage. La cuisine occupe la cour centrale, à ciel ouvert. Les pièces longues et étroites qui la bordent ont toutes une fonction précise. La salle à manger est située à l'entresol, entre la cuisine et les salles de réception du dernier étage, reliées par un escalier astucieux qui laisse filtrer un courant d'air dans la partie la plus fraîche de la

maison. Une porte d'entrée spéciale permet aux invités d'accéder directement à ce niveau sans passer par la cuisine et l'étable. Au dernier étage se trouve également une chambre de prière et une grande pièce de réception aménagée avec des tapis et des coussins.
Page de droite: la salle de réception du dernier étage, au sol recouvert de tapis berbères.

Das Haus ist drei Stockwerke hoch und in den steilen Hang hineingebaut. Der Stall befindet sich im Erdgeschoß, in der Nähe des Brunnens. Als Fenster dienen schmale Schlitze, die sowohl vor Feinden als auch vor der Sommerhitze schützen sollen. Geglättete Lehmstufen führen ins nächste Stockwerk. Die zum Himmel hin offene Küche nimmt den Innenhof in der Mitte ein. Korridorähnliche Zimmer, die davon abgehen, haben jeweils eine bestimmte Funktion. Das Eßzimmer befindet sich auf dem Absatz zwischen Küche und Wohnzimmern im ersten Stock, wo die Treppe so klug konstruiert wurde, daß ein ständiger Luftzug diesen Platz zum kühlsten Ort des Hauses macht. Eine eigene Besuchertür läßt die Gäste auf dieser Ebene ein, so daß sie nicht durch den Stall und die Küche gehen müssen. Im obersten Stockwerk gibt es ein Zimmer zum Beten und einen großen Salon, der mit Teppichen und Kissen ausgelegt ist.
Rechte Seite: das Wohnzimmer im obersten Stockwerk, ausgelegt mit Berberteppichen.

A troglodyte home: the fishermen of Sidi Moussa d'Aglou, above Sidi Ifni on the southwestern coast of Morocco, live in fifty-odd caves that have been hollowed out of the soft stone cliffs. Their amorphic interiors are usually whitewashed and possess rudimentary sleeping and cooking arrangements. The currents are treacherous, so the beaches are deserted. The fishermen's life is regulated by the sea: at 6.30 a.m. they go shrimping, then when the tide goes out they search for mussels and in the late afternoon they go fishing with nets. As the evening draws to a close they kick a football around on the wet sand or play cards, then cook dinner over an outdoor fire.

Une maison troglodyte

Les pêcheurs de Sidi Moussa d'Aglou, sur la côte sud-ouest du Maroc, vivent dans une cinquantaine de grottes creusées dans la pierre tendre des falaises. Les intérieurs, généralement constitués d'une seule pièce, sont simplement blanchis à la chaux et ne contiennent que le strict nécessaire pour cuisiner et dormir. Les courants marins de cette région sont traîtres, aussi les plages restent-elles désertes. La vie des pêcheurs est réglée par la mer: à 6h30, ils partent pêcher la crevette. Puis, à marée basse, ils cherchent les moules. Tard dans l'après-midi, ils lancent leurs filets. En fin de soirée, ils jouent au football sur le sable humide, font des parties de cartes et préparent le dîner au feu de bois.

Eine Höhlenwohnung: Die Fischer von Sidi Moussa d'Aglou oberhalb von Sidi Ifni an der Südwestküste von Marokko leben in etwa fünfzig Höhlen, die in den weichen Fels der Kliffs geschlagen wurden. Die amorphen Innenräume sind gewöhnlich weißgekalkt und haben einfache Schlaf- und Kochgelegenheiten. Wegen der tückischen Meeresströmungen sind die Strände verlassen. Das Leben der Fischer folgt dem Rhythmus des Meeres: Um halb sieben morgens gehen sie auf Krabbenfang, dann, wenn Ebbe ist, suchen sie nach Muscheln, und am späten Nachmittag gehen sie mit Netzen fischen. Abends spielen sie Karten oder ein wenig Fußball auf dem nassen Sand. Später kochen sie sich auf einem Lagerfeuer das Abendessen.

Most of the fishermen at Sidi Moussa d'Aglou live in these caves all year round, although some are beginning to build simple cement constructions (see ill. p. 56 below). Usually brightly painted in contrasting tones these cement constructions are suited for use as family holiday homes during the summer months.

La plupart des pêcheurs de Sidi Moussa d'Aglou vivent toute l'année dans ces grottes, bien que certains d'entre eux aient commencé à se construire de simples bâtisses en ciment (voir ill. p. 56 en bas). Souvent peintes de couleurs vives et contrastées, elles deviennent des maisons de vacances pendant l'été.

Die meisten der Fischer in Sidi Moussa d'Aglou wohnen das ganze Jahr über in diesen Höhlen, obwohl einige damit angefangen haben, einfache Zementbauten zu errichten (s. Abb. S. 56 unten). Sie sind gewöhnlich in leuchtenden, kontrastreichen Farben gestrichen und können von den Fischerfamilien als Ferienwohnung während der Sommermonate genutzt werden.

Provisions or entertainment are a long walk away over the dunes, and the fierce surf keeps tourists away. During the month of August, however, when the nation traditionally takes its holiday, the population of the troglodyte village more than doubles. The tiny caves are crammed with fishermen's families, and the isolation of winter is forgotten.

La route est longue à travers les dunes pour aller faire les provisions ou trouver de quoi se distraire. La violence des rouleaux décourage les touristes. Toutefois, pendant le mois d'août, alors que tout le pays prend des vacances, le village troglodyte voit sa population doubler. Les familles et les amis des pêcheurs s'entassent dans ces grottes minuscules, et on oublie l'isolement de l'hiver.

Proviantbeschaffung und Orte der Unterhaltung sind mit einem langen Fußmarsch über die Dünen verbunden, und die starken Wellen halten Touristen fern. Im August aber, wenn das ganze Land traditionsgemäß Urlaub macht, verdoppelt sich die Bevölkerung des Höhlendorfes. Die winzigen Höhlen sind vollgestopft mit Fischerfamilien, die hier die Isolation des Winters vergessen können.

A town house: life in Tiznit is representative of the smaller towns of southern Morocco. Historically, it has a particular importance. It was once the base of El Hiba, a warlord who conquered Marrakesh and was defeated at Fez in 1913. He was known as the "Blue Sultan" on account of his flowing desert robes and Bedouin followers. The town reflects its history as a military stronghold with over five kilometres of 'pisé' ramparts, neat administrative streets and a considerable garrison. It is a traditional walled town but despite its ancient appearance it was built only a hundred years ago when several existing isolated 'ksour' were simply incorporated into the new street grid. Tiznit is a centre for Berber jewellery, and many of its craftsmen are Jewish. The homes in the mellah reflect the seductive palette of southern Morocco. Ochre walls contrast with doors and windows painted in soft, saturated colours. The small illustration on the left shows a decorative "stencil roller" paint effect, red flowers on a turquoise background, which is very popular. It is used to imitate wall-paper, a commodity perceived as highly desirable but being practically unobtainable.

Une maison de ville

La vie à Tiznit est typique des petites villes du Sud marocain, même si autrefois Tiznit a joué un rôle historique non négligeable. Sa longue tunique du désert et ses partisans bédouins lui valurent le surnom de «Sultan Bleu». Avec ses cinq kilomètres de remparts en pisé, le tracé régulier des rues de son quartier administratif et ses casernes, Tiznit conserve des traces de son passé de place forte militaire. Si elle rappelle les anciennes villes fortifiées, elle n'a pourtant été édifiée qu'il y a cent ans, quand plusieurs ksour des environs ont été incorporés dans le nouveau plan de la ville. Tiznit est un centre important pour le commerce des bijoux berbères et compte un grand nombre d'artisans juifs. Les maisons de la mellâh reflètent la séduisante palette de couleurs du Sud marocain. Les murs ocres contrastent avec les portes et les fenêtres peintes de douces couleurs saturées. La petite illustration à gauche montre les effets de peinture au pochoir, avec des fleurs rouges sur un fond turquoise. Ils sont très prisés et ils imitent le papier peint, un article dedécoration très envié mais souvent inabordable.

Ein Stadthaus: Das Leben in Tiznit ist typisch für die kleineren Städte im Süden Marokkos, obwohl der Ort geschichtlich von besonderer Bedeutung ist. Die Stadt verweist auf ihre Vergangenheit als Militärstützpunkt mit über fünf Kilometer langen Piseewällen, schnurgeraden Verwaltungsstraßen und einer beachtlichen Garnison. Sie war von jeher mit Stadtmauern umgeben, aber die derzeitigen Mauern wurden erst vor hundert Jahren gebaut, als mehrere ›ksour‹ einfach in das neue Straßennetz eingebunden wurden. Tiznit ist ein Zentrum für Berberschmuck, und viele seiner Handwerker sind Juden. Ihre Häuser in der ›mellâh‹ zeugen von der verführerischen Farbenpracht im südlichen Marokko. Ockerfarbene Wände kontrastieren mit Türen und Fenstern, die in sanften, satten Farben gestrichen sind. Die Abbildung oben zeigt einen dekorativen »Schablonen«-Effekt, bei dem rote Blumen auf einen türkisfarbenem Hintergrund gerollt werden. Damit wird eine Tapete imitiert, eine Ware, die als höchst erstrebenswert gilt, aber praktisch unerschwinglich ist.

Essaouira

Speaking of Mogador, (the original name for Essaouira), James Richardson remarked in his "Travels", published in 1860, that the captives who were held there "never attempt to escape, but quietly submit to their destiny." One can quite understand their attitude as this 18th century town, enclosed by battlements, is one of the most attractive sites in Morocco. Its houses are whitewashed and have blue shutters, while the medina is laid out on a French grid pattern: a unique state of affairs explained by the fact that it was designed by a captive architect, Théodore Cornut, on the orders of Sultan Sidi Mohammed Ben Abdallah. Essaouira is celebrated for its relatively untouched beauty, its skilled craftsmen and its Atlantic winds which make it a cool haven from the hot summers of nearby Marrakesh.

Evoquant Mogador – l'ancien nom d'Essaouira – James Richardson note dans ses récits de voyages publiés en 1860, que les captifs qui y étaient retenus prisonniers «ne tentaient jamais de s'évader mais se soumettaient calmement à leur destin». On comprend aisément leur résignation: cette ville fortifiée du XVIIIe siècle est l'un des plus beaux sites du Maroc. Les maisons sont blanchies à la chaux et ornées de volets bleus. Fait unique, la médina est construite sur un plan à la française: en effet, elle a été dessinée par un détenu, l'architecte Théodore Cornut, sous les ordres du Sultan Sidi Mohammed Ben Abdallah. Essaouira est renommée pour sa beauté relativement in- tacte et ses talentueux artisans. Les vents de l'Atlantique en font un refuge frais pendant les mois d'été, lorsque que le soleil torride s'abat sur sa voisine, Marrakech.

Über Mogador – das ist der ursprüngliche Name von Essaouira – bemerkte James Richardson in seinen 1860 veröffentlichten Reisebe- schreibungen, daß die Gefangenen, die dort festgehalten wurden, »nie versuchten zu entkommen, sondern sich still und ergeben in ihr Schicksal fügten«. Man kann ihre Haltung gut verstehen, denn diese Stadt aus dem 18. Jahrhundert, von Befestigungsmauern umschlos- sen, ist einer der attraktivsten Orte in Marokko. Die Häuser sind weißgekalkt und haben blaue Fensterläden. Die Medina ist in einem Schachbrettmuster angelegt. Sie wurde von einem Gefangenen, dem französischen Architekten Théodore Cornut, entworfen, und zwar auf Befehl von Sultan Sidi Mohammed Ben Abdallah. Essaouira ist berühmt für seine relativ unberührte Schönheit, für seine geschickten Kunsthandwerker und für seine atlantischen Winde, die es zu einem kühlen Zufluchtsort vor den heißen Sommern im nahegelegenen Marrakesch machen.

The Danish couple Laise and Soren Adzer Nielsen were immediately attracted to Essaouira when the Moroccan Consul General in Copenhagen first introduced them to his country during a short holiday. They subsequently started looking for a house and came upon the ruined summer residence of the last Pasha of Essaouira. The building, untouched for thirty years, was being used as stabling by a farmer who had no intention of selling. It was only after months of negotiations and difficulties that he finally consented to part with it. The Adzers have been busy restoring and rebuilding ever since. The recent addition of a new wing, centred around the swimmingpool has effectively converted it into a double 'riyâd'. Apart from some good Danish pieces, their home is almost entirely furnished with locally-made objects of their own design.

Laise et Soren Adzer Nielsen

Lorsque le consul du Maroc à Copenhague leur a fait visiter son pays au cours d'un bref séjour, ce couple danois a eu le coup de foudre pour Essaouira. A la recherche d'une maison, ils sont tombés sur la résidence d'été du dernier pacha d'Essaouira. L'édifice, qui tombait en ruines, servait d'étable à un cultivateur et celui-ci n'avait aucune intention de le vendre. Ce ne fut qu'après des mois d'âpres négociations et de difficultés qu'il accepta de s'en séparer. Depuis, les Adzer n'ont cessé de le restaurer et de l'embellir. La récente adjonction d'une nouvelle aile, centrée autour de la piscine, a doublé le ‹riyâd›. Hormis quelques beaux meubles danois, l'intérieur des Adzer est presque entièrement aménagé avec des éléments qu'ils ont dessinés eux-mêmes et fait réaliser localement.

Das dänische Ehepaar Laise und Soren Adzer Nielsen fühlte sich auf Anhieb von Essaouira angezogen, als sie der marokkanische General-konsul in Kopenhagen während eines kurzen Urlaubs zum ersten Mal mit seinem Land vertraut machte. Sie sahen sich nach einem Haus um und stießen dabei auf die Ruine der Sommerresidenz des letzten Paschas von Essaouira. Das Gebäude war seit dreißig Jahren unberührt und wurde von einem Bauern als Stall benutzt, der kein Interesse an einem Verkauf hatte. Erst nach monatelangen Verhandlungen und Schwierigkeiten willigte er schließlich ein, sich davon zu trennen. Die Adzers sind seitdem unermüdlich mit Restaurieren und Umbauen beschäftigt. Der Anbau eines neuen Flügels um den Swimmingpool herum hat die Residenz praktisch in einen doppelten ›riyâd‹ verwandelt. Bis auf ein paar wertvolle dänische Möbel ist ihr Palast fast ausschließlich mit vor Ort gekauften und nach eigenen Entwürfen gearbeiteten Möbeln und Gegenständen eingerichtet.

Left page: a fireplace in a guest bedroom and a colonial sideboard painted "bleu Majorelle". The small table is in the local thuya wood.
Above: another chimney place designed by the Adzers in the room that serves as antechamber to the hammam.
Detail far right: example of Moroccan Kilim upholstery on the furnishings.
Following double page: the kitchen.

Page de gauche: cheminée dans une chambre d'amis et buffet colonial peint en «bleu Majorelle». La table basse est en thuya de la région.
Ci-dessus: une autre cheminée dessinée par les Adzer dans la pièce qui sert d'antichambre au hammam.
Détail à l'extrême droite: un exemple de meubles tapissés de kilims.
Double page suivante: la cuisine.

Linke Seite: ein Kamin in einem Gästeschlafzimmer und eine Anrichte im Kolonialstil, in »Bleu Majorelle« gestrichen. Der kleine Tisch ist aus dem einheimischen Thujaholz.
Oben: ein weiterer von den Adzers entworfener Kaminplatz in dem Raum, der als Vorzimmer zum ›hammam‹ fungiert.
Detail ganz rechts: Beispiel für einen marokkanischen Kelimbezug auf dem Mobiliar.
Folgende Doppelseite: die Küche.

Marrakech

Marrakesh, "El amara" ("the red"), has long been the Southern rival of Fez as the country's imperial capital. It lies low and large on the plain, a metropolis of mud and earth, encircled by seven kilometres of rose-red walls in 'tabiya', a compound of the local pink sand strengthened with lime. The ramparts were constructed in 1126/27 to substitute a stockade of thorn bushes that protected the camp of the first Almoravid settlement. The Almoravids' first subjects included Atlas tribesmen, Saharan nomads, conquered and converted Africans and Maghrebis as well as former slaves. Indeed, Marrakesh is more deeply African than any other of the great cities of the North of Morocco. As Edith Wharton pointed out in 1927: "Marrakesh is the great market of the south; and the south means not only the Atlas with its feudal chiefs and their wild clansmen, but all that lies beyond...: the Sahara of the veiled Tuareg, Dakar, Timbuctoo, Senegal and the Sudan." The site of the rose-red city is breathtakingly beautiful, theatrically set off by the Atlas, the grandest Moroccan mountain range, which is often snow-capped in the hazy distance. Louis de Marmol in the 16th century considered it "a great city, the best situated in all of Africa, in a fine plain ... surrounded by the richest countryside..." At that time the extraordinary irrigation system known as the 'kettara', deep open wells that give the landscape of the Palmeraie a lunar quality, ensured the absolute fertility of the city and reinforced that "oasis" quality that it still has today.

Marrakech, «El amara» («la rouge») est longtemps restée la rivale sudiste de Fès en tant que capitale impériale. Elle s'étend sur la plaine, métropole de boue et de terre, encerclée par sept kilomètres de murailles rose-rouge en ‹tabiya›, un mélange de sable rose local et de chaux. Les remparts furent érigés en 1126/27, pour remplacer la barrière de ronces qui protégeait le premier campement almoravide. Les premiers sujets des almoravides incluaient des tribus de l'Atlas, des nomades du Sahara, diverses peuplades africaines et maghrébines vaincues et converties, et d'anciens esclaves.... De fait, Marrakech est plus africaine que toutes les grandes cités du nord du Maroc, comme l'observait Edith Wharton en 1927: «Marrakech est le grand marché du sud; et le sud ne s'arrête pas aux chefs féodaux et à leurs guerriers sauvages de l'Atlas, mais s'étend bien au-delà: aux Touaregs voilés du Sahara, à Dakar, à Tombouctou, au Sénégal et au Soudan.» Le site de la cité rose-rouge est d'une beauté à couper le souffle avec, en toile de fond, l'Atlas, la plus grande chaîne de montagnes du Maroc, dont on aperçoit souvent les sommets enneigés derrière un rideau de brume. Au XVIe siècle, Louis de Marmol la décrivait comme «une ville superbe, la mieux située de toute l'Afrique, dans une belle plaine... entourée d'un paysage parmi les plus riches...» A l'époque, l'extraordinaire système d'irrigation, les ‹kettara›, de profonds puits ouverts qui donnent à la Palmeraie son aspect lunaire, assurait la grande fertilité de la ville et accentuait cette qualité d'oasis qu'elle conserve encore aujourd'hui.

Marrakesch, »El amara« (»die Rote«), galt lange Zeit als die südliche Rivalin von Fes, die Königsstadt des Landes war. Marrakesch liegt niedrig und ausgedehnt in der Ebene, eine Metropole aus Lehm und Erde, umgeben von einer sieben Kilometer langen rosenroten Mauer aus ›tabiya‹, einem Gemisch aus dem örtlichen rosa Sand und Kalk. Die Stadtmauern wurden 1126/27 gebaut. Sie ersetzten ein Gehege aus Dornbüschen, das das Lager der ersten Almoravidensiedlung schützte. Zu den Untertanen der Almoraviden gehörten Stämme aus dem Atlas, Sahara-Nomaden, besiegte und konvertierte Afrikaner und Mogrebis sowie frühere Sklaven. Marrakesch ist in der Tat wesentlich afrikanischer als die anderen großen Städte des Nordens von Marokko, wie Edith Wharton 1927 zum Ausdruck brachte: »Marrakesch ist der große Marktplatz des Südens; und Süden bedeutet nicht bloß den Atlas mit seinen Stammesfürsten und ihren wilden Clanmitgliedern, sondern auch alles, was jenseits liegt...: die Sahara mit den verschleierten Tuareg, Dakar, Timbuktu, der Senegal und der Sudan.« Die Lage der rosenroten Stadt ist atemberaubend schön vor der Kulisse des Atlas, der grandiosen marokkanischen Gebirgslandschaft, die man oft schneebedeckt in dunstiger Ferne liegen sieht. Louis de Marmol schrieb im 16. Jahrhundert, Marrakesch sei »eine großartige Stadt, die am schönsten gelegene in ganz Afrika, in einer herrlichen Ebene... umgeben von fruchtbarstem Land...« Damals garantierte das hervorragende Bewässerungssystem, das als ›kettara‹ bekannt ist, Fruchtbarkeit und verstärkte den Oasen-Charakter der Stadt, der ihr noch heute eigen ist. Die tiefen offenen Brunnen verleihen der Landschaft der Palmeraie ein mondartiges Gepräge.

On the way to the Tizi n'Test, one of the most spectacular mountain passes in Africa, lies the breathtaking scenery of the Asni valley. It was here, in 1989, where California-based antique dealer Luciano Tempo discovered a caidal casbah in a semi-ruinous state. Now his home, Casbah Tamadot, fitted out with thirteen bedrooms and five drawing-rooms, has become the true expression of Tempo's eclectic style. It reflects his love for ethnic architecture and objects. Every room abounds with juxtapositions of the different cultures he particularly admires. He has an instinctive talent for combining materials from India, Pakistan, Bali or Mexico with indigenous elements, and his imagination has been allowed full rein, with striking results. The dining-room ceiling, for example, is a mosaic of Pakistani carvings, 'zouaked' beams and enamelled pill boxes bought at the 'souk'.

Luciano Tempo

Sur la route de Tizi n'Test, l'un des cols de montagne les plus spectaculaires d'Afrique, s'étend la somptueuse vallée d'Asni. C'est ici qu'en 1989 l'antiquaire californien Luciano Tempo a découvert une ancienne casbah de caïd tombant en ruines. Il en a fait sa demeure. Casbah Tamadot, qui compte treize chambres et cinq salons, est l'expression même de l'éclectisme de Tempo. Elle reflète son amour de l'architecture et de l'art primitif. Chaque pièce est abondamment décorée d'objets venus des quatre coins du monde. Tempo a l'art de marier les matières provenant d'Inde, du Pakistan, de Bali ou du Mexique avec des éléments locaux. Ici, il a donné libre cours à son imagination, avec des résultats impressionnants. Le plafond de la salle à manger, par exemple, est une mosaïque de sculptures pakistanaises, de poutres en ‹zouak› et de boîtes à pilules émaillées chinées au souk.

Auf dem Weg zum Tizi n'Test, einem der spektakulärsten Gebirgspässe Afrikas, liegt das atemberaubende Asni-Tal. Hier entdeckte der in Kalifornien ansässige Antiquitätenhändler Luciano Tempo 1989 eine ›caïd-kasbah‹ in halbzerstörtem Zustand. Kasbah Tamadot, nun sein zweites Zuhause und ausgestattet mit dreizehn Schlafzimmern und fünf Salons, ist zu einem echten Ausdruck von Tempos eklektischem Stil geworden. Sie spiegelt seine Vorliebe für »ethnische« Architektur und Folklore-Gegenstände wider. Jedes Zimmer ist vollgestopft mit einem Nebeneinander verschiedener Kulturen. Tempo besitzt ein intuitives Geschick dafür, Materialien aus Indien, Pakistan, Bali oder Mexiko mit einheimischen Elementen zu verbinden. Dabei hat er seiner Vorstellungskraft freien Lauf gelassen – mit verblüffenden Ergebnissen. Die Decke im Eßzimmer zum Beispiel ist ein Mosaik aus pakistanischer Schnitzereien, in ›zouak‹-Technik bemalten Balken und emaillierten Pillendosen, die er im ›souk‹ gekauft hat.

The large basin containing goldfish is central to the internal structure of the house as the rooms lead off the gallery around it. Luciano Tempo designed the interiors himself and built his home mostly with the sole aid of local craftsmen.

Le vaste bassin rempli de poissons rouges forme le cœur de la maison. Toutes les pièces donnent sur la galerie qui l'entoure. Luciano Tempo a dessiné lui-même l'architecture intérieure et n'a pratiquement eu recours qu'à des artisans locaux.

Das große Bassin mit den Goldfischen bildet den Mittelpunkt im Inneren des Hauses, denn die Zimmer gehen von der umlaufenden Galerie ab. Luciano Tempo hat die Innenräume selbst entworfen und sein Haus fast ausschließlich mit der Hilfe von einheimischen Handwerkern ausgebaut.

Moroccan Interiors   Luciano Tempo   Marrakech

Indian silks are juxtaposed with Moroccan carpets and 'zouak' ceilings. Most of the twenty-five rooms in Tempo's domain, where he spends six months of the year, have extraordinary views of the Asni valley, situated about forty kilometres from Marrakesh.

Des soieries indiennes sont mariées avec des tapis marocains et des plafonds en ‹zouak› peints. La plupart des vingt-cinq pièces de la casbah de Tempo, où il passe six mois de l'année, offrent des vues extraordinaires sur la vallée d'Asni, située à une quarantaine de kilomètres de Marrakech.

Indische Seide wird mit marokkanischen Teppichen und einer ›zouak‹- Zimmerdecke kombiniert. Von den meisten der fünfundzwanzig Zimmer in Tempos Domizil, wo er sechs Monate im Jahr verbringt, hat man einen außergewöhnlich schönen Blick auf das Asni-Tal, das ungefähr vierzig Kilometer von Marrakesch entfernt liegt.

Above: one of the smaller salons, with low Moroccan style seating
and a beautifully carved antique ceiling. The supports for the table in
the shape of elephants were brought back from the Far East.
Right page: the terrace at tea time and its extraordinary view.

Ci-dessus: l'un des petits salons, avec des banquettes basses de style
marocain et un magnifique plafond sculpté. Les éléphants sur lesquels
repose la table basse furent ramenés d'Extrême-Orient.
Page de droite: la terrasse à l'heure du thé et sa vue extraordinaire.

Oben: einer der kleineren Salons, mit niedrigen Sitzmöbeln im ma-
rokkanischen Stil und einer wunderschön geschnitzten alten Decke.
Die Stützen für den Tisch in der Form von Elefanten stammen von
einer Reise in den Fernen Osten.
Rechte Seite: die Terrasse am Nachmittag mit phantastischem
Ausblick.

This 1923 construction is one of the most significant examples of colonial architecture in the whole of North Africa. Boul de Breteuil, the "grande dame" of Marrakesh, who is sadly no longer with us, received the splendid palace as a gift from her mother-in-law the Viomtess de Breteuil. The Viomtess had bought it from the American, Mrs. Taylor, who had originally commissioned its construction by the architect Poisson. He embraced local architecture and techniques at a period when most colonial homes remained unashamedly European. Conceived around two 'riyâds', the ochre walls of the exterior resemble the 'ksour' of the South, and the imposing tower was inspired by the traditional 'tighremt'. Enthroned in her sumptuous domain, Boul became a legendary figure in her lifetime, quintessentially elegant and with a knowledge of all things Moroccan. In the words of Bill Willis (see pp. 150–159), "Boul was the mother of us all."

Boul de Breteuil

Construite en 1923, cette demeure est l'un des plus beaux exemples d'architecture coloniale de toute l'Afrique du nord. Boul de Breteuil, grande dame de Marrakech qui malheureusement nous a quittée, reçut ce splendide palais de sa belle-mère, la vicomtesse de Breteuil. Cette dernière l'avait acheté à Mrs Taylor, une Américaine qui l'avait commandé à l'architecte Poisson. Poisson s'est inspiré de l'architecture et des techniques locales à une époque où la plupart des maisons coloniales étaient résolument européennes. Encerclant deux ‹riyâds›, les façades ocres évoquent les ksours du Sud et l'imposante tour s'inspire du ‹tighremt› traditionnel. Régnant depuis son somptueux domaine, Boul est devenue une figure légendaire grâce à son élégance et sa profonde connaissance de tout ce qui touchait de près ou de loin au Maroc. De la bouche même de Bill Willis (see pp. 150–159): «Boul était notre mère à tous.»

Dieses Gebäude aus dem Jahre 1923 ist eines der bedeutendsten Beispiele für die koloniale Architektur Nordafrikas. Boul de Breteuil, die große Dame von Marrakesch, die leider inzwischen verstorben ist, erhielt den prächtigen Palast als Geschenk von ihrer Schwiegermutter, der Vicomtesse de Breteuil. Die Vicomtesse hatte ihn einer Amerikanerin, Mrs. Taylor, abgekauft, die den Palast ursprünglich bei dem Architekten Poisson in Auftrag gegeben hatte. Poisson orientierte sich dabei an einheimischer Architektur und Bautechniken, und zwar zu einem Zeitpunkt, als sich die meisten Kolonialvillen noch europäisch gaben. Die ockerfarbenen Außenmauern, um zwei ›riyâds‹ herum angelegt, erinnern an die ›ksour‹ des Südens. Der imposante Turm ist von dem traditionellen ›tighremt‹ inspiriert. Über ihr aufwendiges Reich herrschend, wurde Boul wegen ihrer Eleganz und ihrer Kenntnisse Marokkos und alles Marokkanischen bereits zu Lebzeiten zu einer Legende. In den Worten von Bill Willis (s. S. 150–159): »Boul war unser aller Mutter.«

On these pages: *views of the main courtyard and its 'riyââ', overrun with bougainvillaea and other flowering vines. The traditional marble basin, marble and 'zelliges' floor and 'zelliges' fountain add to its charm.*

Ci-dessus, ci-contre et page de droite: *la cour principale et son ‹riyâd› envahi par le bougainvillier et autres plantes grimpantes. La bassin traditionnel en marbre, la fontaine recouverte de carreaux de faïence et le sol dallé de marbre et de ‹zelliges› ajoutent encore au charme des lieux.*

Diese Doppelseite: *der Blick auf den zentralen Innenhof und seinen ›riyâd‹, der mit Bougainvillea und anderen blühenden Rebengewäch-sen bewachsen ist. Das traditionelle Marmorbassin, der Brunnen mit seinen Kachelmosaiken und der mit Marmor und Mosaiken aus-gelegte Boden verleihen dem Ganzen zusätzlichen Charme.*

Above: the salon with its intricate plasterwork and carved and painted ceilings. As in traditional palaces, the walls were mosaicked up to shoulder height with 'zelliges'. Much of the furniture was English, combined with good Moroccan pieces.

Ci-dessus: le salon avec ses délicats entrelacs de stuc et ses plafonds peints et sculptés. Comme dans tous les palais traditionnels, les murs sont tapissés de ‹zelliges› jusqu'à hauteur d'épaule. Le mobilier était principalement anglais, associé à quelques belles pièces marocaines.

Oben: der Salon mit seinen Stuckornamenten und den geschnitzten und bemalten Decken. Wie in alten Palästen wurden die Wände bis auf Schulterhöhe mit ›zelliges‹-Mosaiken ausgelegt. Viele Möbel waren englischer Herkunft, kombiniert mit wertvollen marokkanischen Stücken.

Moroccan Interiors   Boul de Breteuil   Marrakech

Below and above right: the celebrated "Blue Room" and its 'zouak'.
This traditional technique for painting on wood is shown off to its best
result in this intimate sitting-room on the second floor, perched high
above the courtyards. Here, all the furnishings were locally made.

Ci-dessous et ci-dessus à droite: le célèbre «salon bleu» et ses ‹zouak›
Cette technique traditionnelle de peinture sur bois trouve sa plus belle
expression dans ce petit salon intime du second étage, perché au-dessus des jardins. Ici, tout le mobilier a été réalisé localement.

Unten und oben rechts: das berühmte »Blaue Zimmer« und seine
›zouak‹-Bemalung. Diese überlieferte Technik der Holzbemalung
wurde am eindrucksvollsten in diesem intimen Wohnzimmer im zweiten Stock, hoch über den Innenhöfen, angewendet. Alle Möbel in
diesem Raum sind von einheimischen Tischlern angefertigt.

Left page: the bedroom with its intricate 'zouak' work, at its most effective on the 'koubba'.
Above: the bathroom, a homage to twenties and thirties aesthetics. It does not seem out of place in such an expression of pure fantasy as this house is, that has the exterior of a mud fortress, the interior of a Hispano-Moresque palace and the comfort of an English country house.

Page de gauche: la chambre à coucher avec ses ‹zouak› raffinés, particulièrement splendides dans la koubba.
Ci-dessus: la salle de bains, un hommage à l'esthétisme des années vingt et trente. Elle n'est pas déplacée dans cet univers de pure fantaisie qui, vu de l'extérieur, rappelle un château de sable, et de l'intérieur, un palais hispano-moresque pourvu de tout le confort d'une maison de campagne anglaise.

Linke Seite: das Schlafzimmer mit seiner ornamentalen ›zouak‹-Bemalung, am wirkungsvollsten auf der ›koubba‹.
Oben: das Badezimmer, eine Hommage an die Ästhetik der zwanziger und dreißiger Jahre. Es wirkt nicht fehl am Platz in diesem reinen Phantasiegebilde, das von außen wie eine Lehmburg, von innen aber wie ein hispano-maurischer Palast wirkt und den Komfort eines englischen Landhauses besitzt.

Built in 1924 by the artist Jacques Majorelle in a resolutely modern style and flamboyantly painted daubed with the piercing blue that is now referred to by his name, this villa stands amid luxuriant gardens splendidly restored by the present owners. They have lovingly transformed the interior in collaboration with Bill Willis (see pp. 150–159) and Jacques Grange, respecting Majorelle's vision of a neo-Moresque fantasy. This allies the Art Deco motifs which the artist created for his home with an inspired take on the local traditional decorative techniques. Each room takes as its theme one particular incarnation of the orientalist dream, and one of Majorelle's prefered colours fire red, almond green and his famous blue. The result is a pleasure pavilion, aptly baptised "Villa Oasis", that Yves Saint Laurent loves more than any other place on earth and that provides a welcome haven from the frantic pace of the Paris fashion world.

Yves Saint Laurent et Pierre Bergé

Construite en 1924 par l'artiste Jacques Majorelle dans un style résolument moderne et flamboyant, avec ce bleu éclatant qui a désormais pris son nom, cette villa se dresse dans un jardin luxuriant superbement restauré par les propriétaires actuels. Avec l'aide de Bill Willis (voir pp. 150–159) et de Jacques Grange, ils ont minutieusement transformé l'intérieur sans jamais trahir l'esthétique néo-moresque de Majorelle. Les motifs art déco créés par l'artiste ont été combinés avec des éléments inspirés de techniques locales traditionnelles. Chaque pièce incarne un aspect particulier du rêve orientaliste et reprend l'une des couleurs favorites de Majorelle: le rouge incendiaire, le vert amande, et son célèbre bleu. Le résultat est un pavillon de plaisance, baptisé à juste titre «Villa Oasis». C'est le lieu qu'Yves Saint Laurent aime plus que tout autre, son havre de paix après le rythme frénétique du monde parisien de la mode.

Diese Villa, die im Jahre 1924 von dem Künstler Jacques Majorelle in einem entschieden modernen Stil erbaut und in jenem strahlenden Blau gestrichen wurde, das nun »Bleu Majorelle« heißt, steht inmitten prachtvoller Gärten, die von den derzeitigen Besitzern herrlich restauriert wurden. Sie haben auch das Interieur der Villa in Zusammenarbeit mit Bill Willis (s. S. 150–159) und Jacques Grange liebevoll wiederhergestellt, wobei sie sich an Majorelles Vorstellung von einer neo-maurischen Phantasie gehalten haben. Das paßt zu den Art-déco-Motiven, die der Künstler in einer von einheimischen traditionellen Ornamenten inspirierten Version für sein Haus geschaffen hat. Jeder Raum macht sich eine bestimmte Inkarnation des orientalischen Traums zum Thema sowie eine von Majorelles bevorzugten Farben: Feuerrot, Zartgrün und sein berühmtes Blau. Das Ergebnis ist ein Lustpavillon, der »Villa Oasis« getauft wurde und den Yves Saint Laurent mehr als jeden anderen Ort auf der Erde liebt. Er dient ihm als willkommenes Refugium nach der Hektik der Pariser Modewelt.

Page 87: *the 'menzeh', where the ceiling was removed in order to reveal the eaves. This is the most informal room in the house, furnished with forties armchairs in cord and with Art Deco pieces including a desk made for Madeleine Vionnet. It overlooks the splendid gardens.*
On these pages: *the wonderful gardens with pavilion and pond.*

Page 87: *la ‹menzeh›, où la charpente a été mise à nue. C'est la pièce la plus informelle de la maison, meublée avec des fauteuils en corde des années quarante et des pièces Art déco dont un bureau réalisé pour Madeleine Vionnet. Elle donne sur les splendides jardins.*
Ci-contre et ci-dessus: *les magnifiques jardins avec le pavillon et l'étang.*

Seite 87: *die ›menzeh‹, bei der die Decke entfernt wurde, um den Dachstuhl freizulegen. Dies ist der legerste Raum im ganzen Haus, der mit Sesseln mit Seilbespannung aus den vierziger Jahren und Art déco-Möbeln ausgestattet ist, darunter ein Tisch, der für Madeleine Vionnet angefertigt wurde. Von hier blickt man auf die prächtigen Gärten.*
Diese Doppelseite: *die wunderbaren Gärten mit Pavillon und Teich.*

Above: the richly decorated alcove in the entrance hall with 'zouak' and 'djibs' work. It was originally conceived for the musicians at formal receptions.
Right page: other splendid examples of 'zouak' in the niche of the deep-red drawing-room. The painstaking technique caused one craftsman to take nine months to complete the room, conceived to evoke the splendour of 19th-century orientalism as depicted by French writer Pierre Loti. The armchairs, originals from that period, are upholstered with Kilims.

Ci-dessus: l'alcôve richement décorée du hall d'entrée, avec des ‹zouak› et des ‹djibs›. A l'origine, elle accueillait les musiciens lors des grandes réceptions.
Page de droite: d'autres superbes ‹zouak› dans la niche du salon rouge sombre. L'artisan a travaillé neuf mois pour réaliser cette pièce requérant une technique particulièrement délicate. On y retrouve la splendeur de l'orientalisme du XIXe siècle de l'écrivain français Pierre Loti. Les fauteuils, qui datent de cette période, sont tapissés de kilims.

Oben: der reich verzierte Alkoven in der Eingangshalle mit ›zouak‹- und Gipsarbeiten. Er wurde ursprünglich für die Musiker bei feierlichen Empfängen entworfen.
Rechte Seite: weitere prächtige ›zouak‹-Arbeiten in der Nische des dunkelroten Salons. Für diese aufwendige Ausstattung brauchte einer der Handwerker neun Monate. Das Zimmer sollte die Pracht des orientalischen Exotismus aus dem 19. Jahrhundert, den der französische Schriftsteller Pierre Loti vertrat, hervorrufen. Die Sessel, Originalstücke aus jener Epoche, sind mit Kelims bezogen.

Left page: the elaborately decorative fireplace alcove in what is
known as the Art Deco drawing-room on the ground floor.
Above: a detail of the same. The panelling, painted with a free
interpretation of a Moorish motif, was designed by Majorelle. The
leopard armchairs are placed on a patchwork rug.

Page de gauche: une cheminée richement décorée dans l'alcôve du
salon art déco au rez-de-chaussée.
Ci-dessus: un détail des boiseries peintes par Majorelle avec une libre
interprétation d'un motif moresque. Les fauteuils en léopard sont
placés sur un tapis en patchwork.

Linke Seite: der kunstvoll verzierte Kamin-Alkoven in dem Art-déco-
Salon im Erdgeschoß.
Oben: ein Detail des gleichen Zimmers. Die Täfelung, bemalt mit
der freien Variation eines maurischen Musters, wurde von Majorelle
entworfen. Die Leopardensessel stehen auf einem Patchwork-Teppich.

Above: a detail of the "Matisse Room" which is based on a palette of blues. 'Zelliges' in these tones decorate the walls. The console is a thirties piece and the 19th-century vases are Syrian.
Right page: the black marble bathroom which evokes all at once the Art Deco aesthetics of the original interiors of the Hotel Mamounia, the sunken bath of its neighbour, Boul de Breteuil (see pp. 78–85) and, in the words of Jacques Grange, "Egyptian opulence".

Ci-dessus: un détail de la «chambre Matisse», basée sur un camaïeu de bleus. Des ‹zelliges› dans les mêmes tons ornent les murs. Sur une console des années trente, des vases syriens du XIXe siècle.
Page de droite: la salle de bains en marbre noir qui évoque tout à la fois l'esthétique Art déco du décor original de la Mamounia, la baignoire creusée dans le sol de la villa voisine de Boul de Breteuil (voir pp. 78–85) – et, selon les termes de Jacques Grange, «l'opulence égyptienne».

Oben: Detailaufnahme vom »Matisse-Zimmer«, das in verschiedenen Blautönen gehalten ist. ›Zelliges‹ in diesen Farben zieren die Wände. Die Konsole stammt aus den dreißiger Jahren, die Vasen aus dem 19. Jahrhundert sind syrischer Herkunft.
Rechte Seite : Das Badezimmer aus schwarzem Marmor erinnert an die ursprünglichen Art-déco-Interieurs des Hotels Mamounia, an das abgesenkte Bad der Nachbarin Boul de Breteuil (s. S. 78–85) und an, wie Jacques Grange es ausdrückt, »ägyptische Prachtentfaltung«.

This caidal tent, with its characteristic black leather design appliquéd on heavy white canvas, is what is known as a 'makhzen'. They were traditionally erected for travelling dignitaries, as Walter Harris described at the close of the 19th century: "Sultan after Sultan, ever since the Empire of Morocco first came under the dominion of the Arabs, had travelled in exactly the same manner as that in which Moulay Abdul Aziz was making the journey from Marrakesh to Rabat. In no detail had it changed... The very shape and decoration of the tents had never varied, and to such an extent had conservatism been maintained, that so far from travelling with all the luxury that one could imagine, he was forbidden by the unwritten laws of tradition to cover the floor of his state tent, except for three small carpets. The rest of the floor-space must consist of the soil of the country..." Nowadays the court often erects caidal tents as temporary banqueting halls, for which purpose they are often adopted by restaurants.

La tente caïdale

Cette tente caïdale, avec ses motifs caractéristiques en cuir noir appliqués sur une épaisse toile blanche, est appelée ‹makhzen›. Autrefois, elle était érigée pour accueillir les dignitaires en déplacement, comme le décrit Walter Harris à la fin du XIXe siècle: «Depuis que l'Empire du Maroc est tombé sous la domination arabe, chaque sultan voyage exactement comme le faisait Moulay Abdul Aziz quand il se rendait de Marrakech à Rabat. Rien n'a changé depuis». Plus loin, Harris poursuit: «La forme même et la décoration des tentes sont immuables. La tradition s'est maintenue au point que, bien que voyageant dans un luxe inimaginable, des lois tacites interdisent au sultan de couvrir le sol de sa tente officielle de plus de trois petits tapis, le reste du sol devant être constitué du sol du pays traversé». Aujourd'hui, la Cour fait souvent installer ces tentes pour accueillir des banquets et les restaurants y ont souvent recours.

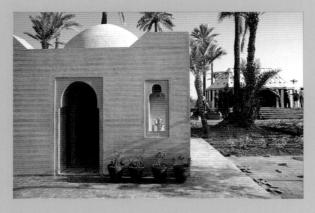

Dieses ›caïdal‹-Zelt mit seinen typischen schwarzen Lederornamenten, die auf die schwere weiße Zeltbahn aufgenäht sind, ist ein sogenanntes ›makhzen‹. Solche Zelte wurden traditionsgemäß für reisende Würdenträger errichtet, wie es Walter Harris am Ende des 19. Jahrhunderts beschrieb: »Seitdem das marrokkanische Reich unter die Herrschaft der Araber geriet, war Sultan um Sultan auf genau die gleiche Weise gereist wie Moulay Abdul Aziz, als er seine Reise von Marrakesch nach Rabat machte... Form und Verzierung der Zelte hatten sich nie verändert, und der Konservatismus war sogar soweit gegangen, daß es dem Sultan, der weit davon entfernt war, in allem nur vorstellbaren Luxus zu reisen, sogar von den ungeschriebenen Gesetzen der Tradition untersagt war, den Boden seines Staatszeltes mit mehr als drei kleinen Teppichen zu belegen. Ansonsten durfte der Boden nur die nackte Erde seines Landes sein...« Heute werden solche Zelte oft vom Hof als zeitweilige Bankettsäle errichtet. Auch Restaurants nutzen sie inzwischen oft für den selben Zweck.

The luxurious version of a caidal tent that the owner of a large estate in the Palmeraie chose to live in while his house was being built.

Une version luxueuse de la tente caïdale où le propriétaire d'un grand domaine dans la palmeraie s'était installé en attendant que sa maison fût construite.

Die Luxusausführung eines ›caïdal‹-Zeltes, in dem der Besitzer eines großen Grundstückes in der Palmeraie wohnte, während sein Haus gebaut wurde.

With the High Atlas mountains outlined in the distance this small house, isolated among date palms, born of the soil, celebrates the beauty of rustic building materials.

Avec le Haut Atlas pour toile de fond, cette petite maison en terre perdue parmi les dattiers célèbre la beauté des matériaux rustiques.

Vor der Silhouette des Hohen Atlas in der Ferne liegt dieses kleine Haus versteckt zwischen Dattelpalmen. Aus heimatlicher Erde gebaut, preist es die Schönheit ländlicher Baumaterialien.

Jacqueline Foissac is the pioneer of 'pisé' and was highly instrumental in adapting this ancient Berber technique to contemporary architecture. She first discovered the Palmeraie of Marrakesh in 1969 when it was completely unexploited, a desert wilderness of date palms and scrub. In this oasis she built herself several homes conjured out of the red earth, turning bourgeois presumptions about luxury upside down. This beautifully graphic construction, a monolithic tribute to the impact of indigenous materials, is the last she is to live in in the Palmeraie. Being something of a nomad herself, she now plans to move to the medina, amid the hustle and bustle of the 'souk', where her building and decorating activities have taken her so often over the years. Her thorough understanding of traditional techniques make her a well-loved figure with the local craftsmen.

Jacqueline Foissac

L'une des premières à prôner le retour au pisé, la décoratrice Jacqueline Foissac a joué un rôle considérable dans l'adaptation de cette technique berbère traditionnelle dans l'architecture contemporaine. Elle a découvert la Palmeraie de Marrakech en 1969 alors que alle-ci complètement inexploitée, n'était plus qu'un désert de dattiers et de buissons. Dans cette oasis, elle a fait surgir comme par enchantement plusieurs maisons de terre rouge que bouleversaient la conception bourgeoise du luxe. Cette bâtisse somptueusement graphique, hommage monolithique à la beauté des matières indigènes, est la dernière habitation de Madame Foissac dans la Palmeraie. Nomade impénitente, la décoratrice vit désormais dans la médina, au sein du tumulte du souk où ses activités professionnelles l'ont si souvent menée au fil des ans. Sa parfaite connaissance des techniques traditionnelles lui valent l'amitié et l'estime des artisans de la région.

Jacqueline Foissac, die Pionierin des Pisee, war wesentlich daran beteiligt, diese alte Berbertechnik für die moderne Architektur nutzbar zu machen. Sie entdeckte die Palmeraie von Marrakesch 1969, als sie noch völlig unkultiviert war, eine Wüstenwildnis aus Dattelpalmen und Büschen. In dieser Oase baute sie sich mehrere Häuser, aus roter Erde gezaubert, wobei sie bürgerliche Vorstellungen von Luxus auf den Kopf stellte. Dieser wunderschöne graphische Bau, ein monolithischer Tribut an die Ausdruckskraft einheimischer Materialien, ist der letzte, den sie in der Palmeraie bewohnen wird. Gleichsam als Nomadin hat sie nun vor, in die Medina zu ziehen, in das Gewimmel des ›souk‹, wohin ihre Bauaktivitäten und Ausstattungsarbeiten sie im Laufe der Jahre so oft geführt haben. Ihr tiefes Verständnis für überlieferte Techniken und Methoden hat dazu geführt, daß die Handwerker vor Ort sie sehr schätzen.

Above: *a view of the terrace with its canvas hangings that provide shelter from the midday sun. These are something of a Foissac trademark along with the extensive use of visible red brick, partly inspired by what was originally a Nubian technique of building domes without reinforcements that was much used in Egypt.*

Ci-dessus: *une vue de la terrasse avec les dais de toile qui protègent du soleil de midi. Elles sont devenues la signature Foissac, tout comme le recours fréquent au briques rouges apparentes, parfois inspiré par une technique nubienne de construction de dômes sans armatures, largement utilisée en Egypte.*

Oben: *Blick auf die Terrasse mit ihren Segeltuchbahnen, die vor der Mittagssonne schützen. Sie sind gewissermaßen ein Markenzeichen für Foissac, ebenso wie ihr ausgedehnter Gebrauch von nacktem roten Backstein; dabei ließ sie sich manchmal von einer ursprünglich nubischen, dann ägyptischen Technik anregen, Gewölbe ohne Abstützung zu bauen.*

Moroccan Interiors   Jacqueline Foissac   Marrakech

Below: the house was conceived for predominantly outdoor living, and the "al fresco" sitting-room shown here epitomises this attitude with its deep, semi-circular canvas-covered sofa for lounging. The alcove, again inspired by Nubian techniques, is the visual reference point for the whole structure and adds texture and variety to the monochromatic pressed-earth walls and floor.

Ci-dessous: la maison est ouverte aux éléments et le petit salon «al fresco» résume bien cet art de vivre au grand air avec son profond sofa semi-circulaire tapissé de toile. L'alcôve, là encore d'inspiration nubienne, est le point de référence visuelle de l'ensemble de la structure et ajoute une note de texture et de variété aux murs et au sol monochromes en pisé.

Unten: Das Haus wurde vornehmlich zum Wohnen im Freien konzipiert. Das abgebildete »al fresco«-Wohnzimmer zeigt dieses Konzept auf kleinerem Raum mit seinem tiefen, halbkreisförmigen, mit Segeltuch bezogenem Sofa, das zum Müßiggang einlädt. Der Alkoven, wiederum von nubischen Techniken inspiriert, ist Blickfang und Fluchtpunkt für den ganzen Bau und verleiht den monochromen Lehmwänden Struktur und Abwechslung.

Left page: throughout the house the high ceilings in brick and decorative ventilation vents allow the air to circulate. The brass bed is a neo-traditional 19th-century piece. The grille over the circular window is a reference to the symbolic "magic triangle" of the Egyptians.
Above: the bathroom with its organic, sensual shapes in 'tadelakt', perfected with the assistance of the Moroccan architect Elie Mouyal (see pp. 114–119).

Page de gauche: dans toute la maison, les haut plafonds en briques et les ouvertures décoratives laissent l'air circuler librement. Le lit en laiton néo-traditionnel date du XIXe siècle. Le motif de la fenêtre ronde est une référence au «triangle magique« symbolique des Egyptiens.
Ci-dessus: la salle de bains, avec ses formes sensuelles et organiques en ‹tadelakt› a été réalisée avec l'aide de l'architecte marocain Elie Mouyal (voir pp. 114–119).

Linke Seite: Im ganzen Haus sorgen die hohen Decken und die dekorativen Ventilatoren dafür, daß die Luft zirkuliert. Das Messingbett stammt aus dem 19. Jahrhundert. Das Gitter vor dem runden Fenster ist eine Anspielung auf das symbolische »magische Dreieck« der Ägypter.
Oben: Das Badezimmer mit seinen organischen, sinnlichen Formen in ›tadelakt‹ wurde mit Hilfe des marokkanischen Architekten Elie Mouyal (s. S. 114–119) vollendet.

This large house, which from a distance gives the impression of something more like a small village enclosed behind the high dusty rose walls, was originally built and decorated by Jacqueline Foissac (see pp. 100–105). Since then its present owner, Tamy Tazi, has given the rustic simplicity of the structure in 'pisé' a more sophisticated allure due to her vast collection of antique Islamic textiles and furnishings, many of which are Ottoman rather than specifically Moroccan. The small illustration on the left shows a detail of the almond-green ceiling in 'tataoui', a traditional technique, originally from the region of Tata in the deep south, that uses slim branches of cedar or laurel to great effect and has been widely adopted in the region of Marrakesh. Originally these were always painted before they were installed giving great scope to interesting plays on colour.

Tamy Tazi

Vue de loin, cette grande maison ressemble à un petit hameau protégé derrière de hauts murs en terre rose. Elle fut initialement construite et décorée par Jacqueline Foissac (voir pp. 100–105). Depuis, sa propriétaire actuelle, Tamy Tazi, a donné à la simplicité rustique de la structure en pisé une allure plus sophistiquée grâce à sa vaste collection de meubles et de tissus islamiques anciens, dont bon nombre sont ottomans plutôt que marocains. La petite illustration à gauche montre un détail du plafond vert amande en ‹tataoui›. Cette technique traditionnelle du plus bel effet utilise de minces branches de cèdre ou de laurier. Bien que venant de la région de Tata, dans le grand sud, elle a été largement adoptée dans la région de Marrakech. A l'origine, les branches étaient toujours peintes avant d'être installées, offrant ainsi d'intéressants jeux de couleurs.

Dieses große Haus, das aus der Entfernung eher den Eindruck eines kleinen Dorfes hinter hohen, staubigen, rosenfarbenen Mauern erweckt, wurde ursprünglich von Jacqueline Foissac (s. S. 100–105) gebaut und ausgestattet. Die derzeitige Besitzerin, Tamy Tazi, hat die rustikale Einfachheit des Piseebaus etwas verfeinert durch ihre umfangreiche Sammlung alter islamischer Stoffe und Möbel, von denen viele allerdings eher ottomanisch als speziell marokkanisch sind. Die Abbildung oben links zeigt einen Auschnitt der zartgrünen Decke in ›tataoui‹, einer traditionellen Technik, die ursprünglich aus dem Gebiet von Tata im tiefen Süden kommt und bei der kleine Zedern- oder Lorbeerzweige erstaunliche Effekte hervorrufen. Diese Technik ist in der Region von Marrakesch weit verbreitet. Ursprünglich wurden diese Zweige immer bemalt, bevor sie in einem interessanten Farbenspiel eingesetzt wurden.

A view of the garden façade and the veranda. The graphic effect of the pillars in raw brick is contrasted by the canvas hangings and the dappled shade cast by the roofing.

Une vue de la façade côté jardin et de la véranda. L'effet graphique des colonnes en briques apparentes est contrasté par les grandes toiles tendues et les taches d'ombre projetées par la toiture en bois.

Blick auf die Gartenfassade und die Veranda. Die graphische Wirkung der Säulen aus rohem Backstein bildet einen Kontrast zu den Segeltuchbahnen und dem gesprenkelten Schatten, der von einer Holzüberdachung geworfen wird.

A view of the swimming pool and the pool pavilion with its canvas hangings and its low balustrade in 'moucharaby'. The mountains of the High Atlas can be seen in the distance.

Une vue de la piscine et de son pavillon, avec des dais et une balustrade en moucharabieh. Au loin, on distingue les cimes du Haut Atlas.

Blick auf den Swimmingpool und den Pool-Pavillon mit seinen Segeltuchbahnen und der niedrigen Balustrade in >moucharabieh<. In der Ferne der Hohe Atlas.

Above: *a corner of the veranda perfectly adapted to the outdoor living that the weather in Marrakesh permits all year long. The carpets and the fabric on the table are woollen Berber weaves.*
Right page: *a detail of the double doors. The outside pair are antique, salvaged from a palace in the medina; the other pair were designed by Jacqueline Foissac around a recurrent Islamic "diamond" motif.*

Ci-dessus: *un coin de la véranda parfaitement adaptée à la vie en plein air que le climat de Marrakech permet tout au long de l'année. Les tapis et le tissu qui recouvre la table sont des tissages berbères.*
Page de droite: *un détail de la double porte. La porte extérieure est ancienne. Elle a été récupérée dans un palais de la médina. La porte intérieure a été réalisée par Jacqueline Foissac à partir d'un motif islamique en «diamant».*

Oben: *eine Ecke der Veranda, perfekt für das Leben im Freien, das das Wetter in Marrakesch das ganze Jahr über möglich macht. Die Berberteppiche und der Berberstoff auf dem Tisch sind aus Wolle gewebt.*
Rechte Seite: *eine Detailaufnahme der Doppeltüren. Das äußere, antike Paar wurde aus einem Palast in der Medina gerettet; das andere Paar – von einem sich wiederholenden islamischen Rautenmuster ausgehend – hat Jacqueline Foissac entworfen.*

Left page: the living-room has ochre walls in 'tadelakt', with a frieze that has been engraved with an Islamic motif. The wall hanging is an Algerian Kilim. The chair and screen are Syrian, both inlaid with mother-of-pearl and ivory.
Above: the bedroom with a pair of 1930s armchairs of Moroccan craftsmanship. The vases over the mantlepiece are part of an extensive collection of Persian enamelled pieces.

Page de gauche: les murs ocres du salon sont en ‹tadelakt›, avec une frise gravée d'un motif islamique. La tenture est un kilim algérien. La chaise et le paravent, incrustés de nacre et d'ivoire, viennent de Syrie.
Ci-dessus: la chambre à coucher avec une paire de fauteuils marocains des années trente. Les vases sur la cheminée font partie de la vaste collection d'objets persans émaillés.

Linke Seite: Das Wohnzimmer hat ockerfarbene Wände in ›tadelakt‹ mit einem Fries, der mit einem islamischen Muster verziert ist. Ein algerischer Kelim dient als Wandbehang. Der Stuhl und der Paravent mit Intarsien aus Perlmutt und Elfenbein sind syrischer Herkunft.
Oben: das Schlafzimmer mit Armsesseln, die in den areißiger Jahren in Marokko gefertigt wurden. Die Vasen über dem Kaminsims stammen aus einer umfangreichen Sammlung persischer Emaillearbeiten.

This house, the first of many to be designed by the young Moroccan architect Elie Mouyal, was born of the red earth of Marrakesh. Mouyal is a passionate advocate of the traditional rustic architecture of Southern Morocco. With this project, conceived twelve years ago, he explored numerous different techniques for building with indigenous materials such as mud, straw and lime. Situated in the Palmerai and laid out around a central courtyard, each elongated rectangle of a room served as a laboratory for methods of employing these raw materials that are so readily available.

Elie Mouyal

Cette maison en terre rouge de Marrakech qui se dresse dans la Palmeraie est la première d'une nombreuse série réalisée par le jeune architecte marocain Elie Mouyal. Ardent défenseur de l'architecture rustique traditionnelle du sud marocain, Mouyal a conçu ce projet il y a douze ans. Il lui a permis d'explorer un vaste répertoire de techniques de construction avec des matériaux indigènes tels que la boue, la paille et la chaux. Chacune des pièces rectangulaires qui donnent sur la cour centrale a servi de laboratoire pour exploiter une nouvelle méthode à l'aide des matières brutes à portée de main.

Dieses Haus, das erste von vielen, die der junge marokkanische Architekt Elie Mouyal entworfen hat, wurde aus der roten Erde von Marrakesch gebaut. Mouyal ist ein leidenschaftlicher Befürworter der traditionellen bäuerlichen Architektur von Südmarokko, und mit diesem Haus, das vor zwölf Jahren entstanden ist, probierte er zahlreiche unterschiedliche Bautechniken mit einheimischen Materialien wie Lehm, Stroh und Kalk aus. Es steht in der Palmeraie und ist um einen zentralen Innenhof herum angelegt, wobei jedes Zimmer – jeweils ein verlängertes Rechteck – als Experimentierfeld für die Anwendung jener leicht zugänglichen Materialien fungierte.

Page 115: *an archway in handmade bricks in the courtyard.*
Above: *different corners of the lounge.*
Right page: *a niche in adobe and red bricks for lazing the days away.*
On the following double page: *the rustic kitchen which appears to be carved out of the raw earth itself.*

Page 115: *dans la cour, une arche en briques faites à la main.*
Ci-dessus: *différents angles du salon.*
Page de droite: *une niche en adobes et en briques rouges pour la sieste.*
Double page suivante: *la cuisine rustique qui semble avoir été creusée directement dans la terre.*

Seite 115: *ein Bogengang aus handgemachten Ziegeln im Innenhof.*
Oben: *verschiedene Ecken der Wohndiele.*
Rechte Seite: *eine Nische aus Lehmziegeln und rotem Backstein zum Müßiggang.*
Folgende Doppelseite: *Die rustikale Küche wirkt, als sei sie aus der nackten Erde herausgemeißelt worden.*

This large villa in the Palmeraie was built by architect Charles Boccara as a family home for his wife and three children. It is an unusual construction, reaching out into the garden, with four different façades; the lawn, swimming pool and pond take on the visual significance of extensions of the house itself. This expansive spirit is something of a turnaround for North African architecture which is traditionally introspective. Terraces, courtyards and a central patio opened to the sky further blur the definition between the interior and the exterior. The use of traditional rural building materials such as 'pisé' and earth bricks or traditional finishes such as 'tadelakt' has long been a characteristic of Boccara's work. Here he has combined his signature style with a play on proportions, choosing to make the interior passageways and staircases particularly narrow. They evoke the humble origins of this Berber-inspired architecture when passageways could never be wider than the palm fronds that they were built from.

Charles Boccara

Cette grande villa dans la Palmeraie a été construite par l'architecte Charles Boccara pour y accueillir sa femme et ses trois enfants. C'est une étrange bâtisse qui s'étend vers le jardin avec quatre façades différentes. La pelouse, la piscine et le bassin constituent autant d'extensions visuelles de la maison. Cet esprit d'ouverture sur l'extérieur est inhabituel dans l'architecture nord-africaine, plus introvertie par tradition. Les terrasses, les cours et le patio central à ciel ouvert achèvent de fondre les limites entre l'intérieur et l'extérieur. L'utilisation de matériaux traditionnels tels que le pisé et les briques en terre cuite, ainsi que les revêtements muraux comme le ‹tadelakt› sont depuis longtemps caractéristiques du travail de Boccara. Ici, son style s'est enrichi d'un jeu sur les proportions, avec des couloirs et des escaliers particulièrement étroits. Ils évoquent les origines humbles de cette architecture d'inspiration berbère, où les passages ne pouvaient jamais être plus larges que les tiges de palmier avec lesquelles ils étaient bâtis.

Diese große Villa in der Palmeraie wurde von dem Architekten Charles Boccara als Wohnhaus für seine Frau und seine drei Kinder gebaut. Es ist ein ungewöhnliches Gebäude mit vier verschiedenen Fassaden, das sich bis in den Garten ausdehnt; der Rasen, der Swimmingpool und der Teich wirken so auf den Betrachter wie Teile des Hauses selbst. Dieser expansive Ansatz ist gleichsam eine Umkehrung der nordafrikanischen Architektur, die ja traditionsgemäß introspektiv ist. Terrassen, Innenhöfe und ein zentraler Patio, der sich zum Himmel hin öffnet, lassen die Grenzen zwischen Innen und Außen verschwimmen. Die Verwendung traditioneller ländlicher Baumaterialien wie Pisee und Lehmziegel oder alter Verputztechniken wie ›tadelakt‹ ist schon seit langem charakteristisch für Boccaras Projekte. Hier hat er seinen typischen Stil mit einem Spiel mit Proportionen, verknüpft wobei Flure und Treppen im Inneren besonders eng sind. Sie erinnern an die ärmlichen Ursprünge dieser von den Berbern inspirierten Architektur, als Flure nicht breiter sein konnten als die Palmwedel, aus denen sie gebaut waren.

Page 120: the façade, with a covered veranda that gives on to the lawn.
Above: the pond and the view towards the house from the gazebo. The pool and the pond are perpendicular to each other and respect the same proportions. The symmetrical floor plan of the house is characteristic of Islamic constructions.
Right page: the view from the façade, that gives onto the swimming pool, as seen from a first-floor terrace. At ground level, a rectangular courtyard that gives onto the pool connects the children's bedrooms.

Page 120: la façade, avec sa véranda couverte qui donne sur la pelouse.
Ci-dessus: le bassin et la maison vus depuis le belvédère. La piscine et le bassin perpendiculaires respectent les mêmes proportions. Le plan de l'ensemble de la maison est symétrique, une caractéristique de l'architecture islamique.
Page de droite: la façade qui donne sur la piscine, vue depuis la terrasse du premier étage. Au rez-de-chaussée, une cour rectangulaire qui s'ouvre sur la piscine relie les chambres des enfants.

Seite 120: die Fassade mit einer überdachten Veranda, die auf den Rasen führt.
Oben: der Teich und der Blick aufs Haus von der Gartenlaube. Der Pool und der Teich liegen im rechten Winkel zueinander und haben dieselben Proportionen. Der Grundriß des Hauses ist symmetrisch, ein Charakteristikum islamischer Architektur.
Rechte Seite: der Blick von der Fassade, die sich zum Swimmingpool öffnet, von der Terrasse im ersten Stock gesehen. Im Erdgeschoß verbindet ein rechteckiger Innenhof, der zum Pool führt, die Schlafzimmer der Kinder.

Moroccan Interiors   Charles Boccara   Marrakech

Left page: the TV-room, an alcove off the living-room, with small Syrian tables and an armchair. The glass painting in the corner is Tunisian. The textiles and the carpet come from Boccara's collection of Moroccan antiques.
Above: the master bedroom on the first floor gives onto a gallery overlooking the pool and courtyard. The bedspread was originally a door curtain in antique embroidery from Rabat. It is a particularly fine piece as all the embroidery is done on very fine tulle, in white and in the strong colours characteristic of Rabat handiwork.

Page de gauche: la salle de télévision, une alcôve communiquant avec le salon, meublée de tables basses et d'un fauteuil syriens. Le sous-verre dans l'angle est tunisien. Les tissus et le tapis font partie de la collection d'antiquités marocaines de Boccara.
Ci-dessus: la chambre des maîtres au premier étage. Elle donne sur une galerie qui surplombe la piscine et la cour. Sur le lit, un ancien rideau de porte brodé provenant de Rabat. C'est une pièce particulièrement précieuse où toutes les broderies sont réalisées sur un tulle très fin, en blanc et dans les couleurs vives typiques de l'artisanat de Rabat.

Linke Seite: Das Fernsehzimmer ist ein Alkoven neben dem Wohnzimmer mit kleinen syrischen Tischen und einem Armsessel. Das Hinterglasbild in der Ecke ist tunesisch. Die Stoffe und der Teppich stammen aus Boccaras Sammlung marokkanischer Antiquitäten.
Oben: Das große Elternschlafzimmer im ersten Stock führt auf eine Galerie, von der aus man den Pool und den Innenhof überblickt. Die Tagesdecke auf dem Bett war ursprünglich ein Türvorhang, eine alte Stickerei aus Rabat; es ist ein besonders schönes Stück, denn alle Stickarbeiten sind auf sehr feinem weißen Tüll ausgeführt und in den kräftigen Farben, die für Handarbeiten aus Rabat charakteristisch sind.

Above: Boccara has designed some of the bathrooms so that even though they look European they can double as hammam, the ancient steam baths that are an essential part of Moroccan life. The dome is of red brick in the spirit of early Nubian architecture from the banks of the Nile.
Right page: the kitchen where the family take their more informal meals.

Ci-dessus: Boccara a conçu des salles de bains européennes en apparence, mais pouvant également servir de hammam, une vieille tradition qui occupe une place importante dans la vie des Marocains. Le dôme de briques rouges est dans l'esprit des premières constructions nubiennes sur les rives du Nil.
Page de droite: la cuisine où la famille prend ses repas quand elle ne reçoit pas.

Oben: Boccara hat einige der Badezimmer so entworfen, daß sie als ›hammam‹ durchgehen können, die Dampfbäder, die ein wesentlicher Teil marokkanischen Lebens sind. Die Kuppel aus rotem Backstein ist von früher nubischer Architektur am Nilufer inspiriert.
Rechte Seite: die Küche, in der die Familie alltags ißt.

The Lévys, although Paris-based, have always spent a good third of the year in their home in the Palmeraie. They bought a small farm at the end of the sixties and have slowly transformed it into a large family home, built around three large courtyards. They have respected the proportions of the rooms and indeed the structure of a Moroccan farmhouse. Everything was built in local materials with just a master builder and his team – no architects were necessary. Left to themselves the masons created the graceful forms of the arches with a natural instinct for harmonious design.

Florence et Bernard Lévy

Bien que basés à Paris, les Lévy passent un bon tiers de l'année dans leur demeure de la Palmeraie. Ils ont acheté une petite ferme vers la fin des années soixante et l'ont lentement transformée en une grande maison de famille bâtie autour de trois grandes cours. Ils ont respecté les proportions des pièces ainsi que la structure des fermes de la région de Marrakech. Tout a été réalisé sans architecte, avec des matériaux locaux et l'aide d'un entrepreneur et de son équipe. Livrés à eux-mêmes, les maçons ont créé d'élégantes arches avec un instinct naturel pour les formes harmonieuses.

Obwohl sie eigentlich in Paris leben, verbringen die Lévys seit jeher ein gutes Drittel des Jahres in ihrem Haus in der Palmeraie. Ende der sechziger Jahre kauften sie einen kleinen Bauernhof und haben ihn allmählich zu einem großen Wohnhaus umgebaut, das um drei große Innenhöfe herum angelegt ist. Die Proportionen der Räume blieben erhalten und damit auch die Struktur eines marokkanischen Bauernhauses. Alles wurde aus einheimischen Materialien gebaut, von einem Baumeister und seinem Team – ein Architekt wurde nicht gebraucht. Mit ihrem natürlichen Gefühl für Harmonie schufen die Steinmetze die anmutigen Formen der Bögen ohne fremde Anleitung.

Previous pages: *details of the rustic architecture of the original structure which was a simple farm in 'pisé'.*

Pages précédentes: *détails de l'architecture rustique de la structure originale, une simple ferme en pisé.*

Vorhergehende Seiten: *Details der bäuerlichen Architektur des ursprünglichen Baus, eines Bauernhauses aus Pisee.*

Left page: the rose garden and the tiled swimming pool.
Below and above: the large terrace for outdoor living.

Page de gauche: la roseraie et la piscine carrelée.
Ci-dessus et ci-dessous: la vaste terrasse pour passer des journées en plein air.

Linke Seite: der Rosengarten und der gekachelte Swimmingpool.
Unten und oben: die große Terrasse für das Leben im Freien.

*The drawing-room that gives onto the large terrace, overlooking the
grove of ancient olive trees. The furniture was all made in the 'souks'.*

*Le salon donnant sur la grande terrasse qui surplombe une ancienne
oliveraie. Tous les meubles ont été fabriqués dans les souks.*

*Das Wohnzimmer, das auf die große Terrasse führt, von der man auf
einen Olivenhain blickt. Die Möbel wurden in den ›souks‹ angefertigt.*

Moroccan Interiors   Florence et Bernard Lévy   Marrakech

The bedroom, where extensive use was made of mud brick. The Lévys built a fireplace in practically every room to counteract the chill of desert nights.

La chambre à coucher, où domine la brique en boue séchée. Les Lévy ont construit une cheminée dans pratiquement toutes les pièces pour se protéger des nuits fraîches du désert.

Das Schlafzimmer, in dem vor allem Lehmziegel verwendet wurden. Die Lévys haben wegen der kalten Wüstennächte fast in jedem Zimmer einen Kamin eingebaut.

Above: the kitchen with a huge functioning fridge from a butcher's shop.
Right page: the guest bathroom with a circular shower in 'zelliges'.

Ci-dessus: la cuisine et son énorme réfrigérateur récupéré chez un boucher.
Page de droite: la salle de bains de la chambre d'ami avec sa douche circulaire tapissée de zelliges.

Oben: die Küche mit einem riesigen, funktionstüchtigen Kühlschrank, der aus einer Metzgerei stammt.
Rechte Seite: das Gästebad mit einer runden Dusche in ›zelliges‹.

This house, home to the American diplomat Frederick Vreeland and his wife, the mosaic artist Vanessa Somers, belongs to the world of fantasy. It has taken over ten years of planning and building to turn an arid corner of the Palmeraie into an expression of their love for the country and their respect for certain ecological prescripts. Built with the help of architects Dominique Michaelis and Zaira de Olivera, the house generates its own solar power. The walls in 'pisé' are 80 cm thick; they have cement reinforcements, and air circulates within the walls ensuring that the house remains cool even during the hottest months. The owners are constantly adding to their house, and all the building materials are handmade from local materials. A a result, its smooth, organic exterior appears to be an extension of the earth itself.

Vanessa Somers et Frederick Vreeland

La demeure du diplomate américain Frederick Vreeland et son épouse, la mosaïste Vanessa Somers, appartient au monde de l'imaginaire. Dix ans d'élaboration et de travaux ont été nécessaires pour transformer ce coin aride de la Palmeraie en l'expression de l'amour du couple pour le pays et de son respect de certains principes écologiques. Construite avec l'aide des architectes Dominique Michaelis et Zaïra de Olivera, la maison génère sa propre énergie solaire. Les murs en pisé font 80 cm d'épaisseur et sont renforcés avec du ciment. L'air circule librement dans les pièces, les maintenant fraîches même pendant les mois les plus chauds. Les propriétaires perfectionnent sans cesse leur intérieur. Tous les matériaux sont faits à la main avec des matériaux locaux. Avec ses façades lisses aux formes organiques, la maison semble être un prolongement de la terre elle-même.

Dieses Haus, das der amerikanische Diplomat Frederick Vreeland und seine Frau, die Mosaikkünstlerin Vanessa Somers, bewohnen, gehört einer Phantasiewelt an. Mehr als zehn Jahre Planen und Bauen gingen voraus, bis eine dürre Ecke der Palmeraie in einen Ausdruck ihrer Liebe zu diesem Land und ihres Respekts für bestimmte ökologische Vorschriften verwandelt war. Das mit der Hilfe der Architekten Dominique Michaelis und Zaira de Olivera gebaute Haus, wird durch selbsterzeugte Solarenergie versorgt. Die Wände aus Pisee sind 80 cm dick; sie sind mit Zement verstärkt, und die Luft kann zwischen den Wänden zirkulieren. So ist dafür gesorgt, daß das Haus auch in den heißesten Monaten kühl ist. Die Vreelands bauen ständig an ihrem Haus weiter. Alle Baustoffe bestehen aus heimischen Materialien; das glatte organische Äußere scheint der Erde entwachsen.

Page 137: the swimming pool in the shape of the characteristic horse-shoe arch. The mosaic by Vanessa Somers represents a secret garden as perceived through this imaginary door.
Above: the roof against the palm trees.

Page 137: la piscine, avec sa forme en ogive caractéristique. La mosaïque, œuvre de Vanessa Somers, représente un jardin secret vu à travers cette porte imaginaire.
Ci-dessus: le toit se détachant sur un fond de palmiers.

Seite 137: der Swimmingpool in der charakteristischen Hufeisenform. Das Mosaik von Vanessa Somers stellt einen verwunschenen Garten dar, wie man ihn durch diese Phantasietür sehen würde.
Oben: das Dach, wie es sich vor den Palmen abzeichnet.

Below: the pressed-mud façade is daubed – Berber-style – with lime. This decorative technique is an adaptation of an ancient custom used to discourage flies.
Following double page: the façade as seen from the first floor terrace. The swimming pool is situated on the first floor out of respect for Islamic traditions.

Ci-dessous: la façade en boue séchée enduite de chaux, dans le style berbère. Cette technique décorative s'inspire d'une ancienne tradition visant à éloigner les mouches.
Double page suivante: la façade vue de la terrasse du premier étage. Par respect des traditions islamiques, la piscine est située au premier étage.

Unten: Die Fassade aus Stampflehm ist nach Berberart mit Kalk bestrichen. Diese dekorative Technik folgt einem uralten Brauch und soll dazu dienen, Fliegen abzuhalten.
Folgende Doppelseite: die Fassade, wie man sie von der Terrasse des ersten Stocks sieht. Der Swimmingpool liegt aus Respekt vor islamischen Traditionen im ersten Stock.

Above: in the entrance hall, white-painted 'moucharaby' and simple wooden Berber pieces are juxtaposed with a door elaborately carved with traditional circular Islamic motifs.
Right page and detail right: the blue bedroom and its 'koubba', reinforced with wooden beams.

Ci-dessus: dans le hall d'entrée, un moucharabieh peint en blanc et de simples meubles berbères en bois sont juxtaposés à une porte richement sculptée de motifs circulaires islamiques.
Page et détail de droite: la chambre bleue et sa koubba soutenue par des poutres en bois.

Oben: In der Eingangshalle stehen weißbemalte ›moucharabieh‹ und schlichte Berbermöbel aus Holz neben einer Tür, die kunstvoll mit traditionellen, kreisförmigen islamischen Motiven verziert ist.
Rechte Seite und Detail rechts: das blaue Schlafzimmer und seine ›koubba‹, die mit Holzbalken abgestützt ist.

Riyâd Boumliha, lost among the labyrinthian lanes of Marrakesh's medina, was originally part of a caidal construction that included a prison, courts, living quarters and a harem. Now beautifully restored and redesigned by the Moroccan architect Chérif, its anonymous façade hides a luxurious interior. The owners, who divide their time between Marrakesh and the countryside outside Paris, have respected the proportions and materials indigenous to Marrakesh, and the 'riyâd' is an exercise in simplicity. The red and ochre tones of the city are reflected in the translucent 'tadelakt' of the walls and the painted and carved wooden ceilings.

Riyâd Boumliha

Perdu dans le dédale de la médina de Marrakech, Riyâd Boumliha faisait autrefois partie d'une casbah de caïd qui incluait une prison, plusieurs cours, des quartiers d'habitation et un harem. Aujourd'hui, magnifiquement restauré et redessiné par l'architecte marocain Chérif, le ‹riyâd› cache une demeure luxueuse derrière ses façades anonymes. Les propriétaires, qui partagent leur temps entre le Maroc et la campagne de la région parisienne, ont respecté les proportions et les matériaux propres à Marrakech. Le ‹riyâd› est devenu un exercice en simplicité. Les tons ocres et rouges de la ville se reflètent sur le ‹tadelakt› translucide des murs et les plafonds en bois peints et sculptés.

Riyâd Boumliha, verborgen in den labyrinthischen Gassen von Marrakeschs Medina, war ursprünglich Teil der Wohnanlage eines ›caïd‹, zu der ein Gefängnis, Höfe, Wohnquartiere und ein Harem gehörten. Es ist von dem marokkanischen Architekten Chérif wunderschön restauriert worden, und hinter seiner anonymen Fassade verbergen sich luxuriöse Innenräume. Die heutigen Besitzer von Riyad Boumliha, die abwechselnd in Marrakesch und in der Nähe von Paris auf dem Lande leben, haben die für Marrakesch typischen Proportionen und Materialien erhalten, und der ›riyâd‹ ist eine Übung in Schlichtheit. Die roten und ockeren Farbtöne der Stadt werden in den durchscheinenden ›tadelakt‹ der Mauern und den bemalten und verzierten Holzdecken aufgegriffen.

Page 145: the jacuzzi in a niche with a carved wooden ceiling, off the courtyard.
Left page: one of the guest bathrooms on the first floor.
Above: the courtyard, heart of the home, with its traditional fountain in 'zelliges'.

Page 145: le jacuzzi dans une niche au plafond sculpté, donnant sur la cour.
Page de gauche: l'une des salles de bains des invités au premier étage.
Ci-dessus: la cour, cœur de la maison, avec sa fontaine traditionnelle recouverte de zelliges.

Seite 145: Der Whirlpool neben dem Innenhof befindet sich in einer Nische mit einer verzierten Holzdecke.
Linke Seite: eines der Gästebäder im ersten Stock.
Oben: der Innenhof, Herz des Hauses, mit dem traditionellen Brunnen in ›zelliges‹.

Above: Moroccan antiques in the large drawing-room where the main decorative element is a majestic fireplace with black columns. There is a fireplace in every room and even in the courtyard.
Left: the stairway to the study and the roof garden.
Right page: a comfortable niche in the drawing-room.

Ci-dessus: des antiquités marocaines dans le grand salon, où le principal élément décoratif est la majestueuse cheminée aux colonnes noires. Il y a une cheminée dans chaque pièce, même dans la cour.
A gauche: l'escalier qui mène au bureau et au jardin sur le toit.
Page de droite: une niche confortable dans le salon.

Oben: marokkanische Antiquitäten in dem großen Salon, dessen beherrschendes dekoratives Element der riesige Kamin mit schwarzen Säulen ist. Jedes Zimmer hat einen Kamin, sogar der Innenhof.
Links: die Treppe zum Arbeitszimmer und zum Dachgarten.
Rechte Seite: eine bequeme Nische im Salon.

Bill Willis, who can in many ways be considered to be the "eminence grise" behind the current trend for all things Moroccan, bought this small palace in the medina of Marrakesh in 1973. Dating from the late 18th century, it appears to have been home to the harem of a lesser member of the ruling dynasty. In an inspired gesture Willis stripped the walls of the ornate plasterwork and 'zelliges'. He considered that these distraced the eye from the exquisite wooden 'koubba' over the central courtyard which is the main feature of the house. He applied 'tadelakt' to the walls in tones of ocre and yellow to create the smooth, luminous surface that is now considered emblematic of his work. In this way he created a space that was evocative of the spirit of Marrakesh interiors well before the import of the over-elaborate decorative techniques of the Hispano-Moresque. He opened up windows, redesigned the floor plan and decorated his home with an intelligent amalgamation of Moroccan craftsmanship and good pieces of furniture acquired during a lifetime of collecting.

Bill Willis

Bill Willis, qui est à maints égards un des pionniers de la redécouverte du Maroc, a acheté ce petit palais dans la médina de 'Marrakech en 1973. Datant de la fin du XVIIIe siècle, le lieu aurait abrité le harem d'un membre mineur de la dynastie qui régnait alors. Dans un élan créatif Willis a dépouillé les murs de leurs stucs et zelliges, estimant qu'ils détournaient l'attention de la superbe koubba en bois qui surplombe la cour centrale. La technique ancienne du ‹tadelakt›, appliquée en tons ocres et jaunes sur les murs, donne des surfaces lisses et lumineuses qui sont devenues emblématiques du travail de Willis. L'espace ainsi créé évoque les intérieurs de Marrakech bien avant l'avènement des techniques ouvragées du style hispano-moresque. Willis a élargi les fenêtres, redessiné les plans de la maison et décoré son intérieur avec un subtil assemblage d'artisanat marocain et de beaux meubles glanés ci et là au cours de toute une vie de collectionneur.

Bill Willis ist in vieler Hinsicht die graue Eminenz des aktuellen Trends für alles, was Marokko anbelangt. Er kaufte diesen kleinen Palast in der Medina von Marrakesch im Jahre 1973. Das Gebäude stammt aus dem späten 18. Jahrhundert und scheint den Harem eines unbedeutenderen Mitglieds der damals regierenden Dynastie beherbergt zu haben. Einem meisterhaften Einfall folgend, befreite Willis die Wände von den aufwendigen Stuckarbeiten und den ›zelliges‹. Er war der Meinung, sie lenkten den Blick vor der exquisiten hölzernen ›koubba‹ über dem mittleren Innenhof ab, die das Hauptmerkmal des Hauses ist. Willis hat für die Wände die alte Technik des ›tadelakt‹ in Ocker und Gelb angewandt, um jene sanft, leuchtende Oberfläche zu schaffen, die typisch für seine Arbeit ist. So hat er einen Raum kreiert, der den Geist von Interieurs in Marrakesch lange vor dem Import der hochelaborierten Ornamentik des spanisch-maurischen Stils reflektiert. Er vergrößerte die Fenster, veränderte den Grundriß und stattete sein Haus mit einer intelligenten Mischung aus marokkanischem Kunsthandwerk und wertvollen Möbelstücken aus, die er im Laufe eines langen Sammlerlebens erworben hat.

Previous pages: a view of the minaret of the neighbouring mosque from the roof terrace and two details characteristic of Willis' love of bizarre juxtapositions.
Above: a view of the courtyard from the first floor.
Right page: the winter garden on the first floor that overlooks the courtyard.

Pages précédentes: le minaret de la mosquée voisine vu depuis la terrasse sur le toit, et deux détails typiques du goût de Willis pour les associations insolites.
Ci-dessus: la cour vue depuis le premier étage.
Page de droite: le jardin d'hiver au premier étage qui surplombe la cour.

Vorhergehende Seiten: der Blick auf das Minarett der benachbarten Moschee von der Dachterrasse aus sowie zwei Details, die charakteristisch sind für Willis' Gefallen an einem bizarren Nebeneinander.
Oben: der Blick auf den Innenhof aus dem ersten Stock.
Rechte Seite: der Wintergarten im ersten Stock, von dem aus der Innenhof überblickt werden kann.

Left page: the main drawing-room situated in what was originally the courtyard. At some point in the 19th century this was covered over with a magnificent dome in carved, sculpted and painted wood. As a result Willis inherited an exceptionally beautiful square room, a very rare occurrence in Morocco where the traditional floor plan includes only rectangular rooms.
Above: in the winter garden, which is an extension of the drawing room, another of Willis' famed fireplaces.

Page de gauche: le grand salon occupe ce qui était autrefois la cour. Au XIXe siècle, celle-ci fut recouverte d'une magnifique coupole en bois sculpté et peint. Willis a ainsi hérité d'un somptueux salon carré, fait exceptionnel au Maroc où les pièces sont traditionnellement rectangulaires.
Ci-dessus: une des célèbres cheminées de Willis dans le jardin d'hiver qui prolonge le salon.

Linke Seite: der große Salon, der an der Stelle des ursprünglichen Innenhofes entstand. Irgendwann im 19. Jahrhundert wurde er mit der großartigen Kuppel aus geschnitztem, behauenem und bemaltem Holz überdacht; so kam Willis zu einem außerordentlich schönen quadratischen Raum, was sehr selten ist in Marokko, wo der traditionelle Grundriß nur rechteckige Räume vorsieht.
Oben: im Wintergarten, der eine Verlängerung des Wohnzimmers ist, ein weiterer von Willis' berühmten Kaminen.

Above: a bedroom with unusual bedposts, a Willis assemblage that
was to inspire his friend, the furniture designer Alessandra Lippini
(see pp. 160–171).
Below: the 'menzeh' with its elaborate niches, also designed by Willis.
Right page: a pile of books in a niche, reflecting Willis' eclectic taste.

Ci-dessus: un lit à baldaquin aux montants peu ordinaires; cet
assemblage de Willis a inspiré son amie Alessandra Lippini (voir pp.
160–171), créatrice de meubles.
Ci-dessous: la ‹menzeh› avec ses niches ouvragées dessinées par
Willis.
Page de droite: une pile de livres dans une niche qui reflète bien
l'éclectisme de Willis.

Oben: ein Schlafzimmer mit ungewöhnlichen Bettpfosten, eine
Willis-Assemblage, die seine Freundin, die Möbeldesignerin Alessandra Lippini (s. S. 160–171), inspiriert hat.
Unten: die ›menzeh‹ mit ihren kunstvoll verzierten Nischen, ebenfalls
von Willis entworfen.
Rechte Seite: Eine bunte Sammlung von Büchern in einer Nische
zeugt von Willis' eklektischem Geschmack.

Above left: *the ochre-red circular bath next to Willis' bedroom. In retrospect it is interesting to note that this use of 'tadelakt' and the smooth organic shapes has given birth to a distinctive "Marrakesh style".*
Above right and right page: *the simply-designed guest bathrooms are in the same recognisable spirit.*

Ci-dessus à gauche: *la baignoire ronde ocre rouge, dans la salle de bains attenante à la chambre de Willis. Avec le recul, il est intéressant de noter que le recours au ‹tadelakt› et à ses formes lisses et organiques a donné naissance à un style typiquement marrakechois.*
Ci-dessus à droite et page de droite: *les salles de bains des invités, décorées dans le même esprit de simplicité.*

Oben links: *das Bad neben Willis' Schlafzimmer in ockerroten Farbtönen. Im nachhinein ist es interessant festzustellen, daß dieser Gebrauch von ›tadelakt‹ und den sanften organischen Formen einen ganz bestimmten »Marrakesch-Stil« kreiert hat.*
Oben rechts und rechte Seite: *Die einfach gehaltenen Gästebadezimmer sind in demselben Stil geschaffen.*

Nadir and Alessandra are part of that international fashion-world elite that hop on a plane at a drop of a hat. As a photographer and stylist team they have spent the last fifteen years wandering around the world's fashion capitals and its most exotic locations. Together they call Bologna home although, over the last few years, their attention has mainly been focused on their Moroccan hideaway, shown on these pages, where they live with their son Felix. Their massive restoration of a classical palace in the medina of Marrakesh has become a wildly creative project revealing not only Nadir's past as an architect but also Alessandra's budding talent as a designer and decorator. They have brought the souvenirs of their vagabond lifestyles to their new home: colours remembered from Mexico, the sensual forms of ethnic African interiors... The result is a delightful fusion of Orientalist fantasy and modern family life.

Alessandra Lippini et Nadir Naldi

Alessandra et Nadir appartiennent à l'élite internationale de la mode, celle qui saute dans un avion comme on prend le métro. Il est photographe, elle est styliste, et tous deux sillonnent depuis quinze ans les quatre coins du globe et les capitales de la mode. Si, à les entendre, leur vrai foyer est à Bologne, ces dernières années toute leur attention s'est concentrée sur leur refuge marocain où ils vivent avec leur fils Félix. Leur restauration extensive d'un palais classique de la médina s'est progressivement convertie en un projet formidablement créatif, témoignant du passé d'architecte de Nadir. Alessandra, elle, s'est découvert un talent caché pour la création de meubles et la décoration. Leur nouvelle demeure abrite les souvenirs de leur vie nomade: couleurs bigarrées du Mexique, formes sensuelles des intérieurs africains... Il en résulte une fusion exquise entre un rêve orientaliste et la vie de famille moderne.

Nadir und Alessandra sind Teil jener internationalen Elite der Modewelt, die mal eben ins Flugzeug steigt, um irgendwohin zu jetten. Als Photograph und Stylistin haben sie sich in den letzten fünfzehn Jahren vor allem in den Modemetropolen der Welt und an ihren besonders exotischen Schauplätzen aufgehalten. Ihr gemeinsames Zuhause ist Bologna, aber in den letzten Jahren gilt ihr Interesse vornehmlich ihrem marokkanischen Zufluchtsort, wo sie mit ihrem Sohn Felix leben. Ihre umfassende Restaurierung eines klassischen Palastes in der Medina von Marrakesch hat sich zu einem Unternehmen ausgewachsen, das alle kreativen Kräfte beansprucht – nicht nur Nadirs Vergangenheit als Architekt, sondern ebenso Alessandras wachsendes Talent als Designerin und Innenausstatterin. Die Souvenirs ihres vagabundierenden Lebensstils haben sie in ihr neues Zuhause eingebracht: Farben aus Mexiko, die ihnen im Gedächtnis geblieben sind, die sinnlichen Formen afrikanischer Innenräume... Das Ergebnis ist eine entzückende Mischung aus orientalischer Phantasie und modernem Familienleben.

Page 161: *life revolves around the traditional courtyard paved with 1001 stars.*
Above: *the "blue" guest bedroom.*
Right page: *the first-floor corridor. The "ethnic" tables and fittings were conceived by Alessandra, who is constantly inspired by the versatility of the artisans in the 'souk'. The interior of the house is entirely surfaced with 'tadelakt', the ancient Moroccan mixture of sand and quicklime. Over the years it becomes veined, like marble.*

Page 161: *toute la vie de la maison tourne autour de la cour traditionnelle pavée de 1001 étoiles.*
Ci-dessus: *la chambre d'amis bleue.*
Page de droite: *le couloir du premier étage. Les tables «ethniques» et les installations ont été dessinées par Alessandra, constamment inspirée par les talents multiples des artisans du souk. Les murs sont entièrement enduits de ‹tadelakt›, un matériau typique du Maroc, constitué d'un mélange de sable et de chaux. Avec le temps, la surface devient craquelée, rappelant la texture du marbre.*

Seite 161: *Das Leben spielt sich um den traditionellen Innenhof herum ab, der mit 1001 Sternen gepflastert ist.*
Oben: *das »blaue« Gästeschlafzimmer.*
Rechte Seite: *der Flur im ersten Stock. Die »ethnischen« Tische und Einrichtungsgegenstände wurden von Alessandra entworfen, die sich immer wieder von der Vielseitigkeit der Kunsthandwerker im ›souk‹ inspirieren läßt. Das Innere des Hauses ist vollständig mit ›tadelakt‹ verputzt, dem alten, in Marokko entwickelten Gemisch aus Sand und ungelöschtem Kalk. Im Laufe der Jahre bildet es Adern und erinnert an Marmor.*

Above: the master bedroom. The bed is an assemblage of
Alexandra's.
Right page: details of the plaster work.
Following pages: two views of a guest bedroom with an African-style
bed put together by Alessandra. The niches are a characteristic of the
house. Some are regular and others have more organic shapes formed
according to the artisan's inspiration. Alessandra first came across the
technique during a trip to Mali and Mauritania.

Ci-dessus: la chambre des maîtres de maison. Le lit est un assemblage
réalisé par Alessandra.
Page de droite: détail des stucs.
Pages suivantes: deux vues d'une chambre d'amis avec un lit
d'inspiration africaine, création d'Alessandra. Les niches sont une des
caractéristiques de la maison. Certaines sont classiques, d'autres, aux
formes plus organiques, sont le fruit de l'inspiration de l'artisan. Alessandra a découvert cet élément architectural au cours d'un voyage au
Mali et en Mauritanie.

Oben: das große Schlafzimmer. Das Bett ist eine Assemblage von
Alessandra.
Rechte Seite: Details verschiedener Stuckarbeiten.
Folgende Seiten: zwei Ansichten eines Gästeschlafzimmers mit
einem von Alessandra entworfenen Bett im afrikanischen Stil. Die
Nischen sind typisch für das Haus: einige sind gleichmäßig, andere
haben eher organische Formen, so wie der Handwerker es gerade
empfand. Alessandra stieß das erste Mal während einer Reise nach
Mali und Mauretanien auf diese Technik.

Above: the rectangular dining-room with traditional Moroccan proportions. It is common usage for rose petals to be strewn on the tables
and the floor for special occasions.
Right page: the kitchen is fitted out with modern equipment as well
as a traditional stove that allows for the slow cooking which so many
Moroccan dishes require. The niches have been conceived to store the
flatware and cooking utensils.

Ci-dessus: la salle à manger rectangulaire, respectant les proportions
traditionnelles marocaines. Les jours de fête, on parsème les tables et
le sol de pétales de roses.
Page de droite: la cuisine avec son équipement moderne, mais aussi
son four traditionnel indispensable pour la cuisson lente que requiè-
rent de nombreux plats marocains. Les niches ont été conçues pour
recevoir la vaisselle et les ustensiles de cuisine.

Oben: das rechteckige Eßzimmer mit den traditionellen marokkanischen Proportionen. Es ist üblich, bei bestimmten Anlässen Rosen-
blätter auf den Tischen und auf dem Boden auszustreuen.
Rechte Seite: die Küche, die mit modernen Geräten, aber auch mit
einem traditionellen Herd ausgestattet ist, auf dem man, wie das für
viele marokkanische Gerichte erforderlich ist, die Zutaten langsam
köcheln lassen kann. Die Nischen wurden so entworfen, daß man
Geschirr und Kochgeräte darin verstauen kann.

Left page: the mosaic swimming pool, lit by tin "star lanterns" from the 'souk'. The pool is built so as to be partly sheltered under the arches of the courtyard. In this way it manages to keep some of its coolness even in the heat of summer.
Above left: the cucumber-green master bathroom, like the rest of the house, is surfaced in 'tadelakt'.
Above right: the "blue" guest-room's adjoining bathroom in deep azure 'tadelakt' and 'zelliges' in a palette of the same tone.

Page de gauche: la piscine en mosaïque, éclairée par des lanternes en fer blanc en forme d'étoiles achetées au souk. Elle est en partie abritée sous les arches de la cour, et reste fraîche même pendant l'été torride.
Ci-dessus à gauche: les murs vert concombre de la chambre des maîtres, enduits de ‹tadelakt› comme le reste de la maison.
Ci-dessus à droite: la salle de bains de la «chambre bleue» en ‹tadelakt› bleu ciel soutenu et carrelée de zelliges dans les mêmes tons.

Linke Seite: der mit einem Mosaik verzierte Swimmingpool, der von »Sternenlaternen« aus dem ›souk‹ beleuchtet wird. Der Pool liegt teilweise geschützt unter dem Gewölbe des Innenhofes. Auf diese Weise bleibt er auch in der Hitze des Sommers etwas kühler.
Oben links: das in Gurkengrün gehaltene große Badezimmer, das wie der Rest des Hauses mit ›tadelakt‹ verputzt ist.
Oben rechts: das Badezimmer neben dem Blauen Gästezimmer in dunkelblauem ›tadelakt‹ und ›zelliges‹ in ähnlichen Farbabstufungen.

Bernard Sanz divides his time between his neo-traditional palace in the medina of Marrakesh and Paris where he designs the menswear collections for Pierre Balmain. He bought it six years ago from Dominique Eluard, the widow of the great French poet. It is an excellent example of the lively adaptation of traditional construction to modern-day living, with no elaborate decorative effects. The courtyard overflows with flowers, including an extravagantly profuse cascade of Jacaranda, and the breakfast marmalade is made from the fruit of the ornamental orange trees. "Dâr Tihour" is named after the birds which are encouraged to bathe in the fountain, filling the courtyard with their gay presence.

Bernard Sanz

Bernard Sanz partage son temps entre Paris, où il dessine des collections masculines pour Pierre Balmain, et son palais néo-traditionnel dans la médina de Marrakech. Il l'a acheté voilà six ans à Dominique Eluard, la veuve du grand poète. C'est l'exemple même de l'adaptation d'une construction traditionnelle aux exigences de la vie moderne, sans effets décoratifs superflus. Les fleurs abondent dans la cour, notamment un superbe jacaranda qui se déverse en cascade luxuriante. La confiture du petit déjeuner est faite avec les fruits des orangers d'ornement. Les oiseaux, auxquels «Dâr Tihour» doit son nom, sont encouragés à venir prendre leur bain dans la fontaine, emplissant la cour de leur joyeux gazouillis.

Bernard Sanz lebt abwechselnd in Paris, wo er die Herrenmode für Pierre Balmain entwirft, und in seinem neotraditionellen Palast in der Medina von Marrakesch. Er kaufte ihn vor sechs Jahren von Dominique Eluard, der Witwe des großen französischen Dichters. Der Palast ist ein hervorragendes Beispiel dafür, wie man einen traditionellen Bau ohne großartige Schnörkel und Effekte auf eine lebendige Weise den Erfordernissen des modernen Lebens anpaßt. Der Innenhof ist mit Blumen überladen, einschließlich einer Kaskade von Jacaranda, und die Frühstücksmarmelade stammt von den Früchten dieses Zier-Orangenbaums. Die Vögel, nach denen »Dâr Tihour« seinen Namen trägt, baden gern im Brunnen und erfüllen den Innenhof mit fröhlichem Leben.

Page 172: *a corner of the study on the ground floor. The tiles are a modern rendering of the ancient technique of 'zelliges'.*
Pages 174 and 175 above: *the covered terrace on the roof, with its heavy canvas curtains and the pleasantly overgrown trellis that provides some welcome shade. Sanz grows a wilderness of honeysuckle, bougainvillaea, tiny perfumed "Marrakesh" roses, begonias, ferns and cacti on his roof.*

Page 172: *un coin du bureau au rez-de-chaussée. Le carrelage est une version moderne des zelliges.*
Pages 174 et 175 en haut: *la terrasse couverte sur le toit, avec ses lourdes tentures de toile blanche et sa pergola croulant sous la verdure qui projette une ombre apaisante. Sanz y cultive une véritable jungle de chèvrefeuille, de bougainvillier, de petites roses parfumées de Marrakech, de bégonias, de fougères et de cactus.*

Seite 172: *eine Ecke des Arbeitszimmers im Erdgeschoß. Die Kacheln sind eine moderne Variante der alten Technik der ›zelliges‹.*
Seite 174 und 175 oben: *die überdachte Dachterrasse mit ihren schweren weißen Segeltuchvorhängen und dem anmutig überwachsenen Spalier, das willkommenen Schatten spendet. Sanz züchtet einen Urwald von Geißblatt, Bougainvillea, winzigen duftenden Marrakesch-Rosen, Begonien, Farnen und Kakteen auf seinem Dach.*

Below right: a detail of the outside gallery on the first floor that acts as a corridor and connects all the rooms.

Ci-dessous à droite: un détail de la galerie extérieure au premier étage qui sert de couloir et relie toutes les chambres.

Unten rechts: Detailaufnahme der Galerie im ersten Stock, die als Flur fungiert und von der alle Zimmer abgehen.

Above: the drawing-room on the ground floor, with a splendid piece of embroidery that centres the space. Much of the furniture is locally made, and Sanz works with local artisans to dream up new pieces as and when they are needed.
Right page: a drawing-room on the first floor lit by a magnificent chandelier in scarlet glass which depicts the Tunisian Beys. The original design on the ceiling has been picked out with fine lines of colour.

Ci-dessus: le salon du rez-de-chaussée. Une somptueuse étoffe brodée occupe l'espace central. La plupart des meubles sont fabriqués dans la région. Sanz travaille avec des artisans locaux pour créer de nouveaux éléments au gré de ses besoins.
Page de droite: un salon du premier étage éclairé par un magnifique lustre écarlate représentant les beys de Tunis. Sur le plafond, les motifs d'origine ont été rehaussés de minces lignes de couleur.

Oben: der Salon im Erdgeschoß, mit einer herrlichen Stickerei, die im Mittelpunkt steht. Viele der Möbel sind aus einheimischen Werkstätten. Sanz arbeitet mit Kunsthandwerkern zusammen, um sich neue Möbel auszudenken, wenn er sie braucht.
Rechte Seite: ein Salon im ersten Stock, der von einem prächtigen Kronleuchter aus scharlachrotem Glas erleuchtet wird, auf denen die tunesischen Beys dargestellt sind. Das Originalmuster an der Decke ist mit zarten farbigen Konturen hervorgehoben worden.

Bert Flint has lived in Marrakesh since 1957 and is a great authority on rural Berber craftmanship. He bought this grand palace twenty years ago to house his extensive collection of rugs, pottery, jewellery and woven cloth. Part of his treasures are on view to the public here, at "Dâr Tiskiwin", near the El Bahia palace. His field work takes him all over the country and in particular to Agadir, where part of his collection is shown, and to Essaouira where he has his sea-side house and can escape from the Marrakesh summers. He lives among rare pieces that he has collected according to his own taste, because he likes them, always discarding a strictly ethnological approach in favour of an instinctive appreciation of colour and shape.

Bert Flint

Installé à Marrakech depuis 1957, grand connaisseur de l'artisanat rural berbère, Bert Flint a acheté ce somptueux palais il y a vingt ans pour y abriter sa vaste collection de tapis, poterie, bijoux et tissages. Une partie de son trésor est exposée au public ici, à «Dâr Tiskiwin», près du palais El Bahia. Ses recherches l'entraînent dans tout le pays, notamment à Agadir où une autre partie de sa collection est présentée, et à Essaouira où se trouve sa maison de bord de mer, son refuge pendant l'été marrakechois. Il vit parmi les objets rares qu'il collectionne par amour, préférant se fier à une appréciation instinctive des formes et des couleurs plutôt que de suivre une approche purement ethnologique.

Bert Flint, der seit 1957 in Marrakesch lebt und eine große Autorität auf dem Gebiet der ländlichen Berberkunst ist, kaufte diesen großartigen Palast vor zwanzig Jahren, um seine umfangreiche Sammlung von Teppichen, Töpferwaren, Schmuck und Webstoffen unterzubringen. Ein Teil seiner Schätze ist hier im »Dâr Tiskiwin«, in der Nähe des El Bahia-Palastes der Öffentlichkeit zugänglich gemacht worden. Durch seine Tätigkeit kommt er im ganzen Lande herum, besonders nach Agadir, wo ein Teil seiner Sammlung ausgestellt wird, und nach Essaouira, wo sein Strandhaus steht, in das er dem Sommer in Marrakesch entfliehen kann. Er umgibt sich mit kostbaren Möbeln, deren Auswahl nur persönlichen ästhetischen Kriterien folgt, d. h. er stellt rein »ethnologische« Kriterien immer zugunsten eines instinktiven Gefallens an Farbe und Form zurück.

Moroccan Interiors   Bert Flint   Marrakech

On the previous double page: *a view of the "salon Marocain" with its modern tiles that imitate 'zeiliges'. Flint decided to buy this house because of the carved cedar ceiling, shown here.*
Left page: *rugs from the Middle Atlas on low seating in a quiet corner.*
Above: *everyday pieces in Flint's bedroom. He enjoys the contrast between simple things and the grandeur of the Hispano-Moresque architecture of the palace.*

Double page précédente: *le «salon marocain» avec son carrelage moderne imitant les zelliges et son plafond en cèdre sculpté. C'est ce dernier qui a décidé Flint à acheter le palais.*
Page de gauche: *des tapis du Moyen Atlas sur des sièges bas dans un petit coin tranquille.*
Ci-dessus: *des objets ordinaires dans la chambre du maître de maison. Bert Flint aime le contraste des formes simples conjuguées à la grandiose architecture hispano-moresque du palais*

Vorhergehende Doppelseite: *Blick auf den »Salon Marocain« mit modernen Kacheln, die ›zelliges‹ imitieren, und einer geschnitzten Zederndecke, Flints Beweggrund, das Haus zu kaufen.*
Linke Seite: *Teppiche aus dem Mittleren Atlas auf niedrigen Sitzgelegenheiten in einer stillen Ecke.*
Oben: *alltägliche Dinge im Schlafzimmer. Flint mag den Kontrast zwischen den einfachen Dingen und der grandiosen spanischmaurischen Architektur des Palastes.*

Fès

Fez is the fountainhead of Morocco's cultural and religious life, the oldest of the imperial cities, dating from the 9th century. Its fascinating medina, classified by the UNESCO as part of World Heritage, defies all attempts at cartography due to the intricacy of its layout which is as curvy and indecipherable as Islamic calligraphy. It is, to my mind, the most seductive of Oriental cities. Like the convoluted imaginings of a hallucinating mathematician, a narrow lane will dissolve into a palm-covered passage, before becoming steps or a dark corridor between walls a metre thick. Like a surrealist theatre set designed by Giorgio de Chirico, high walls and tiny wooden doors, half buried in the ground, hide empty palaces, ballrooms and gardens. Sinuous stairs lead up in half darkness to a white-bright second city on the roofs where the organic contours of the oldest structures evoke Gaudí, where the swallows reign sublime and where the medina rises and falls like waves about you. The demands of the muezzin punctuate the days and the hot fireball of the sun has baked the city sandbrown. Furnished with fountains, mosques, honey-coloured walls and vision after vision of dizzy wonder, Fez is the "Islamic sensation" to beat all others, the prototypical dream scene. Today the city is threatened as its historical centre decays and business is transferred to Casablanca and Rabat. The unthinkable has been proposed: a road through the medina. Indeed, until it becomes generally perceived as desirable to live in the very heart of such beauty, Fez will never breathe as a real city again. A road, penetrating, scarring, destroying, is surely not the answer; it lies with restoration and, most of all perhaps, with a reassessment of values.

Berceau de la vie culturelle et religieuse du Maroc, Fès, la plus ancienne des villes impériales, fut fondée au IXe siècle. Sa fascinante médina, classée «patrimoine mondial» par l'UNESCO, défie toute tentative de cartographie par son tracé aussi complexe et sinueux que la calligraphie islamique. Son charme et son étrangeté en font, à mon sens, la plus séduisante des villes d'Orient. Une allée étroite se perd dans un passage labyrinthique couvert de feuilles de palmiers, avant de devenir escalier ou couloir sombre entre des parois d'un mètre d'épaisseur. Comme dans un décor imaginé par Giorgio de Chirico, de minuscules portes en bois à demi-enfouies au pied de murs gigantesques cachent des palais déserts, des salles de bal et des jardins. Des marches vertigineuses plongées dans la pénombre grimpent vers le ciel et débouchent sur une autre ville d'une blancheur éclatante perchée sur les toits. Là, les contours organiques des bâtiments les plus anciens évoquent Gaudí, les hirondelles règnent en maîtresses des lieux et la médina forme une mer houleuse qui s'étale à vos pieds. Les appels du muezzin ponctuent la journée et les murs cuits par le soleil revêtent des tons de sable. Parsemée de fontaines, de mosquées, de façades couleur de miel, d'une succession de points de vue d'une beauté étourdissante, Fès est «la sensation islamique» par excellence, un décor de rêve jamais égalé. Aujourd'hui, la ville est menacée car son centre historique tombe en ruines et les entreprises déménagent peu à peu pour s'installer à Casablanca ou à Rabat. On a proposé l'inconcevable: une route traversant la médina. De fait, tant que les habitants ne seront pas convaincus du plaisir de vivre au cœur d'une telle beauté, Fès ne pourra se targuer d'être de nouveau une ville à part entière. La solution n'est certes pas dans la construction d'une route pénétrante, défigurante, blessante, mais plutôt dans la restauration et, surtout, dans une redéfinition des valeurs.

Fes ist Quelle und Ursprung des kulturellen und religiösen Lebens in Marokko. Sie ist die älteste der Königsstädte und stammt aus dem 9. Jahrhundert. Ihre faszinierende Medina, von der UNESCO als Teil des Kulturerbes der Welt klassifiziert, widersteht allen Versuchen der Kartographierung, weil sie so kompliziert angelegt ist, so verschlungen und unentzifferbar wie die islamische Kalligraphie. Wegen ihrer Schönheit und Andersartigkeit ist Fes die verführerischste aller orientalischen Städte. Wie die übersteigerten Phantasien eines halluzinierenden Mathematikers verliert sich eine schmale Gasse in eine palmenbedeckte Passage, wird zu einer Treppe oder einem dunklen Gang zwischen meterdicken Wänden. Wie in einem surrealistischen Bühnenbild von Giorgio de Chirico verstecken sich leere Paläste, Tanzsäle und Gärten hinter hohen Mauern und winzigen Holztüren. Gewundene Treppen im Halbdunkel führen hinauf zu einer weiß leuchtenden, zweiten Stadt auf den Dächern, wo die organischen Strukturen der ältesten Bauwerke an Gaudí erinnern, wo die Schwalben souverän regieren und wo sich die Medina rings herum hebt und senkt wie Wellen. Die Mahnungen des Muezzins strukturieren den Tagesablauf, und der heiße Feuerball der Sonne hat die Stadt sandfarben gebrannt. Mit seinen Brunnen, Moscheen und honigfarbenen Mauern ist Fes die größte »islamische Sensation«. Heute ist die Stadt bedroht, weil ihr historisches Zentrum verfällt und das Geschäftsleben nach Casablanca und Rabat verlagert wird. Das Undenkbare ist bereits vorgeschlagen worden: eine Straße durch die Medina. Bis zu dem Zeitpunkt, an dem es allgemein wieder als erstrebenswert gilt, im Herzen einer solch schönen Stadt zu wohnen, wird Fes niemals mehr als echte Stadt atmen. Eine Straße, die durchdringt, Wunden reißt und zerstört, ist sicherlich nicht die Antwort. Diese läge allein in einer Restaurierung und vor allem in der Wiederherstellung alter Wertvorstellungen.

Three families have divided up this gracious palace. It dates from the end of the 18th century and is built in distinctive style of the early Alouite dynasty, from whom the current king, Hassan II, descends. From the roof terrace there is a view of the tanneries (see page 186), where this age-old craft continues to be practised in the same way as in the Middle Ages. The small illustration on the left shows how, for the second time today, Abdulali's mother prepares the bread that he will carry to the communal neighbourhood oven. This chore is routinely the lot of the youngest of the family, often tiny children who stumble along with wooden boards balanced on their heads. The freshly baked loaves invade the narrow streets with their delicious odour.

Dâr Bou Taileb

Trois familles se partagent cet élégant palais construit à la fin du XVIIIe siècle dans le style des premiers souverains alawítes, dont descend le roi actuel Hassan II. Depuis la terrasse sur le toit, on aperçoit les tanneries (voir p. 186), où cet artisanat vieux comme le monde continue d'être pratiqué avec des méthodes quasi médiévales. La petite illustration à gauche montre la mère d'Abdulali préparant pour la seconde fois de la journée le pain qu'il portera au four communal du quartier. Cette corvée revient généralement aux plus jeunes de la famille, souvent des petits enfants qui se frayent un passage dans les ruelles étroites, une planche en équilibre sur la tête, laissant dans leur sillage une délicieuse odeur de pain frais.

Drei Familien haben sich diesen anmutigen Palast aufgeteilt, der vom Ende des 18. Jahrhunderts stammt und in dem unverwechselbaren Stil der frühen Alaouitendynastie gebaut ist, von der auch Hassan II., der derzeitige König, abstammt. Von der Dachterrasse hat man einen Blick auf die Gerbereien (Seite 186), in denen dieses uralte Handwerk weiterhin mit mittelalterlichen Techniken ausgeübt wird. Die Abbildung oben links zeigt, wie Abdulalis Mutter schon zum zweiten Mal heute das Brot zubereitet, das er zum Gemeinschaftsofen des Viertels tragen wird. Diese Arbeit ist gewöhnlich das Los der Jüngsten – oft kleine Kinder noch –, die mit auf dem Kopf balancierten Brettern vorwärtsstolpern, wobei die frischgebackenen Brotlaibe die schmalen Straßen mit ihrem köstlichen Duft erfüllen.

The courtyard, showing the traditional marble fountain and the
customary boldly-striped contemporary canvas door curtains.

*La cour, avec sa fontaine traditionnelle en marbre. Devant la porte, les
rideaux de toile modernes aux rayures vives que l'on retrouve partout.*

*Der Innenhof mit dem traditionellen Marmorbrunnen und den
üblichen breitgestreiften modernen Türvorhängen aus Segeltuch.*

A view of the plaster work and wood carving in the courtyard. Just outside the door is the frantic world of the 'souks', but in this courtyard all is orderly. One of the precepts of Islamic architecture is the inducement of the sensation of peace afforded by this kind of city dwelling, a principle that can be found in most imperial cities.

Une vue des stucs et des bois sculptés de la cour. Ici règnent le calme et l'ordre alors que de l'autre côté de la porte, les souks de Fès grouillent d'une activité frénétique. L'un des préceptes de l'architecture islamique est de créer cette sensation de paix au cœur de la cité, un principe appliqué dans toutes les villes impériales.

Blick auf die Stuckarbeiten und Schnitzereien im Innenhof. Draußen vor der Tür liegt die wilde Welt der ›souks‹, aber in diesem Innenhof ist alles in Ordnung. Eines der Prinzipien islamischer Architektur ist es, ein Gefühl von Ruhe und Frieden zu vermitteln, wie es diese Art von Stadtwohnung bietet, die in den meisten Königsstädten zu finden ist.

This neo-traditional structure, built in 1926, exploits the conventional floor plan of an Islamic home. Since the Koran is an absolute guide to all aspects of life, social as well as spiritual, the range of architectural and decorative arts is strictly disciplined. The individual artist of all epochs is expected to work to an exacting standard within established frameworks of designs and techniques. Structures such as this, built during an expansion of the medina at the beginning of the century, incorporate the use of cement and thus allow more regular finishes and shapes, for instance in the contours of the columns. The house was bought seven years ago and greatly restored and repainted. Six senior members of the family live there now. The fountain in the courtyard benefited from the extraordinary ancient water system of the Islamic city. The silver-plated basin shown is used for ceremonial hand washing before meals; water, often scented with rose petals, is poured over the hands of the guests.

Dâr Skalli

Cet édifice néo-traditionnel construit en 1926 respecte les plans habituels de la demeure islamique. Le Coran étant le guide absolu de tous les aspects de la vie sociale et spirituelle, le champ d'action dans le domaine de l'architecture et des arts décoratifs est strictement régi. L'artiste est toujours censé se conformer à des normes astreignantes à l'intérieur d'une gamme préétablie de motifs et de techniques. Des maisons telles que celle-ci, construites au début du siècle au cours d'une extension de la médina, ont bénéficié du recours au ciment qui permet des finitions et des formes plus régulières, comme les contours des colonnes. Achetée il y a sept ans, la maison a été repeinte et considérablement restaurée. Elle est habitée par six membres âgés de la famille. Dans la cour, la fontaine fonctionne grâce au très ancien et très ingénieux système d'adduction d'eau de la ville islamique. La cuvette en métal argenté sert aux ablutions rituelles avant les repas. On verse de l'eau – souvent parfumée aux pétales de rose – sur les mains des invités.

Dieser neotraditionelle Bau aus dem Jahre 1926 nutzt den üblichen Grundriß eines islamischen Hauses. Da der Koran praktisch zu allen Bereichen des Lebens, sozialen wie spirituellen, klare Anweisungen enthält, ist das Spektrum von Architektur und Design streng begrenzt. Vom einzelnen Künstler jeder Epoche wird erwartet, daß er innerhalb vorgegebener Muster und Techniken anspruchsvollsten Standards genügt. Für Häuser wie dieses, das während einer Erweiterung der Medina zu Beginn dieses Jahrhunderts gebaut wurde, verwendete man auch Zement, was einen ebenmäßigeren Verputz und klarere Formen ermöglicht, zum Beispiel bei den Umrissen der Säulen. Das Haus wechselte vor sieben Jahren den Besitzer und ist seitdem großartig restauriert worden. Sechs ältere Mitglieder der Familie leben jetzt dort. Dem Brunnen im Innenhof kam das hervorragende alte Bewässerungssystem der islamischen Stadt zugute. Das abgebildete Silberbecken dient den rituellen Waschungen vor den Mahlzeiten; mit Rosenblättern parfümiertes Wasser wird den Gästen über die Hände gegossen.

On the previous double page: the preparation of "thé à la menthe" in the courtyard. This is the main living space of the house, usually open to the sky. Here it has recently been covered over to protect the structure from the elements.

Above: a corner in one of the four "salons Marocains" that is also used for sleeping. Traditionally, family members stretch out on the seating, but beds of the European type have become popular. Ornate mirrors of the type shown, often made in Europe specifically for the Arab market during the first half of this century, have also become part of the configuration of these interiors.

Right page: the kitchen has an unusual fixed storage unit.

Double page précédente: la préparation du thé à la menthe dans la cour. Cet espace, d'ordinaire à ciel ouvert, est le lieu le plus fréquenté de la maison. Ici, la cour a été couverte récemment pour la protéger des éléments.

Ci-dessus: un coin de l'un des quatre «salons marocains», qui sert aussi de chambre à coucher. Traditionnellement, les membres de la famille s'étendaient sur les banquettes, mais les lits à l'européenne sont de plus en plus courants. Les miroirs ouvragés comme celui-ci, souvent réalisés en Europe pendant la première moitié de ce siècle spécifiquement pour le marché arabe, sont devenus partie intégrante de ces intérieurs.

Page de droite: la cuisine dispose d'un meuble de rangement peu ordinaire.

Vorhergehende Doppelseite: die Zubereitung des »Thé à la menthe« im Innenhof, der die Hauptwohnsphäre des Hauses ist. Der Hof ist gewöhnlich zum Himmel hin offen, dieser hier wurde aber vor kurzem überdacht, um den Bau vor den Elementen zu schützen.

Oben: eine Ecke in einem der vier »Salons Marocains«, die auch zum Schlafen genutzt wird. Traditionsgemäß strecken sich die Familienmitglieder auf den Sitzgelegenheiten aus, aber Betten vom europäischen Typ sind nun auch populär geworden. Prunkvolle Spiegel wie der abgebildete wurden oft in Europa während der ersten Hälfte dieses Jahrhunderts speziell für den arabischen Markt hergestellt und sind ebenfalls zum festen Bestandteil solcher Interieurs geworden.

Rechte Seite: die Küche hat fest eingemauerte Vorratsschränke, was ungewöhnlich ist.

Rabat

"They call Rabat the Pearl of Morocco. It stands high on the southern bank of the Bou Regreg where the green river lashes the blue sea, above cactus-grown ochre rocks, a long rambling line of white and yellow, everywhere dominated by the huge grey Tower of Hassan." Reginald Rankin, writing in 1908 as war correspondent, was charmed by this peaceful white and blue city. The New Town is a pristine example of Art Deco "à la Moresque". The medina, an essay in straggling whitewashed streets has a vibrant and lively character. The presence of the sea is strongly felt. Down the Rue des Consuls, the only street where, during the 19th century, the foreigners were allowed to live, there are a succession of interesting merchants' 'fondouks', now greatly delapidated and used as workrooms by craftsmen. Through the Bab Oudaïa, considered to be the most beautiful gate in the Moorish world, lies the ancient 'ribât' and original citadel: the Casbah des Oudaïas. This enclosed medina within the city shines bright white in the sun and overlooks Rabat's twin, the port of Salé, previously a pirate republic and the preeminent of the two settlements during the Middle Ages.

«On appelle Rabat la Perle du Maroc. Se dressant sur la rive gauche du Bou Regreg, elle surplombe la rivière verte qui se jette dans le bleu de l'océan, sur des rochers ocres couverts de cactus, formant une longue ligne brisée de blanc et de jaune, partout dominée par l'immense tour grise de Hassan.» Ainsi écrivait Reginald Rankin en 1908, charmé par cette paisible ville blanche et bleue où il était correspondant de guerre. La Ville Nouvelle est un parfait exemple «d'Art déco à la moresque». La médina, un dédale de longues rues irrégulières blanchies à la chaux, déborde de vie. On sent partout la présence de la mer. Dans la Rue des Consuls, la seule rue où, au XIXe siècle, les étrangers avaient le droit de vivre, on peut admirer une succession d'intéressants fondouks, aujourd'hui désaffectés ou repris comme ateliers par des artisans. Au-delà de Bab Oudaïa, considérée comme la plus belle porte du monde moresque, s'étend l'ancien ‹ribât› et la citadelle originale, la Casbah des Oudaïas. Cette médina enfermée à l'intérieur de la ville, resplendissante de blancheur sous le soleil, fait face à la jumelle de Rabat, Salé, autrefois république corsaire et grand port marchand pendant le Moyen-Age.

»Man nennt Rabat die Perle Marokkos. Es erhebt sich am südlichen
Ufer des Bou Regreg, wo der grüne Fluß in das blaue Meer strömt,
über kaktusbewachsenen, ockerfarbenen Felsen, eine lange, verschlun-
gene Kette von Weiß und Gelb, überragt von dem großen, grauen
Hassanturm.« Reginald Rankin, der dies 1908 als Kriegskorrespon-
dent schrieb, war bezaubert von dieser friedlichen, weiß-blauen Stadt.
Die Neustadt ist ein unverfälschtes Beispiel für »Art déco à la
Moresque«. Die Medina mit ihren kreuz und quer verlaufenden weißgekalkten Straßen ist quicklebendig. Die Nähe des Meeres ist überall
zu spüren. An der Rue des Consuls, der einzigen Straße, in der im
19. Jahrhundert Ausländer wohnen durften, gibt es eine Reihe von interessanten ›fondouks‹, die aber verfallen sind und von Handwerkern
als Werkstätten benutzt werden. Wenn man dann durch das Bab
Oudaïa geht, das als schönstes Tor der maurischen Welt gilt, sieht
man den alten ›ribât‹ und die ursprüngliche Zitadelle, die Kasbah des
Oudaïas. Diese von Mauern umgebene Medina in der Innenstadt
leuchtet strahlend weiß in der Sonne und blickt auf Rabats Zwilling,
die Hafenstadt Salé, herab, früher eine Piratenrepublik und im
Mittelalter die bedeutendere der beiden Siedlungen.

*The foundations of the Ksar Tazi, one of Morocco's most imposing
private homes, were laid on five hectares of ground by Haj Omar Tazi
at the beginning of the century. He was a minister to the Sultans
Moulay Abdelaziz and Moulay Youssef and considered to be one of
the richest men of his time. Twelve years of work by the 'maalems' in
plaster, wood, marble and 'zelliges' were needed to complete the
palace, which was then further embellished by Haj Abbès Tazi in the
1950s. Despite its comparatively recent construction, the palace was
laid out along traditional lines which have not suffered substantial
variations for many centuries; it is considered to be one of the first
examples of what is now known as "Neo-Moresque" architecture.
Today, this vast palace is still perfectly maintained. It is built around
two verdant courtyards and seems a world apart, hidden behind an
anonymous wall in the centre of Rabat.*

Ksar Tazi

L'une des plus imposantes demeures privées du Maroc, Ksar Tazi
occupe cinq hectares de terrain. Elle fut construite au début du
siècle par Haj Omar Tazi, ministre des sultans Moulay Abdelaziz et
Moulay Youssef, et l'un des hommes les plus riches de son temps.
Les ‹maalems› ont travaillé pendant douze ans sur les plâtres, le
bois, le marbre et les zelliges avant d'achever le palais, qui a
encore été embelli par Haj Abbès Tazzi dans les années cinquante.
En dépit de sa construction relativement récente, il respecte les
plans traditionnels qui n'ont pas beaucoup varié au cours des
siècles. On le considère comme l'un des premiers exemples de ce
qu'on a appelé depuis le style «néo-moresque». Impeccablement
entretenu, ce vaste palais bâti autour de deux cours verdoyantes
semble aujourd'hui constituer un monde à part caché derrière des
murs anonymes en plein cœur de Rabat.

*Das Fundament für Ksar Tazi, einer der imposantesten Privatvillen
Marokkos, wurde von Haj Omar Tazi am Anfang dieses Jahrhunderts
auf einer Fläche von fünf Hektar gelegt. Tazi war Minister unter den
Sultanen Moulay Abdelaziz und Moulay Youssef und galt als einer
der reichsten Männer seiner Zeit. Die ›maalems‹ arbeiteten zwölf
Jahre lang an Stuck, Holz, Marmor und ›zelliges‹. In den fünfziger
Jahren wurde der Palast dann von Haj Abbès Tazi noch weiter ausge-
schmückt. Obwohl vergleichsweise jüngeren Datums, wurde er nach
traditionellen Gesichtspunkten gebaut, die sich seit Jahrhunderten
nicht wesentlich verändert haben. Er gilt als eines der ersten Beispiele
für eine Bauweise, die man inzwischen »neo-maurisch« nennt. Heute
wirkt dieser nach wie vor perfekt gepflegte Palast, der um zwei grünen
Innenhöfen herum angelegt wurde, wie eine Welt für sich, die verborgen hinter einer anonymen Mauer im Zentrum von Rabat liegt.*

Left page: the intricately decorated summer drawing-room with its Louis XV style furnishings and the billiard table that is popular during family gatherings.
Above: the majestic "salon Marocain" where the family take their meals in the traditional style. The 'zelliges' are as always geometrical and mathematical. Like so much in Islamic art, they draw the attention away from the real world to one of pure form. Away from the chaos of the three-dimensional, physical world, ordered patterns create a clearly defined geometrical order. One point, often hidden, always rules the kaleidoscopic image, a symbol of the one deity.

Page de gauche: le salon d'été richement décoré, avec son mobilier Louis XV et son billard, très apprécié pendant les réunions de famille.
Ci-dessus: le majestueux «salon marocain», où la famille prend ses repas en respectant la tradition. Les zelliges, sont toujours géométriques et mathématiques. Typiques de l'art islamique, ils détournent l'attention du monde réel vers un univers purement formel. A partir du chaos du monde tridimensionnel, les motifs soigneusement agencés créent un nouvel ordre géométrique clairement défini et apaisant. Un point, souvent dissimulé, régit l'image kaléidoscopique, symbole de la Divinité suprême.

Linke Seite: der reich verzierte Sommersalon mit seinen Möbeln im Stile Louis XV. und dem Billardtisch, der bei Familientreffen sehr beliebt ist.
Oben: der majestätische »Salon Marocain«, in dem die Familie ihre Mahlzeiten im traditionellen Stil einnimmt. Die ›zelliges‹ sind wie immer in geometrischen und mathematischen Mustern angelegt; wie so vieles in der islamischen Kunst ziehen sie die Aufmerksamkeit von der realen Welt ab und lenken sie auf eine Welt der reinen Form. Aus dem Chaos der dreidimensionalen, physischen Welt schaffen als wohltuend empfundene, strukturierte Muster eine klar umrissene, geometrische Ordnung. Ein Punkt, der oftmals verborgen bleibt – Symbol für die eine Gottheit – beherrscht das kaleidoskopische Bild.

Above: the central courtyard of one of the palace's many 'douiriya'; these are small independent dwellings, common to most large residences. They are secreted away behind the grand salons and are often where much of the day-to-day living takes place.
Right page: inside the 'douiriya' can be found the private library, consisting of mainly contemporary volumes, belonging to Abdallah Stouky, Hajja Z'hor Tazi's son-in-law, a journalist and book publisher. This library has a very genuine charm as each and every book has been collected and read by Stouky, an avid bibliophile since his adolescence.

Ci-dessus: la cour centrale de l'un des nombreux ‹douiriya› du palais, habitations individuelles à l'abri des regards que l'on trouve dans la plupart des grandes résidences. Elles passent inaperçues derrière les majestueux salons, mais c'est souvent là que se déroule la vie de tous les jours.
Page de droite: la bibliothèque à l'intérieur du ‹douiriya›, abrite principalement des ouvrages contemporains appartenant à Abdallah Stouky, gendre de Hajja Z'hor Tazi, journaliste et éditeur. C'est un lieu plein de charme où chaque livre a été choisi et lu par Stouky, bibliophile vorace depuis son adolescence.

Oben: der zentrale Innenhof von einem der vielen ›douiriya‹ des Palastes. Dies sind kleine, selbständige Wohneinheiten, die für die meisten großen Häuser typisch sind. Sie sind hinter den großen Salons versteckt, und in ihnen spielt sich das alltägliche Leben hauptsächlich ab.
Rechte Seite: die private Bibliothek in der ›douiriya‹, die in erster Linie zeitgenössische Veröffentlichungen enthält. Sie gehört Abdallah Stouky, Hajja Z'hor Tazis Schwiegersohn, einem Journalisten und Verleger. Diese Bibliothek besitzt einen besonderen Charme, da jedes einzelne Buch von Stouky, einem Büchernarr von Jugend an, angeschafft und gelesen wurde.

Tétouan

Tetuan, strikingly beautiful, poised at the top of a steep slope, gleams white in the sun. Its Berber name means "open your eyes", and indeed the architecture of the homes of the medina is overwhelming with its extravagant detail, the stuff of fantasy and orientalist dreams. It is more detailed and intricate than even the architecture of the imperial cities and is evocative of the decorative aspects of the Andalusian Moresque. It is tempting and somehow inevitable to turn to Pierre Loti's sensitive descriptions in his "Journal Intime" that remained unpublished for over a hundred years after his historic journey to Morocco in 1860. Loti found the city arresting: "The white Moorish town is now quite near us. There is no movement around it; at this twilight hour it has the air of a cemetery. Long white walls with even crenellations, recessed doorways whose exquisite, lobed arches, scalloped with stalactites, are outlined under the thick whitewash... And, at last, here are real doors through which we shall enter: low doors, each framed in several bandings of interlaced arabesque ornamentation in a new and different design, doors which succeed each other in a series, as if to better enclose... Inside, many of these houses are magnificent: large courtyards tiled in marble and bordered with scalloped arcades faced in mosaic. In the middle, a sparkling fountain among the orange-trees — it is the Alhambra with the same changing fantasies of honeycomb porticos and cave-like stalactites; an inhabitated Alhambra with hangings, carpets and cushions as though one were entering 'A Thousand and One Nights'. The wonderful courtyard where the sun fell on the arabesques and mosaics was, on the shaded side, covered in brilliant Rabat carpets - and these carpets were strewn with roses and orange flowers."

Accrochée au flanc d'une colline escarpée, la superbe Tétouan est d'une blancheur étincelante. Son nom signifie «Ouvre les yeux» en berbère. De fait, lorsqu'on pénètre dans les ruelles de la médina, on est émerveillé par la richesse des détails qui semblent sortis tout droit d'un rêve orientaliste. Ici, l'architecture est plus ouvragée encore que celle des villes impériales et évoque les aspects décoratifs du style andalo-moresque. Comment ne pas songer aux descriptions pleines de sensibilité de Pierre Loti dans son «Journal Intime»? Rédigées lors de son voyage historique au Maroc en 1860, ces pages ne furent publiées qu'un siècle plus tard: «Voici la blanche ville moresque tout près de nous; aucun mouvement alentour; à cette heure crépusculaire, elle a un aspect de nécropole. Longues murailles blanches à créneaux tout pareils; portes murées dont les ogives exquises, dentelées, festonnées en stalactites, se dessinent encore sous la chaux épaissie... Et enfin voici de vraies portes par lesquelles nous allons entrer; portes basses, encadrées chacune de plusieurs rangs d'arabesques en dentelle, d'un dessin étrange et différent; portes qui se succèdent en série, comme pour mieux enfermer. Au-dedans, plusieurs de ces maisons sont magnifiques: grandes cours dallées de marbre, bordées d'arcades, festonnées, revêtues de mosaïques — avec, au milieu, une fontaine jaillissante entre des orangers — c'est l'Alhambra, avec ses mêmes fantaisies changeantes de portiques dentelés en stalactites de grotte; mais l'Alhambra habité, avec ses tentures, ses tapis, ses coussins... Il me semblait pénétrer dans un rêve des Mille et Une Nuits. La merveilleuse cour, où le soleil tombait sur les arabesques et les mosaïques, était, du côté de l'ombre, recouverte de tapis aux couleurs éclatantes de Rabat — et ces tapis étaient jonchés de roses et de fleurs d'oranger...»

Tétouan, die wunderschöne Stadt oberhalb eines steilen Hanges gelegen, leuchtet weiß in der Sonne. Der Berber-Name bedeutet »Öffne
deine Augen«, und wirklich überwältigt einen die Architektur der
Häuser in der Medina mit ihren extravaganten Details – Stoff für
Phantasien und orientalische Träume. Sie ist detailreicher und ver-
schlungener noch als die Architektur der Königsstädte und erinnert an
die Ornamentik des andalusisch-maurischen Stils. Es ist verlockend
und irgendwie auch unvermeidlich, sich Pierre Lotis sensiblen Be-
schreibungen in seinem Tagebuch »Journal Intime« zuzuwenden, das
nach seiner historischen Marokkoreise im Jahre 1860 noch mehr als
hundert Jahre unveröffentlicht blieb. Loti war gefesselt von Tétouan:
»Direkt vor uns nun die weiße maurische Stadt, ringsum keine Bewe-
gung; um diese Stunde der Dämmerung wirkt sie wie eine Totenstadt.
Langgestreckte weiße Mauern, alle mit den gleichen Zinnen; zuge-
mauerte Türen, deren exquisite, mit Zacken und Stalaktitengirlanden
verzierte Spitzbögen sich noch unter der dicken Kalkschicht abzeich-
nen... Und schließlich vor uns wirkliche Türen, durch die wir gleich
eintreten werden: niedrige Türen, jede von mehreren Reihen Arabes-
ken und Zacken mit fremdartigen, ungewohnten Mustern versehen,
Türen, von denen mehrere aufeinander folgen, als sollten sie etwas
Besonderes gut verschließen... Von innen sind einige dieser Häuser
wunderschön: Weiträumige, mit Marmorplatten gefliese, von girlan-
denförmig verzierten Arkaden umgebene, mit Mosaiken verkleidete
Patios, in deren Mitte zwischen Orangenbäumen ein Springbrunnen
plätschert ... es war, als tauche er in einen Traum aus Tausendund-
einer Nacht ein. Der prächtige Innenhof, in dem die Sonne auf Ara-
besken und Mosaiken fiel, war auf der schattigen Seite mit herrlichen
Teppichen aus Rabat bedeckt – und diese Teppiche waren mit Rosen
und Orangenblüten bestreut ...«

Above: a small reception room on one side of the courtyard. The "toothed" horseshoe arches are a distinctive feature of the architecture of Tetuan that is unique to the city. The heavy neo-gothic armchair and the hoof coat-pegs are unexpected curiosities.
Below: Abdelatif Torres' small office, reading room and library secreted away in a low-ceilinged garret up the backstairs. The desk and chair are very fine pieces, done entirely in true "Morocco" leather work.

Ci-dessus: un petit salon de réception donnant sur la cour. Les arches en ogives dentelées sont un trait distinctif de l'architecture de Tétouan. Le lourd fauteuil néo-gothique et le portemanteau en sabot sont deux curiosités inattendues.
Ci-dessous: le petit bureau de Abdelatif Torres, faisant office de salon de lecture et de bibliothèque, caché dans une mansarde à laquelle on accède par un petit escalier au fond de la maison. Le bureau et la chaise sont des pièces rares d'un raffinement extrême. Elles sont entièrement travaillées à l'ancienne dans du cuir marocain.

Oben: ein kleiner Salon an einer Seite des Innenhofes. Die hufeisenförmigen Torbögen mit ihren »Zähnen« sind ein typisches Merkmal für die Architektur von Tétouan, das sich nur in dieser Stadt so finden läßt. Der schwere neogotische Armsessel und die Mantelhaken aus Hufen sind unerwartete Kuriositäten.
Unten: Das kleine Büro von Abdelatif Torres – sein Lesezimmer und seine Bibliothek – liegt versteckt in einer Dachkammer mit niedriger Decke, die über eine Hintertreppe zu erreichen ist. Der Schreibtisch und der Stuhl, zwei sehr schöne Stücke, sind gänzlich aus echtem marokkanischen Leder gearbeitet.

Moroccan Interiors   Dâr Torres   Tétouan

The Torres are a well-established Tetuan family whose doyen was the politician and intellectual Abdelatif Torres. He established the Istiqlal Party and played an important role in post-independence Moroccan politics. The family home, a neo-traditional palace built along classical lines, reflects the delicate decorative architecture typical of the city. The furniture is a fascinating mixture of traditional pieces supplemented by a potpourri of styles that reflect the taste of the last three generations. The first-floor drawing-room has neo-gothic furnishing that are evocative of the atmosphere of a medieval dining-hall – a reference to the Spanish influence that has long dominated Tetuan.

Dar Torres

Les Torres sont une vieille famille de Tétouan, dont le patriarche était le politicien et l'intellectuel Abdelatif Torres. Il a fondé le parti Istiqlal et a joué un rôle important dans la vie politique marocaine après que le pays eût accédé à l'indépendance. La maison de la famille, un palais néo-traditionnel construit selon des lignes classiques, est typique de l'architecture fleurie de la ville. Le mobilier est un fascinant mélange de meubles traditionnels agrémenté d'un pot-pourri de styles qui reflètent le goût des trois dernières générations. Le salon néo-gothique du premier étage évoque l'atmosphère des grandes salles à manger médiévales, une référence à l'influence espagnole qui a longtemps dominé à Tétouan.

Die Torres sind eine gutsituierte Familie in Tétouan, deren Doyen der Politiker und Intellektuelle Abdelatif Torres war. Er gründete die Partei Istiqlal und spielte nach der Unabhängigkeit eine wichtige Rolle in der marokkanischen Politik. Das Stammhaus der Familie, ein neotraditioneller Palast, wurde nach klassischem Muster erbaut und ist ein Beispiel für die feine, dekorative Architektur, die so typisch für diese Stadt ist. Das Mobiliar besteht aus einer faszinierenden Mischung von traditionellen Möbeln, ergänzt durch ein Potpourri von Stilen, die den Geschmack der letzten drei Generationen widerspiegeln. Der Salon im ersten Stock ist mit neogotischem Mobiliar ausgestattet, das an einen mittelalterlichen Speisesaal denken läßt, eine Hommage an den spanischen Einfluß, der lange in Tétouan vorherrschend war.

Above: a view of the double-depth "salon Marocain" with its finely worked plaster arches and 'zelliges'.
Right page: the traditional brass bed in an alcove of the salon with its fine damask drapes.

Ci-dessus: une vue du double «salon marocain», avec ses arches en stuc ouvragées et ses zelliges
Page de droite: le lit traditionnel en laiton dans une alcôve du salon, avec un baldaquin en damas précieux.

Oben: Blick auf den doppelt angelegten »Salon Marocain« mit seinen schön gearbeiteten Stuckbögen und ›zelliges‹.
Rechte Seite: das traditionelle Messingbett in einem Alkoven des Salons mit seinen edlen Damastvorhängen.

Tanger

"I saw the white roofs of the little port of Tangier sitting right there in the elbow of the land, on the water. This dream of white-robed Africa on the blue afternoon sea, wow, who dreamed it?" So wrote Jack Kérouac, evoking the feeling of unreality that Tangier so often induces. Hercules was Tangier's first hero, ripping Africa and Europe apart and founding a settlement where the water of the Mediterranean and Atlantic mingled. He called it Tanga, in honour of the bewitching woman he loved and whose husband he had murdered. Such myths and legends abound in the city. Hear stories, told with glee by the 'Tangawis', of wicked 19th-century bandits such as Raisuli; of conspirators during the city's hey-day as an international zone, of the dissolute writers of the Beat Generation drinking and drugging, of cosmopolitan aristocracy mixing with the equally cosmopolitan riff-raff... It is an inspiring city and, it would seem, strangely addictive. Truman Capote penned a famous warning: "Before coming here you should do three things: be inoculated for typhoid, withdraw your savings from the bank. say goodbye to your friends – heaven knows you may never see them again. This advice is quite serious, for it is alarming the number of travelers who have landed here on a brief holiday, then settled down and let the years go by."

Evoquant l'impression d'irréalité que Tanger inspire si souvent, Jack Kérouac écrivit: «J'ai vu les toits blancs du petit port de Tanger avançant sur l'eau sur un bras de terre. Ce rêve d'une Afrique drapée de blanc sur la mer bleue de l'après-midi – wow! – qui l'a rêvé?» Hercule fut le premier héros de Tanger. Ecartant l'Afrique et l'Europe, il fonda la première colonie là où se mêlaient les eaux de la Méditerranée et celles de l'Atlantique. Il la baptisa Tanga, en l'honneur de son ensorcelante maîtresse dont il avait tué le mari. C'est du moins ce qu'on raconte, car la ville résonne encore de mille et une légendes. Ici, les tangawis vous parleront pendant des heures des cruels bandits du XIXe siècle tels que Raisuli, des trafiquants en tout genre qui sévissaient à l'époque où la ville jouissait du statut envié de «zone internationale», de la vie dissolue des écrivains de la Beat Generation, puisant leur inspiration dans l'alcool et la drogue, de l'aristocratie cosmopolite frayant avec une pègre venue, elle aussi, des quatre coins du monde… Tanger inspire et, étrangement, envoûte. Truman Capote a pourtant mis en garde le voyageur imprudent: «Avant de venir ici, trois précautions s'imposent: faites-vous vacciner contre la typhoïde, retirez vos économies de la banque et dites adieu à vos amis – qui sait si vous les reverrez un jour? Cet avertissement est très sérieux. Un nombre effarant de voyageurs ont débarqué ici pour un bref séjour et y sont restés définitivement, laissant les années filer.»

»Ich sah die weißen Dächer der kleinen Hafenstadt Tanger, wie sie dort in dieser Krümmung liegt, am Wasser. Dieser Traum vom weißgekleideten Afrika auf dem blauen Nachmittagsmeer, wow, wer träumte den?« schrieb Jack Kérouac und beschwor damit das Gefühl der Unwirklichkeit, das Tanger so oft erweckt. Herkules war der erste Held von Tanger: Er riß Afrika und Europa auseinander und gründete dort eine Siedlung, wo die Fluten des Mittelmeers und des Atlantiks sich vermischten. Er nannte sie Tanga, zu Ehren der bezaubernden Frau, die er liebte und deren Mann er ermordet hatte – so jedenfalls wird es erzählt. Die Stadt wimmelt von solchen Mythen und Legenden. Hören Sie die schadenfrohen Geschichten der Tangawis von den bösen Banditen des 19. Jahrhunderts, wie etwa Raisuli: von Verschwörern während der Blütezeit der Stadt als internationale Zone, von den ausschweifenden Schriftstellern der Beat Generation, die tranken und kifften, von der kosmopolitischen Aristokratie, die sich mit dem gleichfalls kosmopolitischen Gesindel vermischte… Es ist eine anregende Stadt, die, wie es scheint, seltsam süchtig macht. Truman Capote verfaßte eine berühmte Warnung: »Bevor Sie herkommen, sollten Sie drei Dinge tun: sich gegen Typhus impfen lassen, Ihre Ersparnisse von der Bank abheben und Ihren Freunden Lebewohl! sagen – der Himmel weiß, ob man sie jemals wiedersieht. Dieser Rat ist ziemlich ernst gemeint, denn die Zahl der Reisenden ist besorgniserregend, die für einen Kurzurlaub hierhergekommen sind, sich dann niedergelassen und die Jahre haben verstreichen lassen.«

It is a statement open to contention, but perhaps the highest arts in Morocco are the decorative arts. Incorporated into the business of living, they are the arts of reality. Eugène Delacroix, in his thoughts on his stay in Morocco that would prove immensely fruitful and so formative for his career, announced that "the most beautiful pictures I have ever seen are some oriental rugs". Abdellatif Ben Najem, a Moroccan painter, who sells his prolific work in his brother's shop in the 'souk' of Tangier, would no doubt agree. He is self-taught and works from instinct. The bulk of his production is painted on glass and are highly coloured and charmingly naïve renditions of local scenes. His home, a three-story town house in the medina that probably dates from the end of the 19th century, is elaborately decorative, well-preserved and kept as neat as neat can be.

Abdellatif Ben Najem

Sans vouloir porter de jugement définitif, j'estime que les arts décoratifs sont la forme d'art la plus élevée au Maroc: directement liés au quotidien, ce sont les arts de la réalité. Méditant sur son séjour au Maroc, un voyage qui allait se révéler si riche d'enseignements pour son œuvre, Eugène Delacroix déclarait: «Certains tapis d'Orient sont les plus beaux tableaux que j'aie jamais vus.» Abdellatif BenNajem ne le démentirait sans doute pas. Ce peintre marocain expose son œuvre prolifique dans la boutique de son frère dans le souk de Tanger. Autodidacte, il travaille d'instinct. Il peint surtout sur le verre: de charmantes scènes locales vivement colorées et naïves. Sa maison dans la médina, un hôtel particulier de trois étages qui date probablement de la fin du XIXe siècle, est conservée et décorée avec soin. Il y règne un ordre irréprochable.

Über diese Meinung kann man sicher streiten, aber die am höchsten entwickelte Kunst in Marokko ist wahrscheinlich die dekorative. Sie ist die Kunst der Realität, da sie ins Leben integriert ist. Eugène Delacroix verkündete in seinen Betrachtungen über seinen Aufenthalt in Marokko, der sich als so ungeheuer fruchtbar und prägend für seine weitere Entwicklung erwies: »Die schönsten Bilder, die ich jemals gesehen habe, sind ein paar orientalische Teppiche.« Abdellatif Ben Najem, ein außerordentlich produktiver marokkanischer Maler, der seine Werke im Geschäft seines Bruders im ›souk‹ von Tanger verkauft, würde ohne Zweifel zustimmen. Er ist Autodidakt und arbeitet nur seiner Intuition folgend. Die meisten seiner Arbeiten sind Glasmalereien: stark kolorierte und bezaubernd naive Wiedergaben lokaler Szenen. Seine Wohnung, ein dreistöckiges Stadthaus in der Medina, das vermutlich vom Ende des 19. Jahrhunderts stammt, ist aufwendig verziert, gut erhalten und äußerst gepflegt.

Above: *the view over the medina from the impromtu "tent" erected on the roof.*
Right page: *a spectacular traditional brass bed, with a beautifully made canopy that has been embroidered and ruched.*

Ci-dessus: *la vue sur la médina depuis la «tente» improvisée sur le toit.*
Page de droite: *un spectaculaire lit traditionnel en laiton, surmonté d'un superbe baldaquin brodé en nid d'abeilles.*

Oben: *der Blick über die Medina von einem improvisierten »Zelt« aus, das auf dem Dach errichtet wurde.*
Rechte Seite: *ein spektakuläres traditionelles Messingbett, mit einem wunderschön gearbeiteten Baldachin, bestickt und mit Rüschen versehen.*

On the previous double page: *if the definition "Rococo-Moresque"
does not yet exist, it could be invented specially to describe the
neo-traditional decor of the "salon Marocain". The portrait of
Mohammed V, father of the present king, is by Abdellatif.*
Above and right page: *the kitchen.*

Double page précédente: *si le terme «rococo-moresque» n'existe pas
encore, il mérite d'être inventé pour définir le décor néo-traditionnel
du «salon marocain». Le portrait de Mohammed V, père du roi actuel, est d'Abdellatif.*
Ci-dessus et page de droite: *la cuisine.*

Vorhergehende Doppelseite: *Wenn die Bezeichnung »rokoko-
maurisch« noch nicht existiert, sollte man sie erfinden, um das neotraditionelle Dekor dieses »Salon Marocain« zu beschreiben. Das
Portrait von Mohammed V., Vater des derzeitigen Königs, stammt
von Abdellatif.*
Oben und rechte Seite: *die Küche.*

French couturier Jean-Louis Scherrer chose to live in the very heart of the medina in Tangier, as opposed to a villa by the sea, because he was attracted to the energy and vivacity of the popular quarter. The sights and sounds, the ritual of daily life, fascinate him as much as they did Paul and Jane Bowles, or indeed many other artistic expatriates who have chosen to inhabit the medina at different times in Tangier's colourful history. Scherrer set about creating a holiday home to his own design by adapting four existing houses. He built a central courtyard around a simple but elegant fountain, in a pared-down version of the classical Hispano-Moresque architecture. The house is limewashed a luminous white throughout in order to give the illusion of coolness during the summer heat.

Jean-Louis Scherrer

Attiré par l'énergie et la vitalité des quartiers populaires, le couturier Jean-Louis Scherrer a choisi de vivre en plein cœur de la médina plutôt que dans une villa en bord de mer. Les scènes de rue, les bruits, le rituel de la vie quotidienne le fascinent, comme ils ont fasciné avant lui Jane et Paul Bowles ainsi que de nombreux autres expatriés qui se sont installés dans la médina à différentes époques de l'histoire haute en couleurs de Tanger. Scherrer a créé une résidence secondaire à sa mesure en adaptant quatre maisons différentes. Il a construit une cour centrale autour d'une fontaine simple mais élégante, dans une version épurée du style hispano-moresque. Lumineux, l'intérieur de la maison est entièrement blanchi à la chaux afin de donner une illusion de fraîcheur au cours de l'été caniculaire.

Angezogen von der Energie und Vitalität in den volkstümlichen Vierteln beschloß der französische Modeschöpfer Jean-Louis Scherrer, statt einer Villa am Meer im Herzen der Medina von Tanger zu wohnen. Die Eindrücke und Geräusche, die Rituale des täglichen Lebens faszinierten ihn wie vor ihm Jane und Paul Bowles und viele andere ausländische Künstler, die in verschiedenen Phasen von Tangers abwechsluingsreicher Geschichte den Entschluß faßten, in der Medina zu wohnen. Scherrer begann, sich ein Ferienhaus nach eigenen Entwürfen zu bauen, indem er vier bereits vorhandene Häuser miteinbezog. In einer reduzierten Version der klassischen hispano-maurischen Architektur legte er einen zentralen Innenhof um einen einfachen, aber eleganten Brunnen herum an. Das Haus ist in einem leuchtenden Weiß gekalkt, um während der Sommerhitze die Illusion von Kühle zu vermitteln.

Left page: *a view of the salon with its clean lines and its panes of coloured glass in the windows.*
Above: *the bedroom with a traditional brass bedstead and a folding Syrian chair inlaid with mother-of-pearl. From his various terraces Scherrer commands a superb view over the port and across the Straits of Gibraltar. On fine days Spain is visible: a low-lying mass, deep purple in the hazy distance.*

Page de gauche: *une vue du salon, avec ses lignes pures et ses vitres teintées au-dessus des fenêtres.*
Ci-dessus: *la chambre, avec un lit en laiton traditionnel et une chaise pliante syrienne incrustée de nacre. Depuis ses différentes terrasses, Scherrer domine le port et le détroit de Gibraltar. Par beau temps, on aperçoit l'Espagne, une silhouette basse, violette, se dessinant sur la ligne d'horizon.*

Linke Seite: *Blick auf den Salon, mit seinen klaren Linien und den farbigen Fensterscheiben.*
Oben: *das Schlafzimmer mit einem traditionellen Messingbett und einem syrischen Klappstuhl mit Perlmuttintarsien. Von seinen verschiedenen Terrassen aus hat Scherrer einen phantastischen Blick auf den Hafen und die Straße von Gibraltar. An schönen Tagen kann man Spanien sehen, eine geduckte Masse, dunkelviolett in dunstiger Ferne.*

Above: a view of the second-floor salon. The fish sculpture is by
Claude Lalanne.
Right page: a view into the kitchen. All the woodwork and most of the
furnishings were handmade by the artisans of the 'souk' to Scherrer's
specifications. He is something of a Tangier connoisseur when it comes
to finding the best carpenter or antique dealer. It was Scherrer who
first began to collect the work of the painter Abdellatif Ben Najem
(see pp. 212–219).

Ci-dessus: le salon du deuxième étage. La sculpture de poisson est de
Claude Lalanne.
Page de droite: la cuisine. Toutes les boiseries et la plupart des
meubles ont été fabriqués par des artisans du souk suivant les instruc-
tions de Scherrer. Le couturier n'a pas son pareil pour vous indiquer
les meilleurs menuisiers ou antiquaires de Tanger. C'est lui qui, le
premier, a commencé à collectionner les œuvres du peintre Abdellatif
Ben Najem (voir pp. 212–219).

Oben: Blick auf den Salon im zweiten Stock. Die Fischskulptur
stammt von Claude Lalanne.
Rechte Seite: Blick in die Küche. Alle Holzarbeiten und die meisten
Möbel wurden von Kunsthandwerkern aus den ›souks‹ nach Anwei-
sung von Scherrer von Hand angefertigt. Er ist ein Kenner Tangers,
wenn es darum geht, den besten Zimmermann oder Antiquitätenhändler aufzutreiben. Scherrer war der erste, der damit begann, die
Bilder von Abdellatif Ben Najem (s. S. 212–219) zu sammeln.

The summer house: this four storey house surveying the Straits is built around a lightwell that has its architectural origins in the traditional courtyard. It has two exits, one into the tangled lanes of the medina and a second one, probably later, whose steps were hewn into Tangier's massive Portuguese ramparts and lead down into the street. The house is particularly striking because of the original decorative effects dating from the turn of the century. Indeed, the coloured glass panes, folding windows, tiled floors, mosaic 'zelliges' and the intricate stucco work give the house a character all of its own and have been perfectly restored by the house's present European owners.

La Maison d'été

Cette maison de quatre étages qui surplombe le détroit est construite autour d'un puits de lumière qui rappelle la cour traditionnelle. Elle a deux entrées: l'une donne sur l'enchevêtrement des ruelles de la médina, l'autre, sans doute plus tardive, ouvre sur des marches creusées dans la pierre des imposants remparts portugais. L'intérieur frappe surtout par ses éléments décoratifs originaux qui datent du début du siècle. Les vitres teintées, les volets en accordéon, les sol carrelés, les mosaïques de zelliges et les stucs ouvragés confèrent à cette demeure un caractère unique que les propriétaires actuels, des Européens, ont parfaitement su restaurer.

Das Sommerhaus: Dieses vierstöckige Haus, von dem aus man auf die Straße von Gibraltar blickt, ist um einen Lichthof herum angelegt, dessen architektonische Wurzeln im traditionellen Innenhof liegen. Es besitzt zwei Zugänge, einen, der in die verschlungenen Gassen der Medina führt, und einen zweiten, vermutlich späteren, von dem aus Stufen, die in den Stein von Tangers massiven portugiesischen Befestigungsmauern geschlagen wurden, hinunter auf die Straße führen. Besonders eindrucksvoll sind in diesem Haus die ursprünglichen Verzierungen und Ornamente aus der Zeit der Jahrhundertwende. Die bunten Glasscheiben, Klappfenster, mit Fliesen ausgelegten Fußböden, die Kachelmosaike und die feinen Stuckarbeiten verleihen dem Haus einen ganz eigenen Charakter und sind von den gegenwärtigen europäischen Besitzern perfekt restauriert worden.

Following double page and above: the first-floor drawing-room and the gallery from where steep steps lead down to the entrance and up to the guest bedrooms. The stucco work was done by an Italian artisan in the 1880s.

Double page suivante et ci-dessus: la salon du premier étage et la galerie. Un escalier abrupt mène au vestibule du rez-de-chaussée et aux chambres d'amis des étages supérieurs. Les stucs datent des années 1880 et sont l'œuvre d'un artisan italien.

Folgende Doppelseite und oben: der Salon im ersten Stock und die Galerie, von der steile Treppen zum Ausgang hinunter und hoch zu den Gästezimmern führen. Die Stuckarbeiten wurden 1880 von einem italienischen Künstler ausgeführt.

Left page: *a guest room of almost monastic simplicity on the second floor. Here, as in the rest of the house, one can almost always find a breeze as the entire structure has been conceived to avoid the heat of Tangier's fierce summers.*
Above: *another guest room that looks out over the sandy half moon of the beach.*

Page de gauche: *Une chambre d'amis d'une simplicité quasi monacale au deuxième étage. Ici, comme dans toutes les pièces, un léger courant d'air circule en permanence car la maison a été conçue pour éviter la chaleur torride des étés tangérois.*
Ci-dessus: *Une autre chambre d'amis dont la fenêtre s'ouvre sur la plage en forme de croissant de lune.*

Linke Seite: *ein Gästezimmer im zweiten Stock von beinahe mönchischer Schlichtheit. Auch hier findet man immer einen kühlen Lufthauch, da das ganze Haus konzipiert ist, um der brutalen Sommerhitze von Tanger zu widerstehen.*
Oben: *ein weiteres Gästezimmer, von dem aus man den sandigen Halbmond des Strandes überblickt.*

Generally acknowledged as the most beautiful colonial private house in Morocco, Villa Léon l'Africain was named after the Fez scholar of the 16th century who, under the auspices of Pope Leo X, wrote the first comprehensive description of his homeland. His study was to remain unrivalled until the advent of the orientalist vogue of the late 19th century. Situated in the centre of Tangier, the house was built by a French lawyer in 1910, two years before the French were to establish their protectorate. It was directly inspired by a Provençale construction, which was itself copied from on a Louis XVI pavilion. Richard Timewell retired from Sotheby's in 1967, and when he settled in Morocco he brought what he calls his "life's possessions" with him. Indeed, the villa admirably reflects his discriminating taste.

Villa Léon l'Africain

Généralement reconnue comme le plus bel exemple de maison coloniale au Maroc, la villa Léon l'Africain doit son nom à l'érudit originaire de Fès qui, au XVIe siècle, sous les auspices du pape Léon X, rédigea la première description détaillée de sa terre natale. Son ouvrage devait rester sans équivalent jusqu'à l'avènement de la mode orientaliste à la fin du siècle dernier. Située au cœur de Tanger, la maison fut construite par un avocat français en 1910, deux ans avant l'instauration du Protectorat. Elle s'inspirait directement du style Louis XVI provençal. L'historien d'art et esthète Richard Timewell est venu s'y installer en 1967 après avoir pris sa retraite de Sotheby. Il a apporté dans ses bagages «les possessions de toute une vie». De fait, la villa reflète admirablement ses goûts exigeants.

Die Villa Léon l'Africain gilt allgemein als die schönste private Kolonialvilla in Marokko. Sie wurde nach dem aus Fes stammenden Gelehrten des 16. Jahrhunderts benannt, der unter der Schirmherrschaft von Papst Leo X. die erste umfassende Beschreibung seiner Heimat verfaßte. Bis zum Aufkommen der orientalischen Mode gegen Ende des 19. Jahrhunderts blieb seine Studie konkurrenzlos. Das mitten im Zentrum von Tanger gelegene Haus wurde 1910 von einem französischen Rechtsanwalt gebaut, zwei Jahre, bevor die Franzosen ihr Protektorat errichteten. Es war direkt von einem provenzalischen Bau inspiriert, der sich selbst wiederum an einen Pavillon von Ludwig XVI. anlehnte. Richard Timewell gab 1967 seine Stelle bei Sotheby's auf, und als er sich in Marokko niederließ, führte er die ganze »Habe seines Lebens« – wie er es nannte – mit sich. Die Villa reflektiert in der Tat seinen bewundernswert feinen Geschmack.

Page 232: *a view of the neo-classical façade, definitely more Riviera than Africa.*
Above: *the garden façade.*
Right page: *the horseshoe arch, so often employed in colonial architecture, gives onto the manicured garden.*

Page 232: *la façade néo-classique, nettement plus «Côte d'Azur» qu'africaine.*
Ci-dessus: *la façade côté jardin.*
Page de droite: *l'arche en ogive typique de l'architecture coloniale s'ouvre sur un jardin tiré au cordeau.*

Seite 232: *der Blick auf die neoklassische Fassade, mit Sicherheit mehr Riviera als Afrika.*
Oben: *die Gartenfassade.*
Rechte Seite: *Der Torbogen in Form eines Hufeisens, den man so häufig in kolonialer Architektur findet, öffnet sich auf den sorgfältig gepflegten Garten.*

Above and left: the drawing-room and a detail of the chicken wire on the doors of the book-shelves. With its Venetian chandelier and its cosy atmosphere, the room has a decidedly 19th-century feel. While sipping afternoon tea ensconced in a comfortable armchair it seems highly unlikely that Morocco lies just beyond the chintz curtains.
Right page: a view of the emerald-green dining-room with a collection of portraits of British worthies.

Ci-dessus et à gauche: le salon et un détail du grillage «poulailler» de la bibliothèque. Avec son lustre vénitien et son atmosphère douillette, cette pièce a un parfum «fin de siècle». Confortablement enfoncé dans un fauteuil devant une tasse de thé, on a du mal à croire que c'est le Maroc qui s'étend derrière les rideaux en chintz.
Page de droite: la salle à manger vert émeraude et sa collection de portraits de notables anglais.

Oben und links: der Salon und eine Detailaufnahme des Maschendrahts auf den Türen des Bücherregals. Mit seinem venezianischen Kronleuchter und seiner Gemütlichkeit vermittelt das Zimmer eine Atmosphäre wie im 19. Jahrhundert. Wenn man den Nachmittagstee trinkt und sich dabei in einem der bequemen Armsessel niederläßt, kommt es einem ziemlich unwahrscheinlich vor, daß Marokko gleich hinter den Chintzvorhängen liegt.
Rechte Seite: Blick auf das smaragdgrüne Eßzimmer mit einer Sammlung von Porträts britischer Berühmtheiten.

When her husband, the Scottish painter James McBey, eager to indulge his beautiful American bride, suggested motoring down through France and Spain in order to choose her a house, he may or may not have had it in the back of his mind to introduce Marguerite to Morocco. The fact was they ended up there, and she loved it as much as he did. He especially adored Tangier, and his sensitive drawings are a potent testimony to this fascination. His love affair with the country was accompanied by a sense of wonderment: "The whole of the Old Testament might have happened here and most of the New also, except, perhaps, Revelation," he wrote. One morning in the early thirties they did indeed buy a Spanish-style villa high up the mountain in Tangier. An astonishingly elegant figure, Marguerite reigns as gracefully as she has always done over her English-looking interior in mauve and pink.

Marguerite McBey

Lorsque le peintre écossais James McBey, voulant faire plaisir à sa jeune et belle épouse américaine, lui proposa de sillonner les routes de France et d'Espagne en quête d'une maison, il prévoyait peut-être déjà de l'entraîner jusqu'au Maroc. Toujours est-il que c'est là que s'acheva leur voyage et Marguerite fut conquise autant que son époux. James adorait Tanger et ses dessins pleins de sensibilité témoignent de son attachement. Son histoire d'amour avec le Maroc était teintée d'émerveillement: «L'Ancien Testament tout entier et une grande partie du Nouveau auraient pu se dérouler ici, hormis peut-être l'Apocalypse», disait-il volontiers. Un beau matin, au début des années trente, les McBey finirent par acheter une maison: une villa de style espagnol haut perchée sur la montagne de Tanger. Depuis, avec une grâce et une élégance exceptionnelles, Marguerite règne sur son intérieur anglais, mauve et rose.

Der schottische Maler James McBey wollte seiner schönen amerikanischen Braut unbedingt etwas Besonderes bieten. So schlug er ihr vor, mit dem Wagen durch Frankreich und Spanien zu fahren, um ihr ein Haus zu kaufen. Vielleicht hatte er sogar den Hintergedanken, Marguerite Marokko zu zeigen. Jedenfalls landeten sie schließlich dort, und sie liebte das Land ebenso sehr wie er. Er liebte vor allem Tanger, und seine einfühlsamen Bilder sind ein beredtes Zeugnis von seiner Faszination. Seine Liebe zu dem Land wurde von Staunen begleitet: »Alles aus dem Alten Testament und das meiste aus dem Neuen Testament könnte sich hier zugetragen haben, bis auf die Offenbarung möglicherweise«, schrieb er. Eines Morgens in den frühen Dreißigern kauften sie dann wirklich ein Haus, eine Villa im spanischen Stil, hoch auf dem Hügel von Tanger. Marguerite, eine erstaunlich elegante Dame, herrscht so anmutig wie eh und je über ihre englisch wirkenden Interieurs in Mauve und Rosa.

Previous pages: the observatory on the top floor is a study in white-washed simplicity. The house overlooks the scattering of white cubes that is Tangier, punctuated by the proud minarets of the medina.
On these pages: Marguerite lives serenely, surrounded by a garden of semi-wild flowers only slightly tamed.

Pages précédentes: l'observatoire au dernier étage, un bureau aux murs blanchis à la chaux d'une élégante simplicité. La maison domine Tanger, un éparpillement de cubes blancs d'où surgissent les fiers minarets de la médina.
Ci-contre: Marguerite mène une existence sereine au milieu d'un jardin de fleurs à demi sauvages qu'elle tente d'apprivoiser.

Vorhergehende Seiten: das Observatorium im obersten Stockwerk, ein Studierzimmer, weißgekalkt und schlicht. Von hier aus hat man die Aussicht auf die verstreuten weißen Würfel, aus denen Tanger besteht und zwischen denen sich die stolzen Minarette der Medina erheben.
Diese Doppelseite: Marguerite führt ein gelassenes Leben, umgeben von einem Garten voller halbwilder Blumen, die nur leicht zurückgeschnitten werden.

Moroccan Interiors   Marguerite McBey   Tanger

Left page and above: James McBey's studio is a solid masculine
room where Marguerite now paints and draws. The room has an arts-
and-crafts feeling about it even though most of the furniture is made
locally.

Page de gauche et ci-dessus: l'atelier de James McBey, un univers
résolument masculin où Marguerite s'installe désormais pour peindre
et dessiner. Bien que tous les meubles aient été fabriqués à Tanger,
il y règne une atmosphère Arts and Crafts.

Linke Seite und oben: James McBeys Atelier, ein durch und durch
männlicher Raum, in dem jetzt Marguerite malt und zeichnet.
Der Raum erinnert an die Arts-and-Crafts-Bewegung, die meisten
Möbel sind jedoch in Tanger angefertigt worden.

On these pages: Marguerite's bedroom and her salon with an assortment of English pieces and Spanish baroque furniture including an Andalusian mirror. The animal pelt is thought to be a hunting trophy of the last Pasha of Marrakesh.

Ci-dessus et page de droite: La chambre et le salon de Marguerite, qui marient les meubles anglais et le style baroque espagnol, dont un miroir andalou. La peau de panthère serait un trophée de chasse du dernier pacha de Marrakech.

Diese Doppelseite: Marguerites Schlafzimmer und ihr Salon, mit einer Sammlung englischer Möbel und spanischer Barockmöbel, darunter auch ein andalusischer Spiegel. Das Fell soll eine Jagdtrophäe des letzten Paschas von Marrakesch sein.

This house is perched on top of a cliff overlooking the Straits of Gibraltar and the coast of Andalusia. With the help of Stuart Church (see pp. 304–309), architect and decorator, the Shaikha has opened up the structure of the traditional Moorish house with windows and a glass veranda that frames the sea view. The central courtyard with its perfectly proportioned arches gives on to a series of sunny rooms, tiled with hand-cut 'zelliges' specially made in Fez. Unusual pieces picked up in the 'souk' of Tetuan rub shoulders with precious objects and ordinary earthenware bowls. Guests dine by the light of a hundred candles and are entertained on the lawn in the tropical garden that is one of the showpieces of Tangier.

Shaikha
Fatima Al Sabah

Cette maison est perchée au bord d'une falaise qui surplombe le détroit de Gibraltar et la côte d'Andalousie. Avec l'aide de l'architecte et décorateur Stuart Church (voir pp. 304–309), la Shaikha a aéré la structure traditionnelle de la maison mauresque en élargissant les fenêtres et en faisant construire une véranda qui encadre la vue sur la mer. Avec ses colonnes aux proportions parfaites, la cour centrale donne sur une série de pièces ensoleillées, carrelées de zelliges faits sur mesure et taillés à la main à Fès. Des meubles originaux chinés dans le souk de Tétouan côtoient des objets rares et de simples pots en terre cuite. Les invités dînent à la lueur de mille chandelles et se promènent dans le jardin tropical qui fait la fierté de Tanger.

Dieses Haus thront oben auf einer Klippe, von der man über die Straße von Gibraltar auf die Küste Andalusiens blickt. Mit Hilfe des Architekten und Innenausstatters Stuart Church (s. S. 304–309) hat die Shaikha die geschlossene Struktur des traditionellen maurischen Hauses durch Fenster und eine vollständig verglaste Veranda aufgebrochen, die nun den Meeresblick rahmt. Der zentrale Innenhof mit seinen perfekt proportionierten Torbögen führt zu einer Reihe von sonnigen Zimmern, die mit speziell von Hand gefertigten ›zelliges‹ aus Fes gekachelt sind. Ungewöhnliche Möbel und Dinge aus dem ›souk‹ von Tétouan stehen neben kostbaren Gegenständen und gewöhnlichen Tonschalen. Gäste dinieren beim Schein von hundert Kerzen und werden auf dem Rasen bewirtet – in diesem tropischen Garten, der eine der Sehenswürdigkeiten von Tanger ist.

Kilims in the garden for reclining at sunset. Although the Shaikha spends half of her time in America, she was attracted to Tangier because of its cosmopolitan allure – "the Southern-most tip of Europe" is how she defines it.

Des kilims dans le jardin où l'on peut s'allonger pour admirer le coucher de soleil. Bien que passant la moitié de l'année aux Etats-Unis, la Shaikha apprécie l'atmosphère cosmopolite de Tanger, «la ville la plus au sud de l'Europe», comme elle la définit désormais.

Kelims im Garten als Lager bei Sonnenuntergang. Obwohl die Shaikha die Hälfte ihrer Zeit in Amerika verbringt, zieht Tanger sie wegen seiner kosmopolitischen Atmosphäre an – »die südlichste Spitze Europas«, so nennt sie es.

Above: The swimming pool, a deep sea green, is built directly into the rock upon which the house is built. In the background, the recently built 'menzeh'.
On the following double page: the 'tadelakt' interior in the 'menzeh' was engraved with a floral design. The tables are simple Berber pieces in unvarnished wood that Stuart Church is particularly fond of.

Ci-dessus: la piscine, vert océan, creusée dans le rocher sur lequel la villa est construite. Au fond, la ‹menzeh› de construction récente.
Double page suivante: les murs intérieurs enduits de ‹tadelakt› de la ‹menzeh› sont gravés d'un motif fleuri. Les tables sont de simples meubles berbères en bois brut comme les aime Stuart Church.

Oben: Der Swimmingpool in tiefem Seegrün ist direkt in den Felsen gebaut, auf dem auch das Haus errichtet wurde. Im Hintergrund die kürzlich gebaute ›menzeh‹.
Folgende Doppelseite: Das ›tadelakt‹-Interieur der ›menzeh‹ wurde mit einem Blumenmuster verziert. Die Tische sind einfache Berbermöbel aus unbehandeltem Holz, die Stuart Church besonders liebt.

The second son of the Earl and Countess of Pembroke, a darling of the aristocratic "beau monde", David Herbert finally chose Morocco as his home shortly after the Second World War. During extended stays throughout the thirties he had galvanized "tout Tangier" with his wit, sociability and energetic adoption of the contradictory charms of the city. Cecil Beaton in his "Diaries" remembers holidaying with the young Herbert: "After three weeks David has become a complete Tangerino, knows all the local gossip of this oriental Cheltenham and knows every inch of the town." David Herbert has reigned over the international set ever since from his pink house with turquoise shutters perched high on the hill. It is a wonderfully individual creation combining Moroccan architecture with Victorian aesthetics and the fey charm of the 1930s decorator Syrie Maugham. This heady cocktail has heavily influenced Tangier style within the large foreign community.

David Herbert

Second fils du Earl et de la comtesse de Pembroke, enfant chéri du beau monde aristocratique, David Herbert choisit d'élire domicile à Tanger peu après la Deuxième Guerre mondiale. Pendant les années trente, au cours de séjours prolongés, il avait séduit le tout-Tanger par son esprit, son affabilité et son adoption inconditionnelle des charmes contradictoires de la ville dont il était tombé immédiatement amoureux, des impressions et des bruits. Dans son journal, Cecil Beaton se souvient de vacances avec le jeune Herbert: «En trois semaines, David est devenu un parfait Tangérois. Il connaît tous les potins locaux de ce Cheltenham oriental et il n'est pas un centimètre carré de la ville qui ne lui soit familier.» Depuis sa maison rose aux volets turquoise haut perchée sur la colline, David Herbert règne sur la communauté internationale de Tanger. C'est une demeure merveilleusement originale qui associe l'architecture marocaine, l'esthétique victorienne et le charme féerique du décorateur des années trente, Syrie Maugham. Cet enivrant cocktail a fortement influencé le style tangérois au sein de la vaste communauté étrangère.

David Herbert, der zweite Sohn des Earls und der Countess von Pembroke, ein Liebling der aristokratischen »beau monde«, hat kurz nach dem zweiten Weltkrieg Marokko zu seiner Wahlheimat gemacht. Während längerer Aufenthalte in den dreißiger Jahren hatte er bereits »tout Tangier« mit seinem geistreichen Witz, seiner Geselligkeit und seiner schwungvollen Aneignung der widersprüchlichen Reize diese Stadt elektrisiert. Cecil Beaton erinnert sich in seinen Tagebüchern an einen Urlaub mit dem jungen Herbert: »Nach drei Wochen ist David ein vollkommener Tangerino, kennt den ganzen Klatsch dieses orientalischen Cheltenham und jeden Zentimeter der Stadt.« Von seinem rosa Haus hoch oben auf dem Hügel von Tanger aus regiert David Herbert seitdem den internationalen Jet-set. Es ist eine wundervolle individuelle Schöpfung, die marokkanische Architektur mit viktorianischer Ästhetik und dem feenhaften Charme der Innenausstatterin Syrie Maugham aus den dreißiger Jahren verbindet.

On the previous double page: the meticulously well-maintained garden where Herbert keeps an assortment of parrots and other ornamental birds. The name of the house, "Dâr Karroubia", refers to a long departed carob tree. The shells around the door (see p. 253) were arranged by Herbert to give the illusion of entering a Victorian grotto. He inherited his house and his position as arbiter of the Tangier social scene from another fantastic personage, Miss Jessie Green, the quintessential gentlewoman abroad, who first came to Tangier in 1880. In Cecil Beaton's words she "could never be anything but a lady."
Above and below: the apple-green drawing-room with a small sofa by Syrie Maugham in blue and white "toile de Jouy" brought from Herbert's cottage at Wilton, the Pembroke family home. Over the fireplace is a self-portrait by Sir Thomas Lawrence.

Double page précédente: le jardin méticuleusement entretenu où Herbert élève des perroquets et autres oiseaux d'ornement. Le caroubier qui a donné son nom à la villa «Dâr Karroubia» n'existe plus depuis longtemps. Les coquillages autour de la porte (voir p. 253) ont été disposés par Herbert pour créer l'illusion d'une grotte victorienne. Il a hérité de la villa et de son statut d'arbitre de la scène mondaine tangéroise d'un autre personnage haut en couleurs, Miss Jessie Green, la quintessence de la dame anglaise à l'étranger, venue à Tanger en 1880 et qui, selon Cecil Beaton, «n'aurait su être autre chose qu'une lady».
Ci-dessus et à-dessous: le salon vert pomme avec un petit sofa de Syrie Maugham en toile de Jouy bleue et blanche ramené de Wilton, la maison de famille des Pembroke; au-dessus de la cheminée un autoportrait de Sir Thomas Lawrence.

Vorhergehende Doppelseite: der sorgfältig gepflegte Garten, in dem Herbert einige Papageien und andere Ziervögel hält. Der Name des Hauses, »Dâr Karroubia«, bezieht sich auf einen längst verschwundenen Johannisbrotbaum. Die Muscheln an der Tür (s. S. 253) wurden von Herbert angebracht, um die Illusion zu erwecken, man betrete eine viktorianische Grotte. Er erbte das Haus und seine Position als Gebieter der gesellschaftlichen Szene von Tanger von einer anderen phantastischen Persönlichkeit, Miss Jessie Green. Sie kam 1880 nach Tanger und war der Prototyp einer »gentlewoman abroad«. In Cecil Beatons Worten: »Sie konnte nicht anders, als eine Lady zu sein.«
Oben und unten: der apfelgrüne Salon mit einem kleinen Sofa von Syrie Maugham in blau-weißer »Toile de Jouy« aus Herberts Cottage in Wilton, dem Stammsitz der Pembrokes. Über dem Kamin hängt ein Selbstportrait von Sir Thomas Lawrence.

Below: *a fine pair of French provincial Napoleon III arm chairs stand on a carpet from the Middle Atlas, a metaphor for the juxtaposition of local crafts and family heirlooms that constitutes the charm of Herbert's home. The wooden floor was constructed from the packing cases that transported his belongings from Wilton to Morocco in 1950.*

Following pages: *two views of the sky-blue veranda with a series of amusing "trompe l'œil" paintings "vaguely designed" by Herbert and executed by Lawrence Mynott (see pp. 282–285). The white iron garden furniture was also designed by Herbert and made by local craftsmen.*

Ci-dessous: *une jolie paire de fauteuils provençaux Napoléon III sur un tapis du Moyen Atlas, métaphore de l'association de l'artisanat local et des objets de famille qui fait tout le charme de l'intérieur d'Herbert. Le parquet a été réalisé avec les lattes des caisses de son déménagement depuis Wilton en 1950.*

Pages suivantes: *deux vues de la véranda bleu ciel avec une amusante série de trompe-l'œil «vaguement dessinés» par Herbert et peints par Lawrence Mynott (voir pp. 282–285). Les meubles de jardin ont également été dessinés par Herbert et réalisés par un artisan local.*

Unten: *Ein schönes Paar ländlicher Armsessel im Stil der Zeit Napoleons III. steht auf einem Teppich aus dem Mittleren Atlas, beispielhaft für das Nebeneinander von hiesigem Kunstgewerbe und Familienerbstücken, die den Charme dieses Hauses ausmachen. Für den Holzfußboden wurden Gepäckkisten verarbeitet, mit denen Herberts Haushalt 1950 von Wilton nach Marokko geschafft wurde.*

Folgende Seiten: *zwei Aufnahmen von der himmelblauen Veranda mit einer Reihe von amüsanten Trompe l'œil-Gemälden, von Herbert »irgendwie entworfen« und von Lawrence Mynott (s. S. 282–285) ausgeführt. Die weißen Gartenmöbel aus Eisen wurden ebenfalls von Herbert entworfen und von Handwerkern vor Ort angefertigt.*

Moroccan Interiors   David Herbert   Tanger

A villa on the "Old Mountain": the "Old Mountain" is residential district above Tangier, from where the medina and the casbah appear as a higgledy-piggledy assortment of tiny sugar cubes scattered above the blue of the Mediterranean. The gracious villas of the mountain, built by the Spanish and the French colonials, are enchanting. In their exuberant gardens the bustle of the busy city is drowned out by bird-song. In several bursts of building activity during the first half of the century, the house was systematically enlarged and added to from its original configuration as a small Moroccan family home. The architectural influence of the then owners, who were Spanish, could be classified under the imaginary label of "domestic Hispano-Moresque." Today, home to a Tangier "grande dame" and stuffed with Napoleon III furniture and souvenirs of an exotic life, it is wonderfully eccentric and an inspiration for many adopted Tangerinos.

Une villa sur la « Vieille Montagne »

La «Vieille Montagne» est un quartier résidentiel perché sur les hauteurs de Tanger. Vues de là-haut, les maisons de la médina et de la casbah ressemblent à des morceaux de sucre éparpillés sur le bleu de la Méditerranée. Les élégantes villas des colons espagnols et français y sont ravissantes et, dans leurs jardins luxuriants, le vacarme de la ville est étouffé par le chant des oiseaux. A l'origine, cette villa était une petite maison de famille marocaine. Elle a été agrandie à plusieurs reprises au cours de la première moitié de ce siècle. Le style architectural des propriétaires d'alors, des Espagnols, méritait le qualificatif inédit de «hispano-moresque familial». Aujourd'hui demeure d'une «grande dame» de Tanger, remplie de meubles Napoléon III et de souvenirs d'une vie peu ordinaire, elle est merveilleusement excentrique et a inspiré de nombreux Tangérois d'adoption.

Eine Villa auf dem »Alten Berg«: Der »Alte Berg« ist ein Wohnviertel oberhalb von Tanger, von dem aus die Medina und die Kasbah wie ein wildes Durcheinander von winzigen Zuckerwürfeln aussehen, die oberhalb des blauen Mittelmeers verstreut sind. Die Villen auf dem Berg, die von spanischen und französischen Kolonisten erbaut wurden, sind bezaubernd, und in ihren überquellenden Gärten wird der Lärm der Stadt vom Gesang der Vögel übertönt. In mehreren Etappen wurde dieses ursprünglich kleine marokkanische Familienhaus während der ersten Hälfte des Jahrhunderts systematisch vergrößert. Den architektonischen Einfluß der damaligen, spanischen Besitzer könnte man mit dem inoffiziellen Begriff »einheimisches Hispano-Maurisch« zusammenfassen. Heute gehört das Haus einer »grande dame« Tangers. Vollgestopft mit Möbeln im Stile Napoleons III. und den Souvenirs eines exotischen Lebens, ist es eine Inspirationsquelle für viele, die sich hier niedergelassen haben.

Page 261: the view from the entrance hall through the blue salon and into the pink drawing-room where the mistress of the house reclines on her celebrated leopard-print velvet sofa when she receives for tea or cocktails.

Left page: the bedroom with its imposing Napoleon III bed, in the style known as "Chinoiserie" with Far-Eastern motifs inlaid in lacquer and mother-of-pearl.

Above left: the Napoleon III boudoir on a theme of flowers. The Japanese engravings are of the imperial family dressed in western garb. The two sofas, c. 1880, are in characteristic "petit-point" embroidery.

Above right: the "salon Marocain", a corner in the drawing-room with the traditional low sofas, here upholstered in antique fabrics.

Page 261: vus depuis le vestibule, le salon bleu et le petit salon rose, où la maîtresse de maison reçoit pour le thé ou les cocktails allongée sur son célèbre sofa en velours «panthère».

Page de gauche: la chambre à coucher avec son imposant lit Napoléon III de style «chinoiserie», avec des motifs extrême-orientaux en incrustations de laque et de nacre.

Ci-dessus à gauche: le boudoir Napoléon III sur un thème fleuri. Les estampes japonaises représentent la famille impériale vêtue à l'occidentale. Les deux sofas, datant de 1880, sont tapissés en petit point.

Ci-dessus à droite: le «salon marocain», dans un angle du grand salon, avec les sofas bas traditionnels recouverts de tissus anciens.

Seite 261: der Blick von der Eingangshalle durch den blauen Salon in das rosa Wohnzimmer, wo die Hausherrin sich auf ihr berühmtes Samtsofa mit Leopardenmuster bettet, wenn sie Gäste zum Tee oder Cocktail empfängt.

Linke Seite: das Schlafzimmer mit seinem imposanten Napoleon III.-Bett in dem als »Chinoiserie« bekannten Stil, mit fernöstlichen Motiven aus Lack- und Perlmuttintarsien.

Oben links: das Napoleon III.-Boudoir mit Blumenmotiven. Die japanischen Stiche zeigen die Kaiserfamilie in westlicher Kleidung. Die beiden Sofas mit charakteristischer Petit-point-Stickerei sind um 1880 entstanden.

Oben rechts: der »Salon Marocain«, eine Ecke im Wohnzimmer mit den traditionellen niedrigen Sofas, die hier mit alten Stoffen bezogen sind.

Moroccan Interiors   Dâr Oualu   Tanger

On the edges of the casbah of Tangier stands Dâr Oualu. Suspended on the hillside, it is a pink and blue dream looking out over the Mediterranean from Africa to Spain. A traditional 'dâr', hidden behind a small iron-studded door in an alleyway with a deep well of a courtyard at its heart, it has been transformed into a Moorish fantasy by decorator Jean-Louis Riccardi. He is often invited, and every time he comes to stay he adds to the wealth of magic clutter with his finds in the remarkable antique shops of Tangier. The steady north light, reflected off the blue walls, is a subtle and unexpected element infusing the house with mystery even when the sun relentlessly beats down on Tangier's white roofs.

Dâr Oualu

Dâr Oualu se dresse en lisière de la casbah de Tanger. Accrochée à flanc de colline, c'est une fantaisie rose et bleue qui domine la Méditerranée de l'Afrique à l'Espagne. Avec sa profonde cour centrale, ce ‹dâr› traditionnel caché dans une allée derrière une petite porte en fer a été transformé en rêve moresque par le décorateur Jean-Louis Riccardi. Il y est souvent invité et, à chaque visite, il enrichit encore le bric-à-brac magique de ses trouvailles dans les merveilleuses boutiques d'antiquités de la ville. Elément de décor subtil et inattendu, la lumière du Nord se reflète sur les murs bleus en plongeant la maison dans une aura de mystère même quand le soleil cogne sans répit sur les toits blancs de Tanger.

Am Rande der Kasbah von Tanger steht Dâr Oualu, an den Hang geschmiegt, ein Traum in rosa und blau, von dem man übers Mittelmeer von Afrika nach Spanien schaut. Es ist ein traditionelles ›dâr‹, verborgen hinter einer kleinen eisenbeschlagenen Tür in einem Gäßchen, mit einem tiefen Brunnen im zentralen Innenhof, und wurde von dem Innenausstatter Jean-Louis Riccardi in eine maurische Phantasie verwandelt. Jedes Mal, wenn Riccardi zu Besuch kommt, fügt er der Fülle magischen Krimskrams noch etwas hinzu, einen neuen Fund aus den bemerkenswerten Antiquitätenläden von Tanger. Das ruhige nördliche Licht, das von den blauen Wänden reflektiert wird, ist ein subtiles und unerwartetes Element, das dem Haus etwas Geheimnisvolles verleiht, auch wenn die Sonne erbarmungslos auf Tangers weiße Dächer brennt.

Page 264: *a view of the gallery in the drawing-room. Riccardi enlarged the windows that give onto the Straits of Gibraltar, allowing light and air into the house.*
Above: *part of the drawing-room in what used to be the courtyard that was open to the elements.*
Right: *view from the ground-floor up to the first-floor gallery.*

Page 264: *la galerie du petit salon. Riccardi a fait élargir les fenêtres qui donnent sur le détroit de Gibraltar, laissant la lumière et l'air pénétrer dans la maison.*
Ci-dessus: *un angle du petit salon où se trouvait autrefois une cour ouverte aux éléments.*
A droite: *la galerie du premier étage vue du rez-de-chaussée.*

Seite 264: *Blick auf die Galerie im Salon. Riccardi vergrößerte die Fenster, die sich auf die Straße von Gibraltar öffnen, um Licht und Luft ins Haus zu lassen.*
Oben: *ein Teil des Salons in dem ehemaligen Innenhof, der nicht überdacht war.*
Rechts: *Blick vom Erdgeschoß auf die Galerie im ersten Stock.*

Right: a motley and gaudy collection of crowns and tiaras, placed in a niche in the dining-room.
Below: the powder-pink and baby-blue gallery overlooking what was the courtyard. The gallery is well lit and pleasant for studying, reading or just relaxing. The bedrooms, bathrooms and the dressing-room lead out from it, as does the stairway, to the rooftop terrace.

A droite: dans l'encadré, une collection bigarrée de couronnes et de tiares exposée dans une niche de la salle à manger.
Ci-dessous: la galerie rose pâle et bleu pastel dominant l'ancienne cour. Bien éclairée, elle est idéale pour lire, étudier ou simplement se détendre. Les chambres, les salles de bains et le dressing donnent sur la galerie, comme l'escalier qui mène à la terrasse du toit.

Rechts: ein kunterbuntes Durcheinander von Kronen und Tiaren in einer Nische im Eßzimmer.
Unten: die puderrosa und babyblaue Galerie, die einen Blick auf den ehemaligen Innenhof gewährt. Die Galerie ist gut beleuchtet und ein angenehmer Platz zum Studieren, Lesen oder einfach bloß Entspannen. Die Schlafzimmer, Badezimmer und das Ankleidezimmer führen davon ab, wie auch die Treppe zur Dachterrasse.

On the previous double page: the dining area tiled in pink and blue, with an appliquéd Moroccan wall-hanging, ocelot velvet cushions and a collection of baroque and bejewelled candelabras.
On these pages: bathrooms, the dressing room and the ground-floor kitchen with its ox-blood and emerald colour scheme.

Double page précédente: le coin salle à manger carrelé de rose et de bleu, avec une tapisserie marocaine aux motifs appliqués, des coussins en velours ocelot et une collection de chandeliers baroques incrustés de pierreries.
Ci-dessus, ci-dessous et page de droite: les salles de bains, le dressing et la cuisine du rez-de-chaussée dans une gamme de couleurs sang-de-bœuf et vert émeraude.

Vorhergehende Doppelseite: der rosa und blau gekachelte Eßbereich, geschmückt mit einem marokkanischen Wandteppich mit Applikationen, Samtkissen mit Ozelotmuster sowie mit einer Sammlung von barocken und mit Edelsteinen besetzten Kandelabern.
Diese Doppelseite: die Badezimmer, das Ankleidezimmer und die Küche im Erdgeschoß mit ihrer Farbgebung in Ochsenblut und Smaragd.

High up on the mountain overlooking Tangier a gate in Matisse blue opens onto a luxuriant garden created by Italian writer Umberto Pasti and Milan-based French fashion designer Stephan Janson. It shelters a magnificent collection of irises, which are Umberto's pride and joy, and two small villas overgrown with mermaid roses and passionflower. These villas are decorated with a colourful "assemblage" of carefully chosen clutter from the dusty wastes of Tangier's flea market and the local 'souks' and bazaars. The brightly coloured walls were inspired by nearby neighbour David Herbert (see pp. 252–259). The eclectic assortment of local objects echoes Tangier's raffish past and the inspiration is all at once colonial, Spanish, forties elegance and sixties hippie.

Villa Tebareh Allah

Sur le haut de la montagne qui domine Tanger, un portail bleu Matisse s'ouvre sur un jardin luxuriant créé par l'écrivain italien Umberto Pasti et le styliste français basé à Milan Stephan Janson. Sa magnifique collection d'iris fait la fierté d'Umberto. Au cœur du jardin, noyées sous les roses sirènes et les passiflores, deux petites villas ont été décorées avec un assemblage coloré et soigneusement choisi d'objets glanés sur les étals poussiéreux du marché aux puces de Tanger ou dans les souks et les bazars de la région. Les couleurs vives des murs s'inspirent du décor voisin de David Herbert (voir pp. 252–259). Cet assortiment éclectique d'objets locaux témoigne du passé mouvementé de Tanger. L'atmosphère y est tout à la fois coloniale, espagnole et hippie, avec une touche de l'élégance des années quarante.

Hoch oben auf dem Berg über Tanger führt ein Matisse-blaues Tor in einen luxuriösen Garten, der von dem italienischen Schriftsteller Umberto Pasti und dem in Mailand ansässigen französischen Modeschöpfer Stephan Janson geschaffen wurde. Er beherbergt eine prachtvolle Sammlung von Iris, Umbertos ganzer Stolz. Außerdem gibt es zwei kleine Villen, die ganz mit kleinen Rosen und Passionsblumen überwachsen sind. Sie sind mit einer bunten Sammlung sorgfältig ausgesuchter Dinge aus den staubigen Winkeln von Tangers Flohmarkt und den hiesigen ›souks‹ und Basaren angefüllt. Die leuchtenden Wandfarben wurden von Nachbar David Herbert (s. S. 252–259) angeregt. Die eklektische Sammlung von einheimischen Dingen spiegelt Tangers verwegene Vergangenheit wider. Die Anregungen stammen aus der Kolonialzeit, aus Spanien, den eleganten Vierzigern und der Hippiezeit der sechziger Jahre ...

On the previous double page: *a view of the guest pavilion, added in the late fifties by the then owner, writer Sanche de Gramont.*
Left page and above: *the study that adjoins the master bedroom and looks over the semi-tropical stepped garden. With the aid of local craftsmen the house has been completely transformed. Mohammed, the housekeeper for over thirty years, enthusiastically entered into the spirit of the flamboyant changes, and Umberto claims "an almost telepathetic understanding" with him. Together, they resuscitated the neglected garden.*

Double page précédente: *le salon du «pavillon des invités», construit dans les années cinquante par l'ancien propriétaire, l'écrivain Sanche de Gramont.*
Page de gauche et ci-dessus: *le bureau contigu à la chambre à coucher principale qui donne sur le jardin semi-tropical. La maison a été entièrement transformée avec l'aide d'artisans locaux. Mohammed, qui y est majordome depuis trente ans et avec qui Umberto affirme avoir une «entente quasi télépathique», a suivi avec enthousiasme tous les changements extravagants. Ensemble, ils ont redonné vie au jardin abandonné.*

Vorhergehende Doppelseite: *der Gästepavillon, der in den späten fünfziger Jahren von dem damaligen Besitzer, dem Schriftsteller Sanche de Gramont, angebaut wurde.*
Linke Seite und oben: *das Arbeitszimmer, das an das große Schlafzimmer anschließt und von dem aus man den halbtropischen, in Terrassen angelegten Garten überblickt. Mit der Hilfe hiesiger Handwerker wurde das Haus vollständig umgebaut. Mohammed, der seit über dreißig Jahren dem Haushalt vorsteht, hat sich enthusiastisch auf die gewaltigen Veränderungen eingelassen, und Umberto behauptet, daß sie sich fast »telepathisch verstehen«. Gemeinsam haben sie den vernachlässigten Garten wieder zum Leben erweckt.*

Above and right page: *two of the guest bedrooms with their whimsical furnishings and colour schemes, at the disposal of Stephan and Umberto's large "family of friends". These are often fashion and artistic luminaries and their sybaritic sojourns are, fittingly, a modern-day version of the adventures of the international aesthetes who have peopled the house since it was first built for the eccentric Ottilie Cannon in the twenties.*

Ci-dessus et page de droite: *deux des chambres d'amis avec leurs couleurs vives et leur mobilier plein d'humour, à la disposition de la «grande famille» d'amis d'Umberto et Stephan – un aréopage de sommités du monde des arts et de la mode dont les séjours sybarites perpétuent une tradition lancée par les esthètes internationaux qui ont peuplé la villa depuis sa construction dans les années vingt par l'excentrique Ottilie Cannon.*

Oben und rechte Seite: *zwei der Gästezimmer mit ihren witzigen Möbeln und Farben, die für Stephans und Umbertos große »Familie von Freunden« zur Verfügung stehen. Diese sind oft Koryphäen der Mode- und Kunstwelt, und ihre hedonistischen Aufenthalte sind, passenderweise, eine moderne Version der Abenteuer internationaler Ästheten, die das Haus bevölkert haben, seit es in den zwanziger Jahren für die exzentrische Ottilie Cannon gebaut worden war.*

Above: *a view of the guest pavilion.*
Left: *a quiet corner in the madly fertile garden.*
Right page: *the terrace of the guest pavilion, where most of the festive lunch and dinner parties take place.*

Ci-dessus: *le pavillon des invités.*
A gauche: *un petit coin tranquille dans un jardin exubérant.*
Page de droite: *la terrasse du pavillon des invités, où sont pris la plupart des déjeuners et dîners.*

Oben: *der Blick auf den Gästepavillon.*
Links: *eine stille Ecke in dem wild wuchernden Garten.*
Rechte Seite: *die Terrasse des Gästepavillons, wo sich die meisten festlichen Mittagessen und Dinnerparties abspielen.*

The painter and illustrator Lawrence Mynott first came to Tangier as an extra in a "Vogue" fashion shoot. He returned for Malcolm Forbes' seventieth birthday party: a party of such extravagance that it has already assumed mythological proportions in the memory of most Tangerinos, on par with the famed soirées of Barbara Hutton in the sixties. That's when he decided to move here. For the last six years the Mynotts have lived on the top floor of a 1941 apartment building in a predominantly Spanish section of the New Town. Mynott has not been unduly tempted by the opportunities for recreating on orientalist fantasy but rather has amused himself by composing a series of "tableaux" that have transformed the apartment into an essay on "trompe l'œil".

Anthea et Lawrence Mynott

Le peintre et illustrateur Lawrence Mynott est venu pour la première fois à Tanger comme figurant à l'occasion d'un reportage de mode pour «Vogue». Il y est revenu pour célébrer les soixante-dix ans de Malcom Forbes au cours d'une réception d'un tel luxe qu'elle a pris des proportions mythiques dans la mémoire des Tangérois, au même titre que les célèbres soirées de Barbara Hutton dans les années soixante. C'est alors qu'il a décidé de s'installer ici, dans un appartement au dernier étage d'un immeuble construit en 1941 dans un quartier à prédominance espagnole de la Nouvelle Ville. Ne cédant pas à la tentation de recréer un décor de rêve orientaliste, Mynott s'est amusé à composer une série de tableaux qui ont transformé son intérieur en un traité sur le trompe-l'œil.

Der Maler und Illustrator Lawrence Mynott kam das erste Mal als Komparse für Modeaufnahmen für die Zeitschrift »Vogue« nach Tanger, das nächste Mal, als Malcolm Forbes seinen siebzigsten Geburtstag feierte: eine Party von solcher Extravaganz, daß sie in der Erinnerung der meisten Tangerinos schon fast mythische Ausmaße angenommen hat – ebenso wie die berühmten Soirees von Barbara Hutton in den sechziger Jahren. Damals beschloß er hierherzuziehen. Seit sechs Jahren wohnen die Mynotts nun im obersten Stockwerk eines 1941 erbauten Appartementhauses in einem vornehmlich spanischen Teil der Neustadt Tangers. Mynott hat die Chance, eine orientalische Phantasie zu rekreieren, nicht übermäßig verlockt. Dafür hat er sich damit amüsiert, eine Reihe von Trompe l'œil-Tableaus zu malen.

Above and right page: two details of the drawing-room. The vibrant colour scheme was inspired by a shirt by designer Richard James that juxtaposed bonbon pink and pistachio green. The idea behind the decor was a dream-like nostalgia of "what Tangier was and still can be in the imagination", which depicts the most exuberant cross-cultural fantasy.

Ci-dessus et page de droite: deux détails du petit salon. La palette de couleurs vibrantes lui a été inspirée par une chemise du styliste Richard James qui juxtaposait le rose bonbon et le vert pistache. La décoration repose sur le concept nostalgique de ce que Tanger «fut et peut encore être pour l'imagination», se traduisant par un exubérant mélange de cultures d'une liberté et d'une fantaisie absolues.

Oben und rechte Seite: zwei Details vom Salon. Die dynamische Farbgebung wurde von einem Hemd des Designers Richard James inspiriert, mit Bonbonrosa neben Pistaziengrün. Die zugrundeliegende Idee hinter diesem Dekor war die traumähnliche, nostalgische Erinnerung an das, »was Tanger einmal war und in der Vorstellung immer noch sein kann«. Und das ist für ihn gleichbedeutend mit einer außerordentlich mitreißenden multikulturellen Phantasie.

Twenty years ago, when John Gairdner first came to Tangier from London on a holiday, he thought he was flying to the desert. Tangier and the verdant hillside of Jamma el Mokra, where his friend Tessa Coddrington lives, took him by storm. He fell in love with the deserted beaches, the food, the people themselves. One day he went for a solitary walk down the lane behind Tessa's house and stumbled on this cottage. The farmer who owned it had lived there since the thirties, fathered five sons and then moved on. Hippies had then squatted there, but when John discovered it, it was quite empty. The decision was made on the spot, and John scribbled a plan for his wild, raggedly romantic garden on a bit of paper the very day of the sale. Nowadays, seriously agricultural, it boasts the smallest, sweetest tomatoes in the whole of Tangier as well as a riot of vibrantly coloured blooms.

John Gairdner

En débarquant pour la première fois à Tanger il y a vingt ans, John Gairdner s'attendait à trouver un désert. Tanger et la colline verdoyante de Jamma el Mokra où vit son amie Tessa Coddrington l'ont laissé pantois. Il est aussitôt tombé amoureux des plages désertes, de la nourriture et des habitants... Un jour, au cours d'une promenade solitaire dans l'allée derrière chez Tessa, il est tombé sur cette petite maison. Son propriétaire, un agriculteur qui y avait vécu dans les années trente, y avait élevé ses cinq fils avant de poursuivre sa route. Ensuite, la maison avait été squattée par des hippies. Lorsque John l'a découverte, elle était vide. Sa décision fut prise sur le champ. Le jour même de la vente, il griffonnait déjà des plans pour transformer le jardin en potager tout en lui conservant son petit air sauvage. Aujourd'hui, il peut s'enorgueillir d'avoir les tomates les plus succulentes de Tanger ainsi qu'une abondance de fleurs de toutes les couleurs.

Als John Gairdner vor zwanzig Jahren das erste Mal aus London nach Tanger kam, um Urlaub zu machen, dachte er, er fliege in die Wüste. Dann eroberten Tanger und die grünen Hänge von Jamma el Mokra, wo seine Freundin Tessa Coddrington wohnt, sein Herz im Sturm. Er verliebte sich in die verlassenen Strände, das Essen, die Menschen... Eines Tages schlenderte er allein die Gasse hinter Tessas Haus hinunter und stieß auf dieses Cottage. Der Bauer, dem es gehörte, hatte dort seit den dreißiger Jahren gewohnt, fünf Söhne bekommen und war dann woanders hingezogen. Danach hatten Hippies dort gehaust, aber als John es entdeckte, war es praktisch leer. Der Entschluß fiel auf der Stelle, und noch am Tag des Kaufs kritzelte John einen Plan für seinen wilden, zerklüfteten und romantischen Garten auf ein Stück Papier. Heute ist er, wie ein ernsthafter Landwirt, stolz auf die kleinsten, süßesten Tomaten in ganz Tanger und auf ein Meer von Blumen in pulsierenden Farben.

On the previous double page: *a view of the main room. All the furniture is locally made; the two-tone palm matting is of the type used in mosques.*
Above left and right: *fruit and vegetables in the kitchen and the pastel-pink fireplace bedecked with flowers from the garden.*
Right page: *the kitchen table and local bounty.*

Double page précédente: *la pièce principale. Tous les meubles viennent de la région. Le tapis bicolore en feuilles de palmier est du type de ceux utilisés dans les mosquées.*
Ci-dessus à gauche et à droite: *des fruits et des légumes dans la cuisine. Sur la cheminée rose pastel, des fleurs du jardin.*
Page de droite: *la table de la cuisine et des produits de la région.*

Vorhergehende Doppelseite: *Blick auf das große Zimmer. Alle Möbel stammen aus einheimischer Produktion. Die zweifarbigen Palmmatten sind von der Art, wie sie in Moscheen benutzt werden.*
Oben links und rechts: *Obst und Gemüse in der Küche, daneben der pastellrosa Kamin, geschmückt mit Blumen aus dem Garten.*
Rechte Seite: *der Küchentisch und einheimische Ernte.*

Above: *John has created a very informal atmosphere. He even decided to keep the mural painted by the hippies during the seventies, before he acquired the house. It now graces the walls of what has become his bedroom.*
Right page: *the improvised dressing-room in bamboo.*

Ci-dessus: *John a su créer une atmosphère nonchalante. Il a conservé la fresque peinte par des squatters hippies dans les années soixante-dix avant qu'il n'achète la maison. Elle orne à présent les murs de sa chambre.*
Page de droite: *le dressing improvisé avec des bambous.*

Oben: *John hat eine sehr lockere Atmosphäre geschaffen. Er hat sogar das Wandgemälde behalten, das die Hippies während der siebziger Jahre gemalt haben, bevor er das Haus erwarb. Es ziert die Wände des Zimmers, das nun sein Schlafzimmer ist.*
Rechte Seite: *die improvisierte Garderobe aus Bambus.*

The noted London collector and antiquarian Christopher Gibbs loves Morocco with a passion. He escapes to Tangier as often as possible, where he lives in a three-room hideaway halfway up the "Old Mountain". His "pied-à-terre", simply decorated with a few very good pieces, can claim an unglorious role in Tangier's literary history. It was previously part of the former hostel that sheltered the Bowles and a good many of their friends at various stages of penury. In the words of Tennessee Williams: "For reasons of economy… we put up at a perfectly ghastly hotel called El Far-Har (rhymes with horror) at the top of a very steep hill over the ocean. Spectacular view: every possible discomfort!" In Gibbs' attractive rooms only the view remains the same, hypnotic, beautiful, unchanging.

Christopher Gibbs

Le célèbre collectionneur et antiquaire londonien Christopher Gibbs est un passionné du Maroc. A la moindre occasion, il se réfugie dans sa tanière tangéroise sur les flancs de la «Vieille Montagne». Ses trois pièces, sobrement décorées avec quelques objets de grande qualité, sont entrées dans l'histoire littéraire de Tanger par des voies détournées: elles faisaient autrefois partie d'un hôtel bon marché qui a accueilli les Bowles et bon nombre de leurs amis lorsqu'ils traversaient des périodes difficiles. Tennessee Williams a évoqué ainsi ces temps héroïques: «Pour des raisons d'économie, …nous nous sommes installés dans un hôtel parfaitement sordide baptisé El Far-Har (qui, en anglais, rime avec ‹Horreur›) au sommet d'une colline qui surplombe l'océan. La vue y est spectaculaire, le confort, inexistant.» De cette époque ne subsiste que la vue: hypnotique, superbe, immuable.

Der bekannte Londoner Sammler und Antiquitätenhändler Christopher Gibbs liebt Marokko leidenschaftlich. Er zieht sich so oft wie möglich nach Tanger zurück, wo er in einem Drei-Zimmer-Refugium am Hang des »Alten Berges« wohnt. Seine drei Zimmer, schlicht eingerichtet mit einigen wenigen kostbaren Möbeln, können den zweifelhaften Ruhm für sich in Anspruch nehmen, eine entschieden unrühmliche Rolle in Tangers literarischer Geschichte gespielt zu haben. Sie waren einmal Teile der früheren Herberge, die den Bowles und einer ganzen Menge ihrer Freunde in Zeiten der Not Unterkunft gewährte. In den Worten von Tennessee Williams: »Aus finanziellen Gründen … übernachteten wir in einem absolut grauenvollen Hotel names El Far-Har (reimt sich auf Horror) oben auf einem sehr steilen Hügel über dem Meer. Spektakulärer Ausblick: jeder nur erdenklichen Un-Komfort!« In den stillen Räumen von Gibbs ist nur der Ausblick derselbe geblieben: hypnotisch, wunderschön, unveränderlich.

Above: the salon, with a traditional 'haiti' wall-hanging made of
strips of appliquéd fabric. The cushions are in delicate Fez embroidery.
Right page: the bedroom with a woven cover and a local carpet.

Ci-dessus: le salon avec une tapisserie ‹haiti› traditionnelle faite de
bandes de tissus appliqués. Les coussins sont recouverts de délicates
étoffes brodées de Fès.
Page de droite: la chambre à coucher avec un dessus-de-lit en laine
et un tapis de la région.

Oben: der Salon, mit einem traditionellen ›haiti‹-Wandbehang
aus Stoffstreifen mit Applikationen. Die Kissen sind mit feiner Fes-
Stickerei verziert.
Rechte Seite: das Schlafzimmer mit einer gewebten wollenen Decke
und einem einheimischen Teppich.

This "Blue House" on the mountain of Tangier belongs to Roland
Beaufre and serves as holiday home for a family from Paris. It
started off as a "play house" when, as teenagers, Roland and his
sister badgered their parents into letting them rehabilitate the fifties
gatehouse of the family holiday home for their own use. Then they
set about decorating it with local materials and artifacts. A visit to
Chechaouen, a sacred village perched high in the Rif mountains
whose houses are all painted with an ice-blue limewash, provided the
inspiration. The very light in Chechaouen, bouncing off the walls of
the mountain medina, is surprisingly but undeniably blue and the
same effect was created not only by painting every surface pale blue,
but also by fitting blue panes in the windows.

La Maison Bleue

Cette «Maison Bleue» sur la montagne de Tanger appartient à
Roland Beaufre, mais une famille rivant à Paris y passe toutes ses
vacances. Tout a commencé lorsque, adolescents, Roland et sa
sœur ont harcelé leurs parents jusqu'à ce qu'ils les laissent aména-
ger cette maison de gardiens des années cinquante dans la pro-
priété familiale. Ils l'ont décorée avec les moyens du bord et de
l'artisanat local. Une visite à Chechaouen leur a fourni l'inspiration
de base. Dans ce village sacré perché au sommet du Rif, les façades
sont enduites de chaux pigmentée de bleu glacier. Pour retrouver
la lumière aux reflets bleus qui se répercute sur les murs de la
médina de Chechaouen, toutes les surfaces de la maison ont
été peintes en bleu pâle et des vitres bleutées ont été posées aux
fenêtres.

Dieses »Blaue Haus« auf dem Hügel von Tanger gehört Roland
Beaufre und dient einer Familie aus Paris als Urlaubsdomizil. Es
begann als eine Art »Spielhaus«: Roland und seine Schwester bear-
beiteten als Teenager ihre Eltern, damit sie ihnen erlaubten, das
Pförtnerhäuschen zu einem Ferienhaus aus den fünfziger Jahren für
ihren eigenen Gebrauch wiederherzustellen. Dann begannen sie, es
mit einheimischen Stoffen, Möbeln und Gegenständen einzurichten
und auszustatten. Ein Abstecher nach Chechaouen, einem heiligen
Dorf hoch im Rif-Gebirge, dessen Häuser alle mit einem eisblauen
Kalkanstrich getüncht sind, brachte die entscheidene Inspiration. Das
Licht in Chechaouen wird von den Wänden der Gebirgs-Medina blau
reflektiert; der gleiche Effekt wurde hier dadurch erzielt, daß nicht nur
jede Oberfläche blaßblau gestrichen wurde, sondern auch dadurch,
daß die Fenster blaue Scheiben erhielten.

The "salon Marocain" with its low table and seating. The white wool rugs, embroidered with sequins, are characteristic of Riffian handiwork. The gaudy modern embroidered satin cushions, appreciated for their kitsch value, come from local shops. Much of the furniture was picked up at Tangier's famously cheap flea market Casa Barata.

Le «salon marocain», avec sa table et ses banquettes basses. Les tapis de laine blanche, brodés de paillettes, sont typiques de l'artisanat du Rif. Les coussins en satin brodés, appréciés pour leur kitsch, viennent des boutiques locales. Une grande partie du mobilier provient de la célèbre mine aux bonnes affaires, le marché aux puces de Tanger, Casa Barata.

Der »Salon Marocain« mit seinen niedrigen Tischen und Sitzgelegenheiten. Die weißen Wollteppiche, mit Pailletten bestickt, sind typisch für Handarbeiten aus dem Rif-Gebirge. Die knalligen, bestickten Satinkissen, die wegen ihres Kitscheffekts sehr geschätzt werden, kommen aus Läden der Gegend. Ein großer Teil der Möbel wurde auf Tangers berühmtem billigen Flohmarkt Casa Barata erworben.

The guest bedroom is located past the salon on the ground floor. The cushions, low sofas and industrial matting on the floor continue the monochromatic theme. The bed, a family heirloom in which his father was born, was decorated by Roland. The light filtered through the blue glass of the windows creates an illusion of coolness, even during the hot and humid Tangier summer.

La chambre d'amis donne sur le salon, au rez-de-chaussée. Les coussins, les canapés bas et le tapis industriel assurent la continuité de la palette chromatique. Le lit, un meuble de famille qui a vu naître son père, a été peint par Roland. La lumière qui filtre par les vitres bleutées donne une illusion de fraîcheur, même pendant les étés chauds et humides de Tanger.

Das Gästezimmer geht vom Salon im Erdgeschoß ab. Die Kissen, die niedrigen Sofas und die maschinell hergestellten Matten auf dem Fußboden nehmen die monochrome Farbgebung wieder auf. Das Bett, ein Familienerbstück, in dem sein Vater geboren wurde, wurde von Roland verziert. Das Licht, das durch die blauen Fensterscheiben gefiltert wird, verschafft die Illusion von Kühle, selbst während des heißen und schwülen Sommers in Tanger.

On these pages: *two views of the sunny main room on the first floor. It is an informal library and salon that gives onto a large terrace. The white carpets and striped fabric are finely woven in wool and contribute to the summery atmosphere and pale palette.*

Ci-dessus et page de droite: *deux vues de la grande pièce toujours ensoleillée au premier étage. Donnant sur une grande terrasse, elle fait également office de bibliothèque et de salon. Les tapis blancs et les tissus rayés, de fins tissages de laine, ajoutent encore à l'atmosphère estivale et à la palette pastel de la maison.*

Diese Doppelseite: *zwei Ansichten von dem sonnigen Salon im ersten Stock. Es ist ein gemütlicher Salon mit Bibliothek, der auf eine große Terrasse führt. Die weißen Teppiche und gestreiften Stoffe sind aus feingesponnener Wolle gewebt und tragen zu der sommerlichen Atmosphäre in Pastelltönen bei.*

Painter, architect, jewellery and furniture designer – the American expatriate Stuart Church is a true Tangerino. Tall and distinguished, usually dressed in flowing robes and with his characteristic bushy white beard, he is a striking figure. He arrived in the city somewhere between the Beat Generation and the Hippy Era and never left. He has designed some of the most interesting interiors in Tangier and is one of the most ardent champions of a pared-down ethnic style that could almost be qualified as "Moroccan minimalism". He has been influential in the re-evaluation of simple Berber wooden furniture and is a specialist in traditional techniques.

Stuart Church

Peintre, architecte, dessinateur de bijoux et de meubles, l'Améri-cain Stuart Church est un vrai Tangérois dans l'âme. Grand et dis-tingué, généralement vêtu d'une tunique longue, portant une barbe blanche broussailleuse, c'est un personnage haut en couleurs. Il a débarqué à Tanger entre la Beat Generation et le mouvement hip-pie et il y est resté. Il a réalisé certaines des décorations d'intérieur les plus intéressantes de la ville et c'est un ardent défenseur d'un style «ethnique» épuré que l'on pourrait presque qualifier de «minimalisme marocain». Spécialiste des techniques tradition-nelles, il a contribué à réhabiliter la simplicité des meubles berbères en bois.

Maler, Architekt, Schmuck- und Möbeldesigner – der Amerikaner Stuart Church ist ein echter »Tangerino«. Groß und distinguiert, normalerweise in fließende Gewänder gekleidet und mit seinem cha-rakteristischen buschigen weißen Bart ist er eine auffallende Erschei-nung. Er kam irgendwann zwischen der Beat Generation und den Hippies nach Marokko und blieb da. Einige der interessantesten Inte-rieurs in Tanger sind von ihm entworfen worden. Stuart ist ein glühenden Verfechter eines reduzierten ethnischen Stils, den man bei-nahe »marokkanischen Minimalismus« nennen könnte. Er spielte eine wesentliche Rolle bei der Aufwertung von schlichten Berber-möbeln und ist ein Kenner überlieferter Techniken und Methoden.

Page 305: Stuart's work table with an unfinished portrait of Shaikha Fatima Al Sabah (see pp. 246–251).
On these pages: Much of the year is spent outdoors: Stuart's view down to the sea unrolls before the eyes, a 'koubba' adding an element of mystery.

Page 305: la table de travail, avec un portrait inachevé de Shaikha Fatima Al Sabah (voir pp. 246–251).
Ci-contre: Stuart passe le plus clair de son temps à l'extérieur: la vue sur la mer s'étend à l'infini, un koubba ajoutant une touche de mystère.

Seite 305: Stuarts Arbeitstisch mit einem noch nicht beendeten Portrait von Shaikha Fatima Al Sabah (s. S. 246–251).
Diese Doppelseite: Ein Großteil des Jahres wird im Freien verbracht. Die Aussicht aufs Meer entfaltet sich vor den Augen. Eine ›koubba‹ gibt dem Ganzen etwas Geheimnisvolles.

Moroccan Interiors   Stuart Church   Tanger

Stuart has chosen to live in the countryside on a hillside outside
Tangier. His little hut is isolated, and he has no phone or electricity.
This solitude he considers his true luxury. He goes down to town every
few days, where his friend Rachel Muyal of the celebrated bookshop
Librairie des Colonnes keeps him in touch with the rest of the world.

Stuart a choisi de vivre à la campagne sur une colline près de Tanger.
Dans son petit refuge isolé, il n'y a ni téléphone ni électricité. Cette
solitude est son vrai luxe. Il descend régulièrement à la ville où
son amie Rachel Muyal, qui tient la célèbre Librairie des Colonnes,
l'informe de ce qui se passe dans le reste du monde.

Stuart hat sich für ein Leben auf dem Lande außerhalb von Tanger
entschieden. Seine abgelegene kleine Hütte liegt an einem Hang und
hat weder Telefon noch Elektrizität. Er hält diese Abgeschiedenheit für
einen wahren Luxus. Alle paar Tage geht er in die Stadt hinunter, wo
ihn seine Freundin Rachel Muyal von der Buchhandlung Librairie des
Colonnes auf dem laufenden hält über das, was in dem Rest der Welt
vorgeht.

Left page and below: *the uncluttered white-washed space is punctuated by two simple fireplaces and several large rugs. The large windows flood the unstructured rooms with light.*

Page de gauche et ci-dessous: *l'espace dépouillé blanchi à la chaux est ponctué de deux sobres cheminées et plusieurs grands tapis. Les larges fenêtres baignent de lumière les pièces non structurées.*

Linke Seite und unten: *Die Akzente in diesem schlichten weißgekalkten Raum werden von zwei einfachen Kaminen und mehreren großen Teppichen gesetzt. Durch die großen Fenster strömt Licht in die unstrukturierten Zimmer.*

Reminiscent of a scene in a Wim Wenders movie, this cabin sits stranded, miles from anywhere, on the edge of a deserted white beach. The Atlantic surf breaks only a few metres from the front door. The cabin is painted bright blue, as is the well, the only source of water. The overall impression is decidedly surreal. This effect is enhanced when you discover that the interior is in fact beautifully put together with an upbeat palette of pastels and lots of simple seaside furniture. The juxtaposition of the fierce natural elements – such as the rough sea, burning sun and empty sky – with the domesticity of the interior is stunning.

Anna McKew et Ahmed Maïmouni

Comme dans un arrêt sur image extrait d'un film de Wim Wenders, cette cabane est échouée à des kilomètres de tout, au bord d'une plage blanche et déserte, les vagues de l'Atlantique venant mourir à quelques mètres de sa porte. Elle est peinte en bleu vif, comme le puits, l'unique point d'eau. L'impression d'ensemble est résolument surréaliste. Cet effet est encore accentué quand on découvre l'intérieur magnifiquement aménagé avec des meubles simples de bord de mer et une gamme joyeuse de tons pastels. Le contraste entre les éléments naturels bruts – mer houleuse, soleil torride et ciel immuablement bleu – et le confort douillet de la maison est saisissant.

Wie in einem Wim-Wenders-Film, liegt diese Hütte kilometerweit von allem entfernt wie angespült am Rande eines einsamen, weißen Strandes, während sich die atlantischen Wellen nur wenige Meter vor der Haustür brechen. Sie ist hellblau gestrichen, genauso wie der Brunnen, der die einzige Wasserquelle ist. Der erste Eindruck ist eindeutig surreal und wird noch verstärkt, wenn man entdeckt, daß das Interieur wirklich wunderschön zusammengestellt wurde, mit einer fröhlichen Palette von Pastellfarben und vielen schlichten Strandmöbeln. Der Kontrast der natürlichen Elemente in ihrer Wildheit – das rauhe Meer, die brennende Sonne und der leere Himmel – und des friedlichen Innern des Hauses ist eindrucksvoll.

Page 311: the front door, with the amusing absurdity of a street number in this isolated spot, offers a view into this brilliantly conceived interior that is based on a succession of brightly-coloured rooms.
On these pages: Anna McKew has an innate sense of colour and indeed of style. Every little eccentric detail of the furnishing contributes to the integrity of the whole. The house is used mostly as a base from which to spend long days on the beach, the owners preferring to return to their other home in Tangier-proper most evenings.

Page 311: un numéro de rue au-dessus de la porte dans cet endroit perdu et une vue de l'intérieur brillamment conçu, basé sur une enfilade de pièces vivement colorées.
Page de gauche, ci-dessus et ci-dessous: Anna McKew a un sens inné de la couleur et du style. Chaque petit détail excentrique contribue à la cohérence de l'ensemble. La maison sert surtout de base pour venir passer la journée à la plage, ses propriétaires préférant rentrer à Tanger le soir.

Seite 311: die Haustür mit der amüsant-absurden Hausnummer an dieser abgelegenen Stelle. Der Blick ins Innere zeigt die brillante Gestaltung der aneinandergereihten, in leuchtenden Farben gehaltenen Innenräume.
Diese Doppelseite: Anna McKew hat einen angeborenen Sinn für Farben und eben auch für Stil. Jedes kleine exzentrische Detail trägt zu dem Gesamteindruck und der Harmonie des Ganzen bei. Das Haus wird hauptsächlich als Ausgangspunkt für lange Tage am Strand benutzt, da die Besitzer es meist vorziehen, abends in ihr Haus in Tanger zurückzukehren.

Above: *the bedroom for sybaritic siestas during the hottest part of the day.*
Right page: *the salon at the back of the house where guests can do likewise.*

En haut: *la chambre à coucher, pour des siestes indolentes pendant les heures les plus chaudes de la journée.*
Page de droite: *le salon à l'arrière de la maison, où les invités peuvent se reposer dans l'après-midi.*

Oben: *das Schlafzimmer für hedonistische Siestas während der heißesten Stunden des Tages.*
Rechte Seite: *der Salon an der Rückseite des Hauses, wo auch die Gäste Siesta halten können.*

Above: the kitchen is primarily used for putting together cheerful summer lunches or candlelight picnics.
Right page: all the water has to come from the well, so the shower is a fairly primitive affair.

Ci-dessus: la cuisine sert surtout pour préparer de joyeux repas pendant l'été ou des pique-niques aux chandelles.
Page de droite: le puits étant la seule source d'eau, la douche est relativement rudimentaire.

Oben: In der Küche werden in erster Linie fröhliche Sommerlunches oder Picknicks bei Kerzenlicht vorbereitet.
Rechte Seite: Alles Wasser kommt aus dem Brunnen, und so ist die Dusche eine ziemlich primitive Angelegenheit.

Glossary of Arabic and Moroccan terms / Glossaire des termes arabes et marocains / Glossar der arabischen und marokkanischen Begriffe

The glossary uses the French transcription of Arabic and Moroccan words. Otherwise, the English transcription of these words, according to the Oxford English Dictionary, is used.

La transcription française que nous avons utilisée pour les termes arabes et marocains est celle du dictionnaire Petit Robert, lorsque le mot y est référencé.

Das Glossar benutzt die französische Transkription der arabischen und marokkanischen Wörter. Ansonsten wird im deutschen Text die Schreibweise verwendet, wie sie der Duden vorgibt, sofern das Wort dort aufgeführt ist.

agadir
fortified building used for storing harvests

grenier-citadelle utilisé pour entreposer le produit des récoltes

befestigter Vorratsspeicher für Feldfrüchte

arabesque
particular type of Islamic decoration derived from ancient designs of plant-like scrolling; motifs of vegetal origin – leaves, flowers, buds and stems – laid out in geometric patterns

type de décor spécifiquement islamique qui est dérivé des décors antiques de rinceaux végétaux; des motifs d'origine végétale – feuilles, fleurs, bourgeons et tiges – se trouvent agencés dans des compositions géométriques qui restent sousjacentes

spezifisch islamische, von antiken Laubfriesen abgeleitete Ziermuster; pflanzliche Motive wie Blätter, Blüten, Knospen und Stiele sind einem zugrundeliegenden geometrischen Muster folgend angeordnet

arganier
tree found in southern Morocco whose fruit is used for animal feed; the oil extracted from the kernel is valued and used in Morocco for cooking, soap-making and lighting

arbre du Sud marocain dont le fruit est utilisé comme nourriture pour les ruminants; de l'amande renfermée dans le noyau on extrait une huile appréciée au Maroc dans la cuisine, pour la savonnerie et pour l'éclairage

südmarokkanischer Baum, dessen Früchte als Futter für Wiederkäuer verwendet werden; die im Kern eingeschlossene Nuß wird zu einem Öl verpreßt, das in der marokkanischen Küche beliebt ist und darüber hinaus in der Seifenherstellung und als Lampenöl Verwendung findet

bab
gate or door

porte

Tür

bahou
rectangular niche centred in the long wall of a room opposite the entrance; it is large enough to accommodate one or more couches

niche murale rectangulaire située au centre du long côté de la salle,
en face de l'entrée; elle est de taille suffisante pour pouvoir y installer un ou même plusieurs sièges

Nische, die in die der Tür gegenüberliegende Wand eingelassen ist; die Größe reicht für einen oder sogar mehrere Sitzplätze

bayt
room, sometimes flat

pièce d'habitation, parfois aussi appartement

Wohnraum, gelegentlich auch Wohnung

bled
village, rural community or district in the Maghreb

villages et agglomérations rurales du Maghreb

Dorf, ländliche Siedlung im Maghreb

caïd
Muslim chief responsible for justice and administration

chef musulman responsable de la justice et de l'administration

für Justiz und Verwaltung zuständiger moslemischer Würdenträger

casbah
fortified rural dwelling; also a fortified residence of the ruler in the medina

maison rurale fortifiée; désigne également la résidence fortifiée du souverain dans la médina

befestigtes ländliches Wohnhaus, auch Bezeichnung für die befestigte Residenz des Herrschers in der Medina

chamachât
little vaulted windows of sculpted plaster above doors

petits claustras de plâtre sculpté cintrés situés au-dessus des portes

kleine Belüftungssteine oberhalb der Türen in Form von Rundbögen aus skulptiertem Gips

dâr
house

maison

Haus

djebel
mountain

montagne

Berg

djibs
plaster, gypsum

plâtre

Gips, Stuck

douiriya
"small house"; annexes of the main house comprising of kitchen, oven, hammam and stores around a small, central courtyard

«petite maison»; constructions annexes de la maison principale, regroupant cuisine, four, hammam et magasins autour d'une courette centrale

»kleines Haus«; Nebengebäude eines Haupthauses, mit Küche, Backofen, ›hammam‹ und Vorratsräumen, die um einen kleinen Innenhof herum liegen

fondouk
hostelry, commercial centre, warehouse

auberge, centre de commerce, entrepôt de marchandises

Herberge, Handelszentrum und Warenlager

haiti
the lining of a tent; a panel in wood, plaster of cloth

doublure d'une tente; panneau de bois, tissu plâtré

Unterfütterung für Zelte, bestehend aus Holzplatten oder mit Gips verstärktem Stoff

hammam
Arabic word for baths; traditional baths in the Islamic world are steam baths

terme arabe pour bain; les bains traditionnels du monde islamique sont des bains de vapeur

arabisches Wort für Bad; traditionell finden sich in der islamischen Welt Dampfbäder

harem
the part of the house reserved for women, and a term for the women themselves

partie de la maison qui est réservée aux femmes, et ensemble de ces femmes

der Teil des Hauses, der den Frauen vorbehalten ist; auch Bezeichnung für diese Frauen selbst

harira
traditional soup usually consumed during Ramadan

soupe traditionnelle consommée habituellement à l'époque du Ramadan
traditionelle Suppe, die gewöhnlich während des Ramadans gegessen wird

kettara
underground irrigation canal

canal d'irrigation souterrain

unterirdischer Bewässerungskanal

kilim
woven carpet

tapis tissé

Webteppich

koubba
dome constructed over a ceremonial room or the tomb of a saint

coupole surmontant une salle d'apparat ou le tombeau d'un saint

Kuppel über einem Prunksaal oder dem Grab eines Heiligen

ksar (pl. ksour)
palace, fortress; in southern Morocco a fortified complex sheltering a village community

terme arabe pour palais, forteresse; au Sud du Maroc: agglomération fortifiée abritant une communauté villageoise

arabisches Wort für Palast, Festung; im Süden Marokkos: befestigte Siedlung einer Dorfgemeinde

maalem
master-craftsman

maître artisan

Handwerksmeister

Maghreb
western part of the Arab world comprising of Morocco, Algeria and Tunisia

partie occidentale du monde arabe comprenant le Maroc, l'Algérie et la Tunisie

westlicher Teil der arabischen Welt mit Marokko, Algerien und Tunesien

makhzen
originally: store, reserves, wealth; in Morocco it also means everything relating to the royal family or governing body

à l'origine: dépôt, réserves, richesse; au Maroc ce terme désigne en même temps tout ce qui se rapporte à la famille royale, c'est-à-dire aussi une partie de l'administration du pays
ursprüngliche Bedeutung: Lager, Vorräte, Reichtum; in Marokko bezeichnet dieser Begriff zugleich alles, was mit der Königsfamilie zu tun hat, d. h. auch einen Teil der Verwaltung des Landes

medersa
traditional higher school comprising of classrooms, often student lodgings and prayer-room; rarely a minaret

école supérieure traditionnelle, comprenant des salles de cours, souvent aussi des chambres d'étudiants et une salle de prière, beaucoup plus rarement un minaret

traditionelle höhere Schule mit Unterrichtsräumen, oft auch mit Zimmern für die Studenten und einem Betsaal, seltener einem Minarett

médina
in Arabic "town"; also used nowadays in Western parlance for the traditional districts of Arab towns

mot arabe pour ville, actuellement utilisé, dans les langues occidentales, pour les quartiers traditionnels des villes arabes

im Arabischen »Stadt«; in den westlichen Sprachen sind heute die traditionellen Viertel der arabischen Städte gemeint

mellâh
Jewish quarter of a medina

le quartier juif de la médina

jüdisches Viertel in der Medina

menzeh
pavilion in a garden with a view

pavillon de jardin offrant une belle vue

Gartenpavillon mit schöner Aussicht

moucharabieh
balustrade in wood openwork which can be seen out of, but not into; used particularly to protect windows, balconies and walkways reserved for women

balustrade ajourée en bois, permettant de voir sans être vu et utilisée notamment pour protéger fenêtres, balcons et estrades réservées aux femmes

aus Holz geschnitzte Brüstung, durch die man hinausschauen kann, ohne selbst gesehen zu werden; vorwiegend vor Fenstern, Balkonen und Estraden, die den Frauen vorbehalten sind

mukarnas
ornate honeycomb or stalactite vaulting

motif décoratif en nid d'abeilles

Stalaktitengewölbe, Wabenmuster

nouala
tents or huts of nomads

tente de nomades

Nomadenzelt

pisé
sun-dried earth (used especially for walls) which can include lime or straw

terre battue (utilisée notamment pour des murs) qui peut comporter de la chaux ou des fragments de paille

Stampflehm, aus dem vor allem Wände errichtet werden; er kann Kalk oder Stroh enthalten

ribât
a stronghold erected in Islamic border regions and intended for the holy war; it shelters the combatants and comprises of a prayer-room, meeting-rooms, stores and stables

place forte érigée dans les régions frontalières de l'islam et destinée à la guerre sainte; il abrite les guerriers et comporte une salle de prière, des salles de réunion, des magasins et des écuries

Festung in den Grenzgebieten des Islam, die dem Heiligen Krieg dient; meist sind Soldaten untergebracht; zudem gibt es einen Betsaal, Versammlungsräume, Lager und Pferdeställe

riyâd
inside garden or courtyard

jardin clos privé

umfriedeter privater Garten

sahrìdj
fountain or basin

fontaine ou bassin

Brunnen oder Wasserbecken

setwan
entrance corridor leading to the courtyard of a house

corridor d'entrée précédant l'accès à la cour d'une maison

Korridor, der zum Innenhof eines Hauses führt

souk
market, bazaar; the word is used to denote the whole of a town's traditional commercial centre, specific parts of it or simply streets lined with shops

marché; le mot est utilisé pour l'ensemble du centre commercial traditionnel d'une ville, pour des parties spécifiques de cet ensemble, ou simplement pour des rues marchandes bordées de boutiques

Markt; bezeichnet das gesamte traditionelle Handelszentrum einer

Stadt, spezielle einzelne Teile davon oder einfach eine von Geschäften gesäumte Einkaufsstraße

sultan
an Islamic princely title which implies spiritual and temporal power

un titre princier islamique qui implique à la fois pouvoir spirituel et pouvoir temporel

islamischer Fürstentitel, der zugleich geistliche und weltliche Herrschaft beinhaltet

tabiya
compound of pink sand and strengthened lime

mélange de sable rose et de chaux renforcée

Mischung aus rosa Sand und Kalk

tadelakt
Moroccan wall and occasionally floor treatment comparable to Italian stucco, made of sand and quicklime and polished by stone and black soap

enduit à la chaux, coloré, ciré et lissé au savon noir, similaire au stucco italien, utilisé pour les murs et quelquefois les sols

in der Art von italienischem Stuck gefertigter Kalkputz, der mit Stein und schwarzer Seife geglättet und gefärbt wird; für Wand- und gelegentlich auch Bodenflächen verwendet

tagguebbast
sculpted plaster cornice

revêtement de plâtre ciselé

mit fein ausgeschnittenen Mustern versehener Stucküberzug

tajine
Moroccan traditional stew, also the name of the dish with a conical top in which it is cooked

plat traditionnel cuisiné au four; désigne aussi le plat de terre cuite et son couvercle de forme conique

traditionelles Eintopfgericht; auch Bezeichnung für den Tontopf mit konisch zulaufendem Deckel, der für die Zubereitung verwendet wird

tangawi
inhabitant of Tangier

habitant de Tanger

Einwohner von Tanger

tataoui
painted reeds laid between the beams of a ceiling forming a geometrical pattern

roseaux peints assemblés et entrecroisés entre les poutres d'un plafond, formant un décor géométrique

bemalte Schilfstreifen, die zwischen den Deckenbalken in dekorativen geometrischen Mustern verlegt und verflochten werden

testir
geometrical interlaced pattern radiating out from a central star

entrelacs géométriques irradiant autour d'une étoile centrale

von einem Stern ausstrahlende geometrische Flechtmuster

thuya
variety of wood specifically used by the craftsmen of Essaouira

essence de bois travaillée plus spécialement par les artisans d'Essaouira

Holzart, die vor allem von den Handwerkern in Essaouira verarbeitet wird

tighremt
complex both for the household and its animal lifestock

habitation où vivent plusieurs familles et leurs animaux domestiques

Wohnkomplex für mehrere Familien und deren Haustiere

tourik
interlaced, plant-like ornaments

ornements de caractère végétal

Pflanzenornamente

wast ad-dar
"centre of the house"; central courtyard of the house

«centre de la maison»; terme utilisé pour la cour centrale de la maison

»Zentrum des Hauses«; Bezeichnung für den Innenhof

zelliges
mosaic of tiles

mosaïque de faïence

Mosaik aus Fayencekacheln

zouak
traditional technique of painting on wood

technique traditionnelle de peinture sur bois

traditionelle Technik der Holzbemalung

Bibliography / Bibliographie

Barber, Neville: Morocco, Londres: Thames & Hudson, 1965

Benkirane, Narjess; Phillipe Saharoff: Marrakech, Demures et Jardins Secrets, ACR Editions

Bidwell, Margaret et Robin: Morocco, the Traveler's Companion, Tauris Publishers

Bowles, Jane: Out in the World: Selected Letters 1935–1970, ed. par Millicent Dillon, Santa Barbara (CA): Black Sparrow Press, 1985

Bowles, Paul: The Sheltering Sky, Londres: John Lehmann, 1949
– The Spider's House, New York: Random House, 1955
– Without Stopping, New York: Ecco Press, 1972
– Points in Time, Londres: Peter Owen, 1982
– Let it Come Down, Londres: Arena, 1985
– Their Heads Are Green, Londres: Peter Owen, 1985
– A Hundred Camels in the Courtyard, San Francisco (CA): City Lights Books, 1986

Brives, Abel: Voyages au Maroc, Alger, 1909

Bryans, Robin: Morocco, Land of the Farthest West, Londres: Faber & Faber, 1965

Burroughs, William: The Naked Lunch, Londres: Paladin, 1986
– Junky, Londres: Penguin, 1977

Caillie, René: Travels through Central Africa to Timbuctoo and across the Great Desert to Morocco, performed in the years 1824–28, Londres, 1830 (repr. 1968)

Canetti, Elias: The Voices of Marrakesh, Londres: Marion Boyars, 1978

Capote, Truman: A Capote Reader, Londres: Hamish Hamilton, 1987
– Answered Prayers, New York: Plume, 1988

Dennis, Lisl et Landt: Morocco, New York: Potter Clarkson Publishers, 1992

Dillon, Millicent: The Little Original Sins: The Life and Work of Jane Bowles, Londres: Virago Press, 1988

Ellingham, Mark; Mc Veigh, Shaun: The Rough Guide to Morocco, Londres: Harrap-Columbus, 1988

Elsner, Eleanor: The Present State of Morocco, Londres, 1928

Enderlein, V.: Islamische Kunst, Dresde, 1990

Finlayson, Iain: Tangier, City of the Dream, Flamingo Publishers, 1993

Fischer, Rudolf: Marokko, Fribourg-en-Brisgau: Herder, 1986

Flint, Bert: Tapis et Tissage, vol. 2 de «Formes et Symboles dans les Arts Maghrebis», Tanger: Imprimie E.M.I., 1974

Fodor's North Africa, New York: Fodor's Travel Publications, Inc., 1988

Foucauld, Vicomte Charles de: Reconnaissance au Maroc en 1883–1884, Paris, 1888

Gallotti, Jean: *Moorish Houses and Gardens of Morocco*, vol. 1, New York: William Helburn 1926

Grove, Lady Agnes: *Seventy-one Days Camping in Morocco*, Londres: Longmans, Green and Co., 1902

Le Guide du Routard Maroc, Editions Hachette

Harris, Walter: *Morocco That Was*, Londres: Eland Books, 1983

Helfritz, Hans: *Marokko, Berberburgen und Königsstädte des Islam*, Cologne: DuMont, 1980

Herbert, David: *Second Son*, Londres: Peter Owen, 1972
– *Engaging Eccentrics*, Londres: Peter Owen, 1990

Hoag, J.: *Islamische Architektur*, Stuttgart, 1970

Ingram, Jim: *Land of Mud Castles*, Londres, 1952

Innes, Miranda: *Ethnic Style*, Conran Octopus, 1994

Lewis, Wyndham: *Journey into Barbary*, Penguin Travel Library

Loti, Pierre: *Au Maroc*, Edition du Centenaire/Christian Pirot (édition allemand: *Pierre Loti: Im Zeichen der Sahara*, Brême: Manholt Verlag, 1991)

Maugham, Robin: *North African Notebook*, Chapman & Hall

Maxwell, Gavin: *Lords of the Atlas*, Londres: Longmans, Green and Co., 1966

Miège; Bousquet; Denarnaud; Beaufre: *Tanger*, ACR Editions

Musallam, Basim: *The Arabs*, Collins/Harvill, 1983

Les Orientalistes, 3 volumes, ACR Editions

Paccard, André: *Le Maroc et l'artisanat traditionnel islamique dans l'architecture*, Paris: Edition Atelier 74, 1979

Pepys, Samuel: *The Tangier Papers of Samuel Pepys*, publié par The Naval Records Society, Londres, 1935

Rice, David Talbot: *Islamic Art*, Londres: Thames & Hudson, New York: Oxford University Press, 1975

Rogerson, Barnaby: *The Cadogan Guides: Morocco*, Chester (CT): The Globe Pequot Press, 1989

Souvenirs de Voyages, catalogue pour l'exposition du Louvre, Réunion des Musées Nationaux, 1992

Tharaud, Jerôme et Jean: *Fés, ou le bourgeois de l'Islam*, Paris, 1930
– *La Chaîne d'or*, Paris, 1950

Vickers, Hugo: *Cecil Beaton*, Londres: Weidenfeld & Nicholson, 1985

Wharton, Edith: *In Morocco*, Londres: Century, 1984

Wilson, Eva: *Islamic Design*, British Museum Publications, 1988

Wolfert, Paula: *Couscous and other good food from Morocco*, Harper-Perennial, 1987

Acknowledgements / Remerciements / Danksagung

I would like to dedicate this book to my daughter and her Moroccan family who helped stimulate my love for the country and its people. The photographic shoots were styled by the following people: The Berber Tent and Elie Mouyal styled by Jean-Pascal Billaud; Luciano Tempo styled by Isabel da Silva Ramos; Stuart Church styled by Marie-France Boyer; Shaikha Fatima Al Sabah, Jean-Louis Scherrer styled by Alexandra d'Arnoux. The stories on the Caidal Tent, Jacqueline Foissac, Tamy Tazi, Vanessa Somers and Frederick Vreeland, Marguerite McBey were styled by Valentine de Ganay. Both the Bill Willis and Boul de Breteuil layouts involved the work of several stylists. Many thanks to them all. Riyâd Boumliha and Dâr Lévy were styled by Chris O'Byrne. All the others were styled by myself on location in Morocco.
I would also like to thank the various magazines, such as "Elle Decoration", "Marie Claire Maison", "Maison et Jardin" and several others, that previously published these stories.
Sophie Baudrand, who was responsible for the photographic co-ordination of the whole project, applied herself far beyond the call of duty: gratitude is also due to Thiana Ljubojevic, Karen Jaegel and Patricia Boving. Roland Beaufre was unfailing in his support and generous in sharing his thorough knowledge of the country, as well as being an excellent travelling companion. Tiggy Maconochie was a staunch supporter throughout and a faithful friend. Karim Atiya was of great help during the many trips this book required.
The Maroc Hotel Group and in particular Mr. Benarrosh and the staff at their Paris office were of invaluable assistance in organizing most of the accomodations. I would also like to thank Sabine Poirrier of Bouzy Voyages for organizing the travels.
In Tangier, my greatest debt is to Boubker Temli who was a prodigious source of information, and a wonderful advisor. Abdelatif from "Le Coin de l'artisanat Berbère" and Magid were also particularly helpful. Mr. and Mrs. Amati allowed us the use of their wonderful house in the medina which greatly facilitated our task. Madame Beaufre also deserves warmest thanks.
In Fez, our most sincere thanks must go to the management of the Palais Jamais, one of the most wonderful hotels in the country and the kind offices of Mr. Ben Arafa, its General-Director. Abdulali was an essential factor in our complicated house-hunting activities in the medina, as was the architect Hassan Redouane, from the ADER-FES. In Casablanca, our thanks must go to the director and staff of the luxurious Riad Salam Hotel of the Maroc Hotel Group where we had a very pleasant stay and to Francoise d'Orgé who proved a source of excellent advice.
In Marrakesh, our first thought is for the Mamounia, undoubtedly the most famous hotel in Morocco. Mr. Bergé, the director, and Mr. Constanza were unfailingly hospitable for the length of our stay with them, Zahra was an inexhaustible source of information. Mr. Lancs, Director of the charming Tickha Hotel of the Maroc Hotel Group, was also truly supportive and our stay at his beautiful hotel was one of the highlights of our time in Marrakesh. Alessandra Lippini, Francoise Lafont and Jacqueline Foissac were most helpful as was Jacques Grange.

Lisa Lovatt-Smith